Life with Kevin®

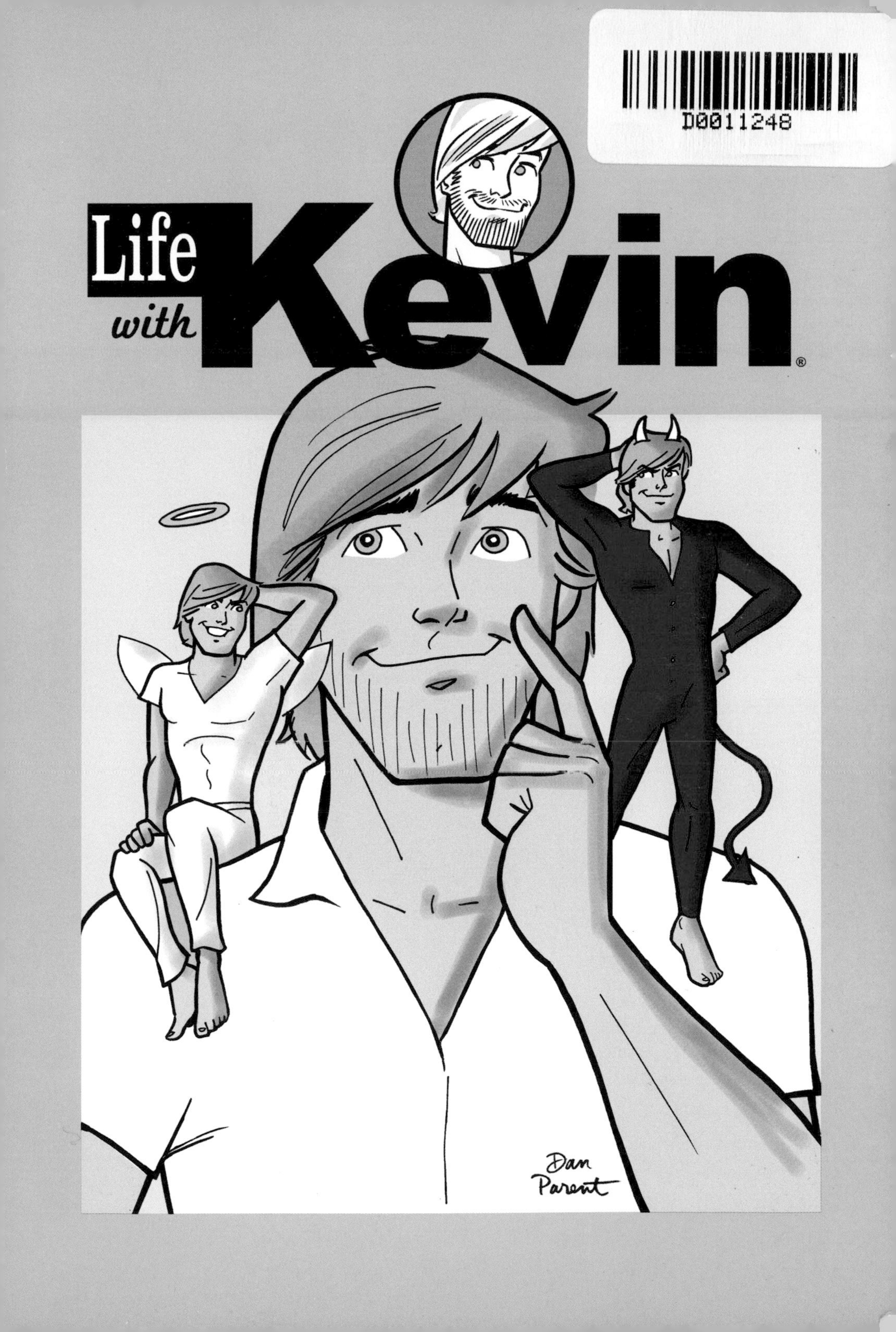
Dan Parent

Life with Kevin

SCRIPT, PENCILS & COLORS:
DAN PARENT

INKS:
J. BONE

LETTERS:
JACK MORELLI

ASSOCIATE EDITOR:
STEPHEN OSWALD

ASSISTANT EDITOR:
JAMIE LEE ROTANTE

EDITOR/CO-PRESIDENT:
ALEX SEGURA

CO-PRESIDENT:
MIKE PELLERITO

CO-PRESIDENT/EDITOR-IN-CHIEF:
VICTOR GORELICK

PUBLISHER/CO-CEO:
JON GOLDWATER

Meet Kevin Keller.

He's just out of college and ready to make a name for himself in the Big Apple! Kevin is the son of Kathy and US Army Colonel Thomas Keller. Kevin, along with his parents and his two younger sisters Denise and Patty, traveled around the world before finally settling down in Honesdale at the start of his high school career.

It was at this time that Kevin realized he was gay. He rose above adversity and even helped his fellow schoolmates fight against bullying. The Keller family then made one final move during Kevin's junior year of high school: to a welcoming little town known as Riverdale! Upon his arrival he immediately caught the eye of the beautiful, rich Veronica Lodge who was determined to leave her boyfriend Archie Andrews in the dust while she pursued a romance with the gorgeous new kid. Little did she know Kevin was one of the only guys in Riverdale who *wasn't* interested in her! Kevin and Veronica soon after became BFFs—for better or for worse!

While at Riverdale High, Kevin's interest in journalism grew and he worked on the school paper, joined the debate team and even became class president! Kevin made a lot of new friends along the way (even some famous friends— can you say "Oh My!"?) as well as accruing a few romantic interests!

But high school is now well over and with his college years just behind him, Kevin is ready to make another big move: to New York City! With a major in Journalism and a new internship, he's ready to take the news world by storm. But as the saying goes, anything can change in a New York minute...

CHAPTER 1

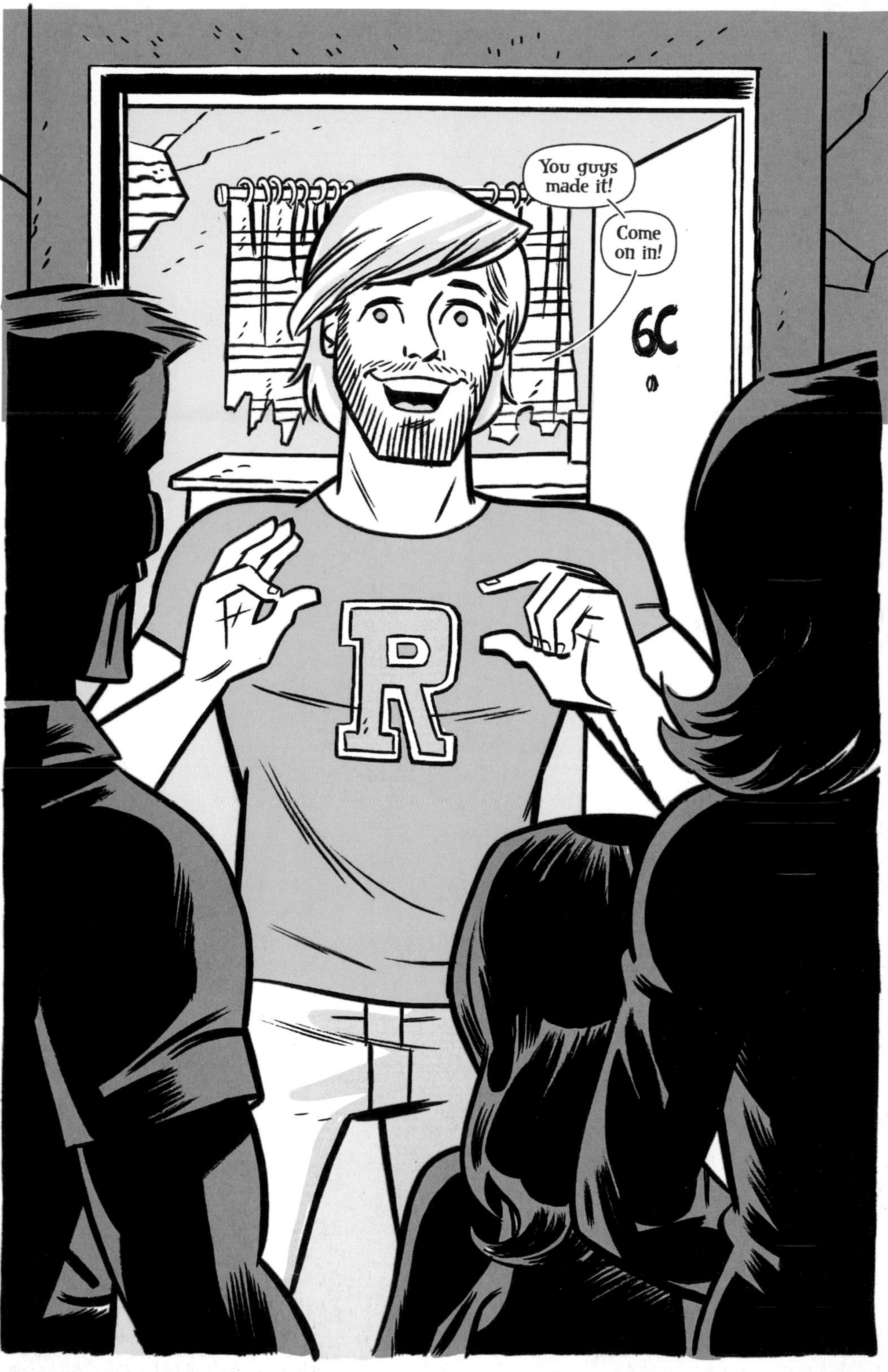
You guys made it!
Come on in!
6C

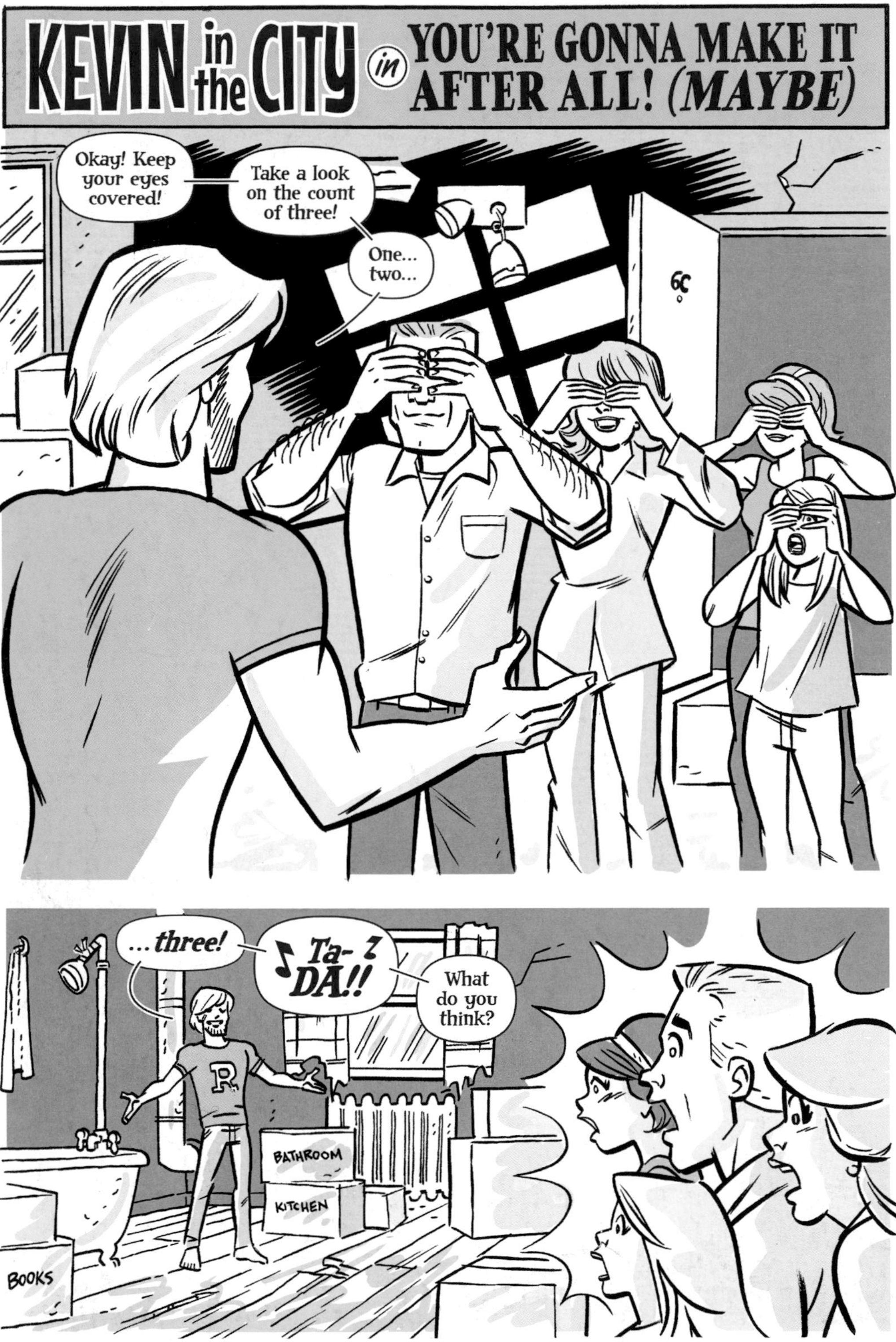
KEVIN in the CITY in YOU'RE GONNA MAKE IT AFTER ALL! (MAYBE)
Okay! Keep your eyes covered!
Take a look on the count of three!
One... two...
6C
...three!
Ta-DA!!
What do you think?
BATHROOM
KITCHEN
BOOKS

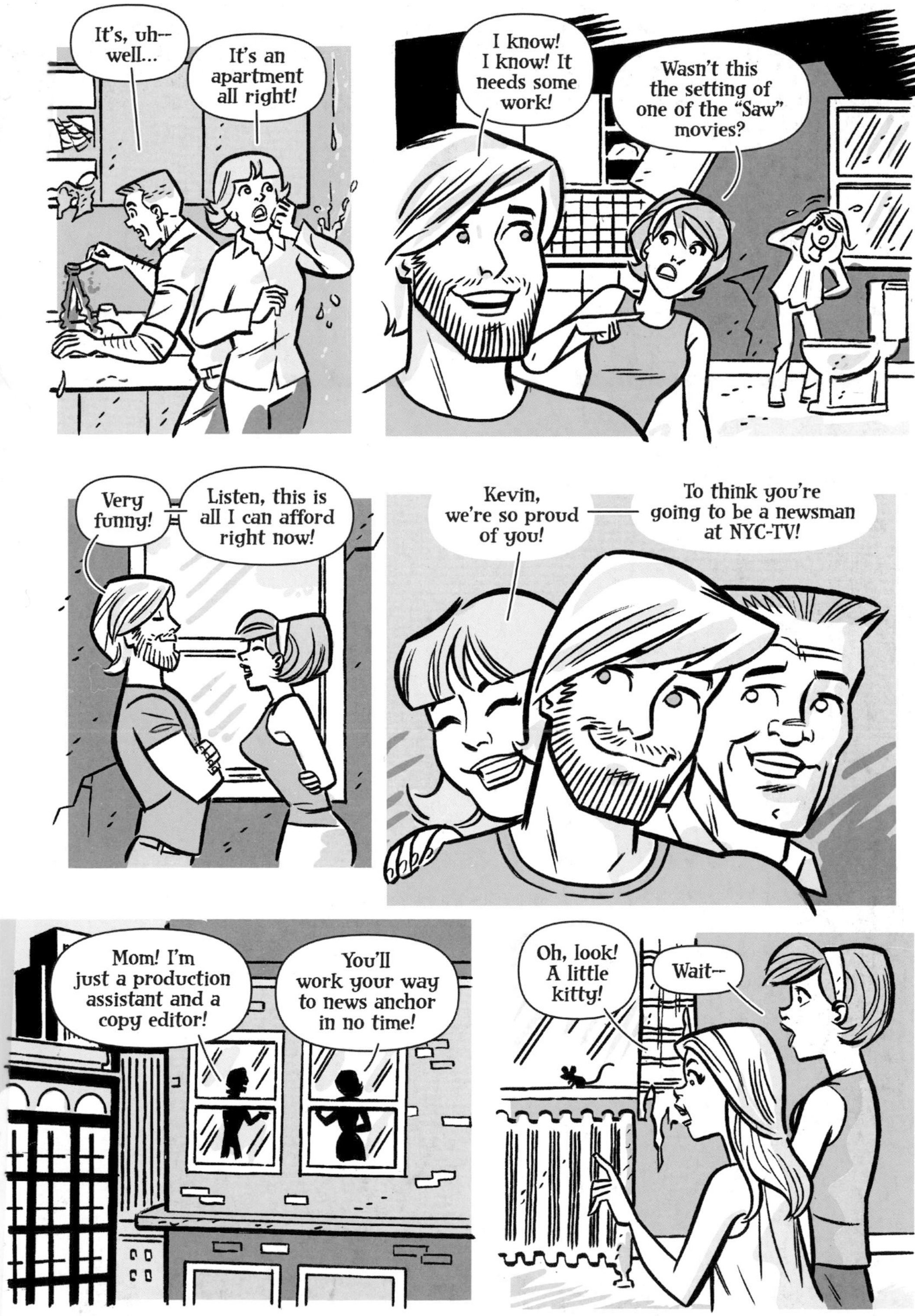
It's, uh-- well...
It's an apartment all right!
I know! I know! It needs some work!
Wasn't this the setting of one of the "Saw" movies?
Very funny!
Listen, this is all I can afford right now!
Kevin, we're so proud of you!
To think you're going to be a newsman at NYC-TV!
Mom! I'm just a production assistant and a copy editor!
You'll work your way to news anchor in no time!
Oh, look! A little kitty!
Wait--

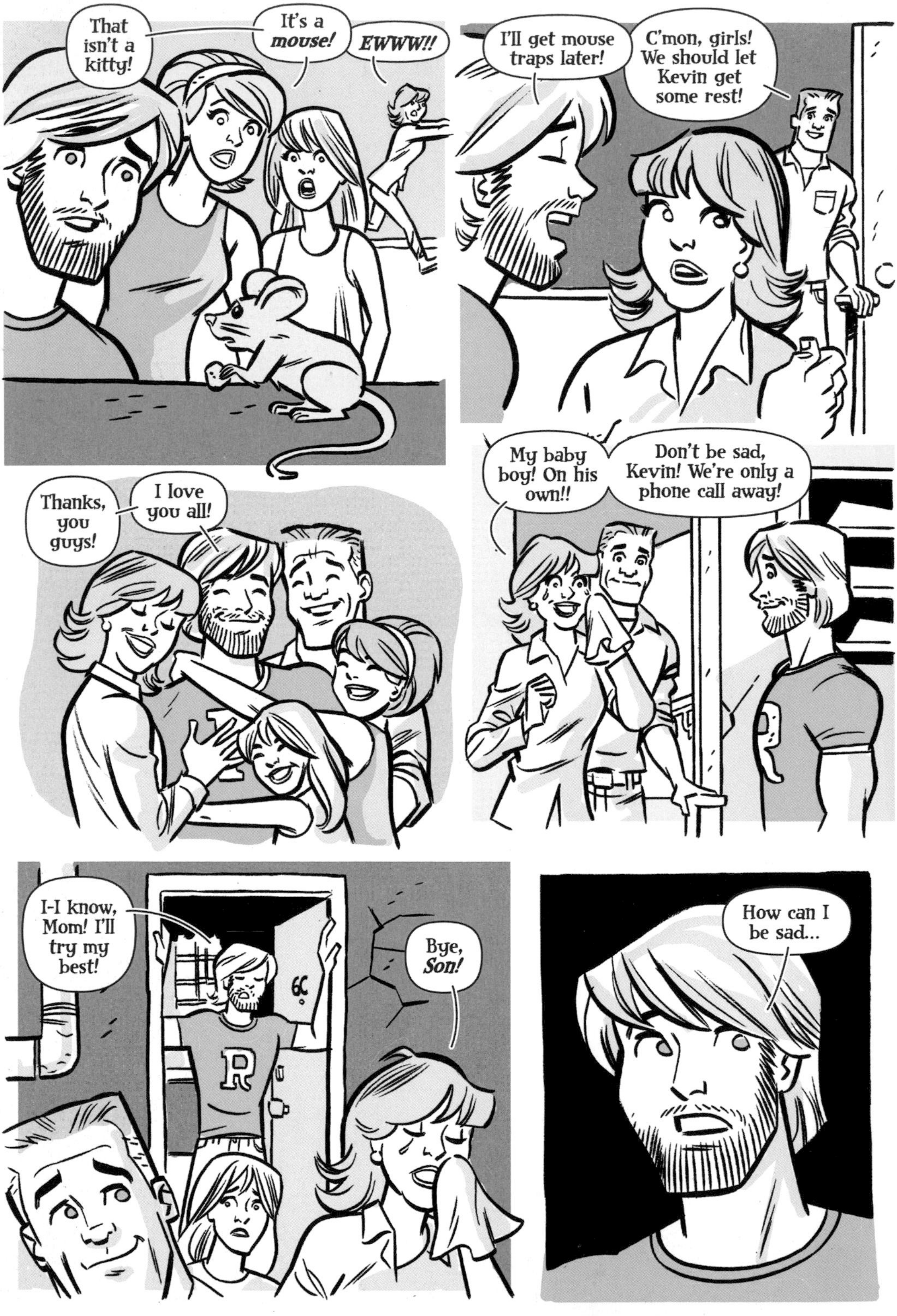
That isn't a kitty!
It's a *mouse!*
EWWW!!
I'll get mouse traps later!
C'mon, girls! We should let Kevin get some rest!
Thanks, you guys!
I love you all!
My baby boy! On his own!!
Don't be sad, Kevin! We're only a phone call away!
I-I know, Mom! I'll try my best!
Bye, *Son!*
How can I be sad...

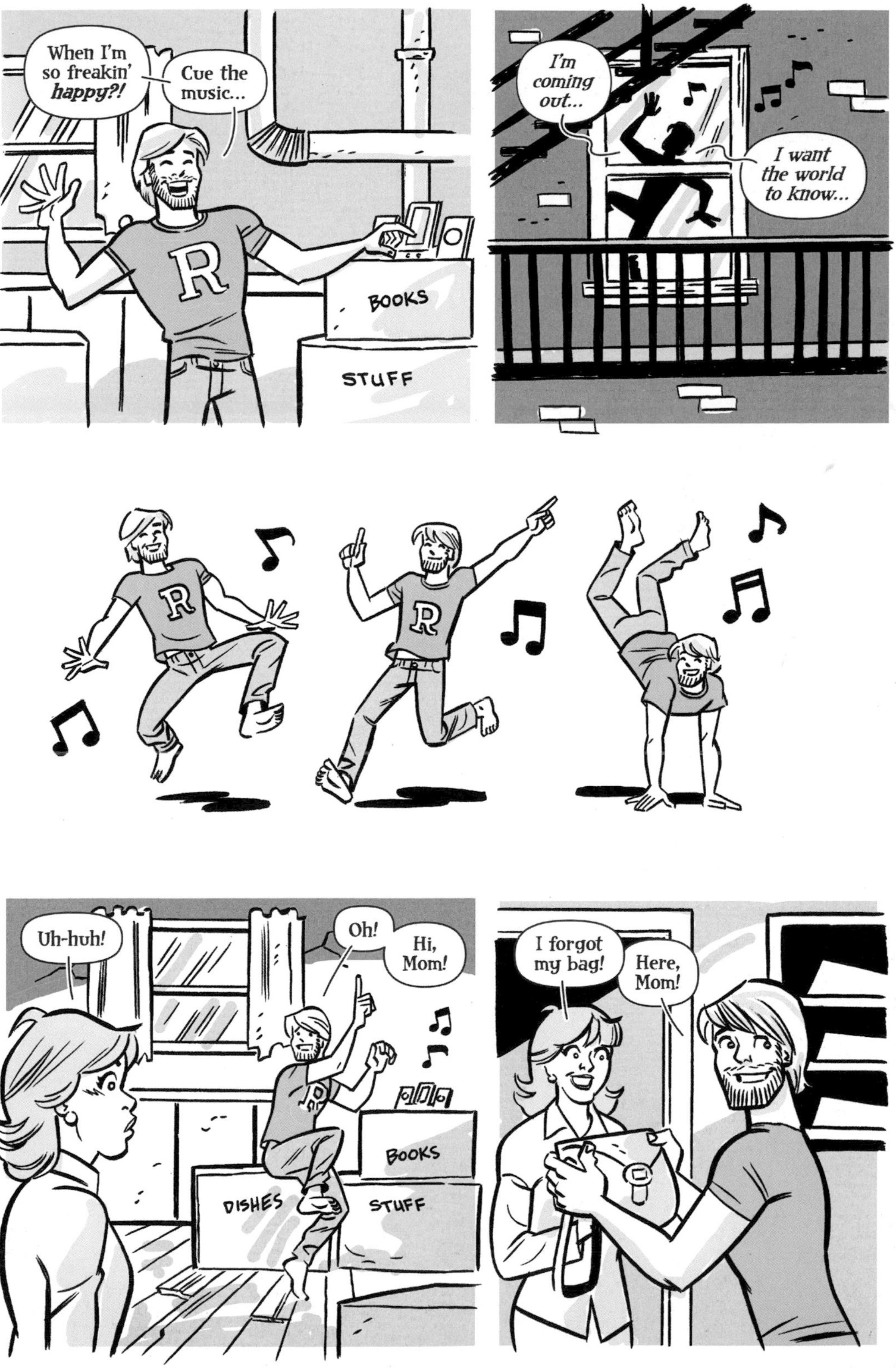
When I'm so freakin' ***happy?!***
Cue the music...
I'm coming out...
I want the world to know...
BOOKS
STUFF
Uh-huh!
Oh!
Hi, Mom!
BOOKS
DISHES
STUFF
I forgot my bag!
Here, Mom!

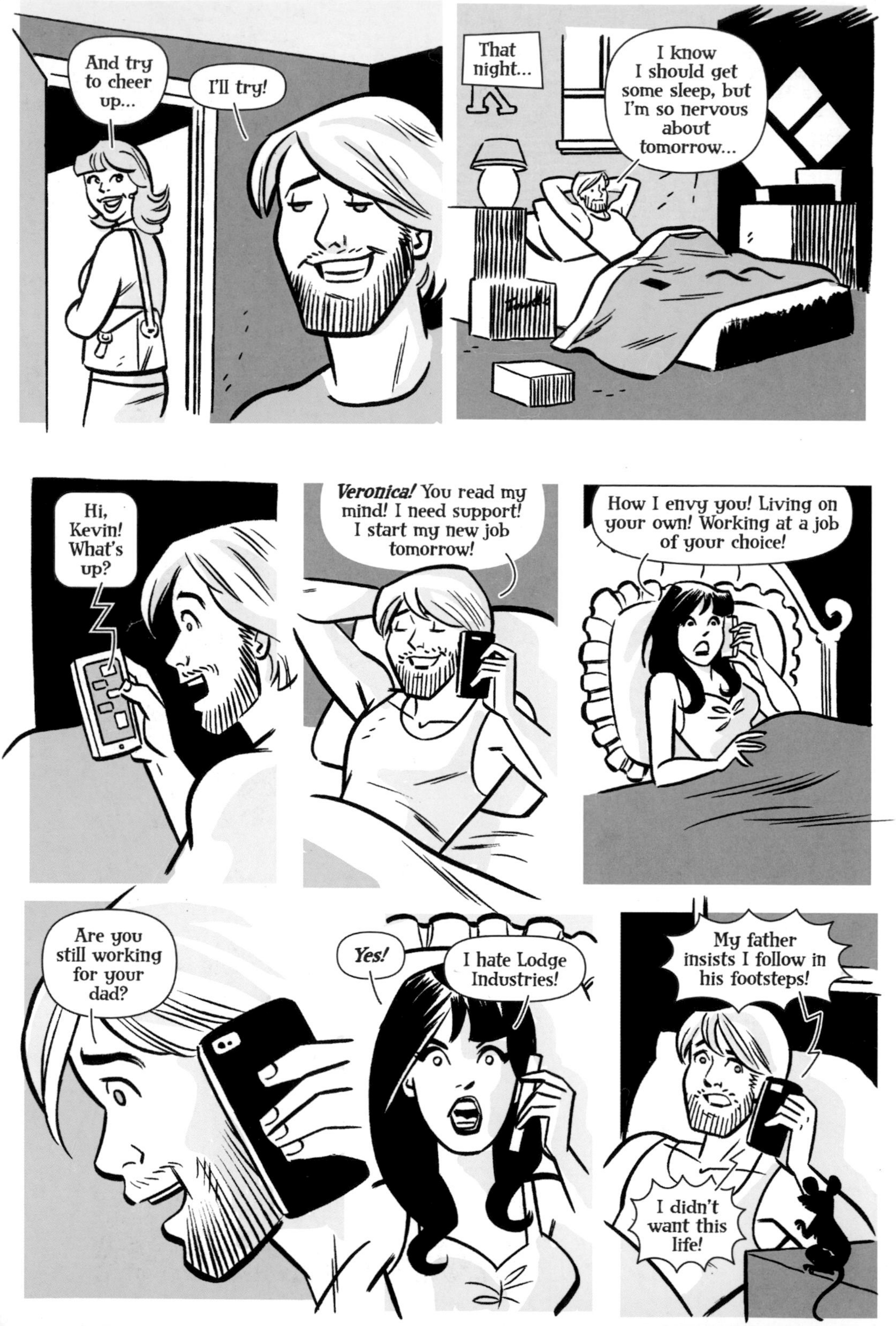
And try to cheer up...
I'll try!
That night...
I know I should get some sleep, but I'm so nervous about tomorrow...
Hi, Kevin! What's up?
Veronica! You read my mind! I need support! I start my new job tomorrow!
How I envy you! Living on your own! Working at a job of your choice!
Are you still working for your dad?
Yes!
I hate Lodge Industries!
My father insists I follow in his footsteps!
I didn't want this life!

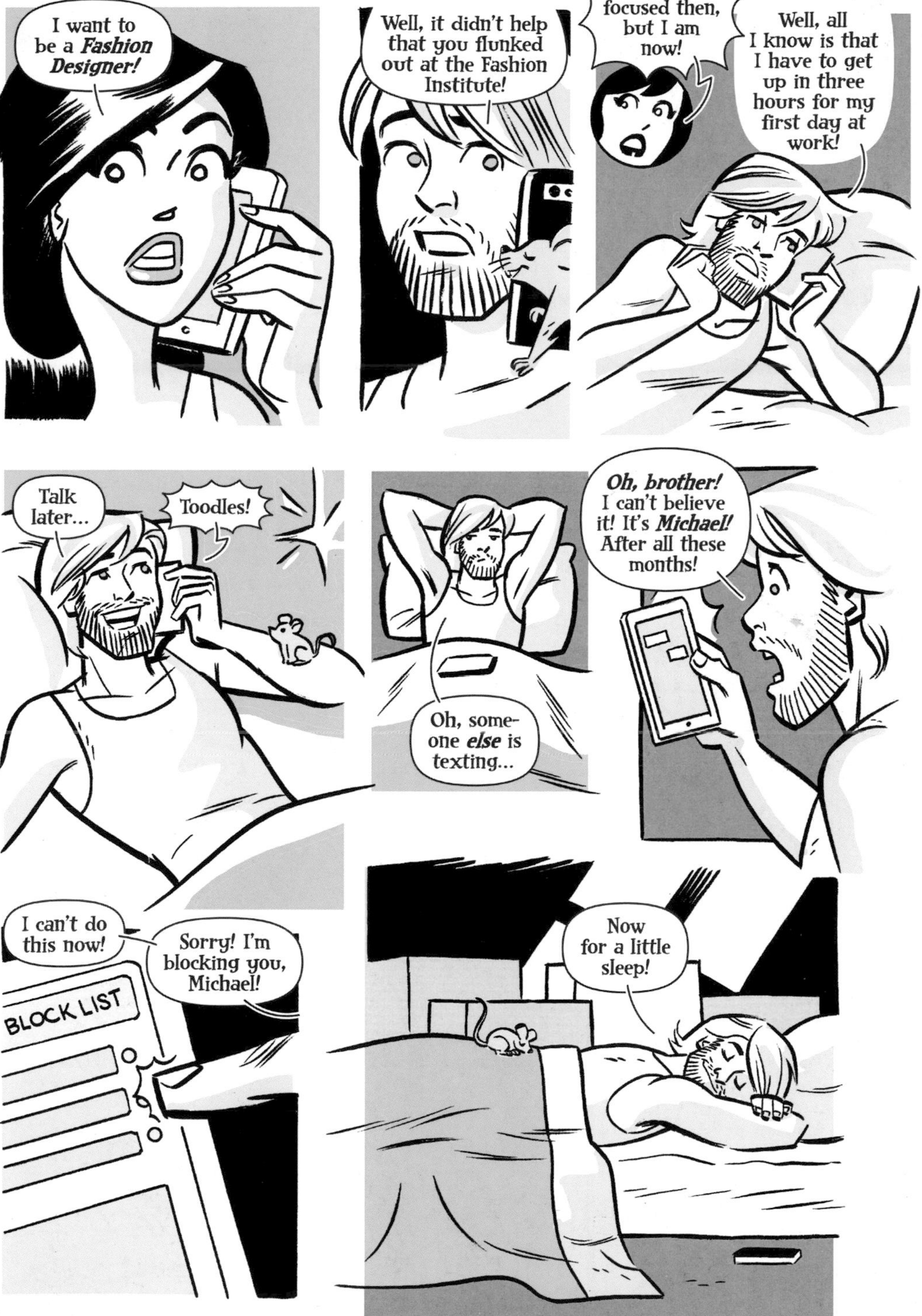
I want to be a *Fashion Designer!*
Well, it didn't help that you flunked out at the Fashion Institute!
I wasn't focused then, but I am now!
Well, all I know is that I have to get up in three hours for my first day at work!
Talk later...
Toodles!
Oh, some-one *else* is texting...
Oh, brother! I can't believe it! It's *Michael!* After all these months!
I can't do this now!
Sorry! I'm blocking you, Michael!
BLOCK LIST
Now for a little sleep!

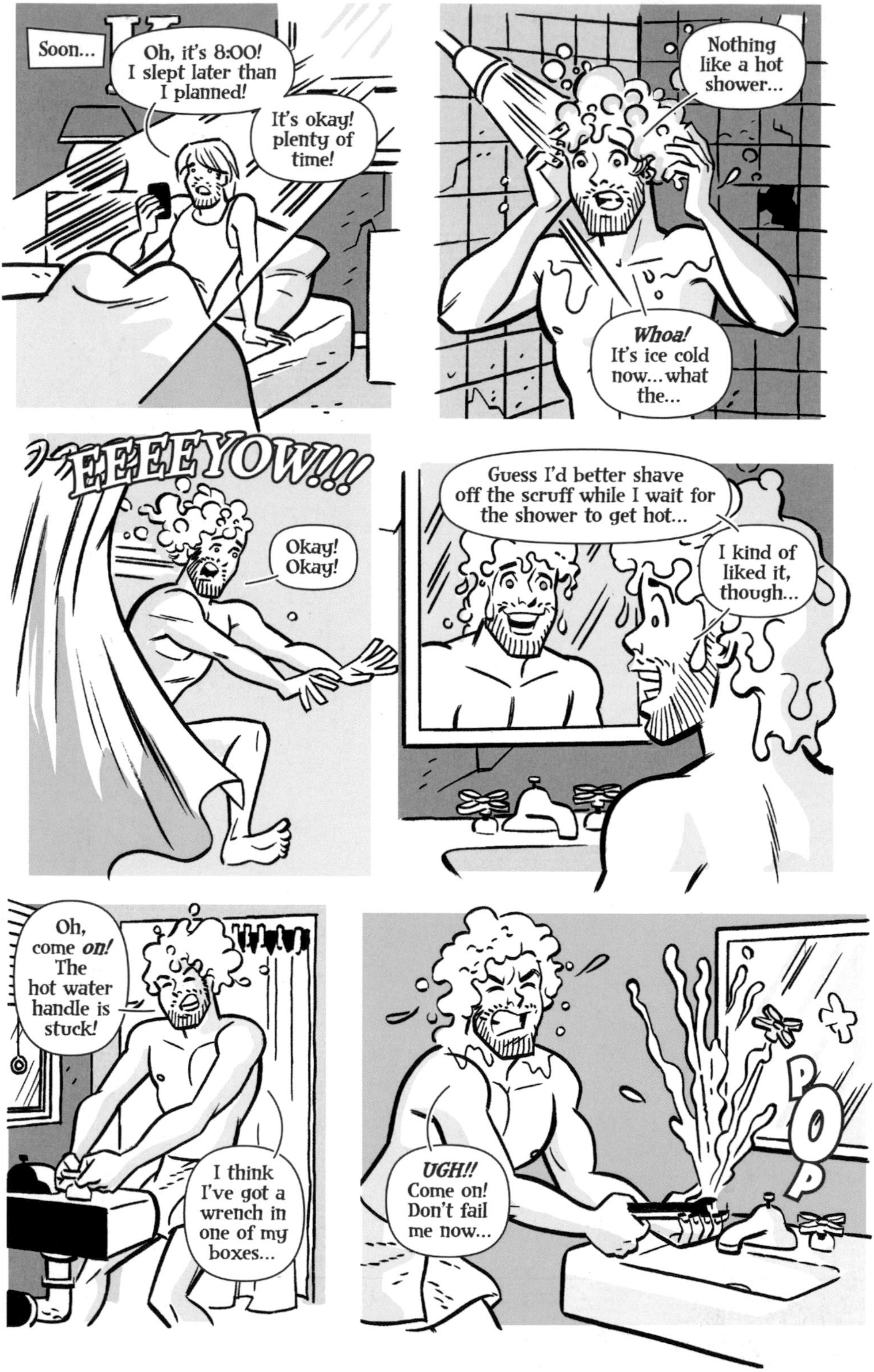
Soon...
Oh, it's 8:00! I slept later than I planned!
It's okay! plenty of time!
Nothing like a hot shower...
Whoa! It's ice cold now...what the...
EEEEYOW!!!
Okay! Okay!
Guess I'd better shave off the scruff while I wait for the shower to get hot...
I kind of liked it, though...
Oh, come on! The hot water handle is stuck!
I think I've got a wrench in one of my boxes...
UGH!! Come on! Don't fail me now...
POP

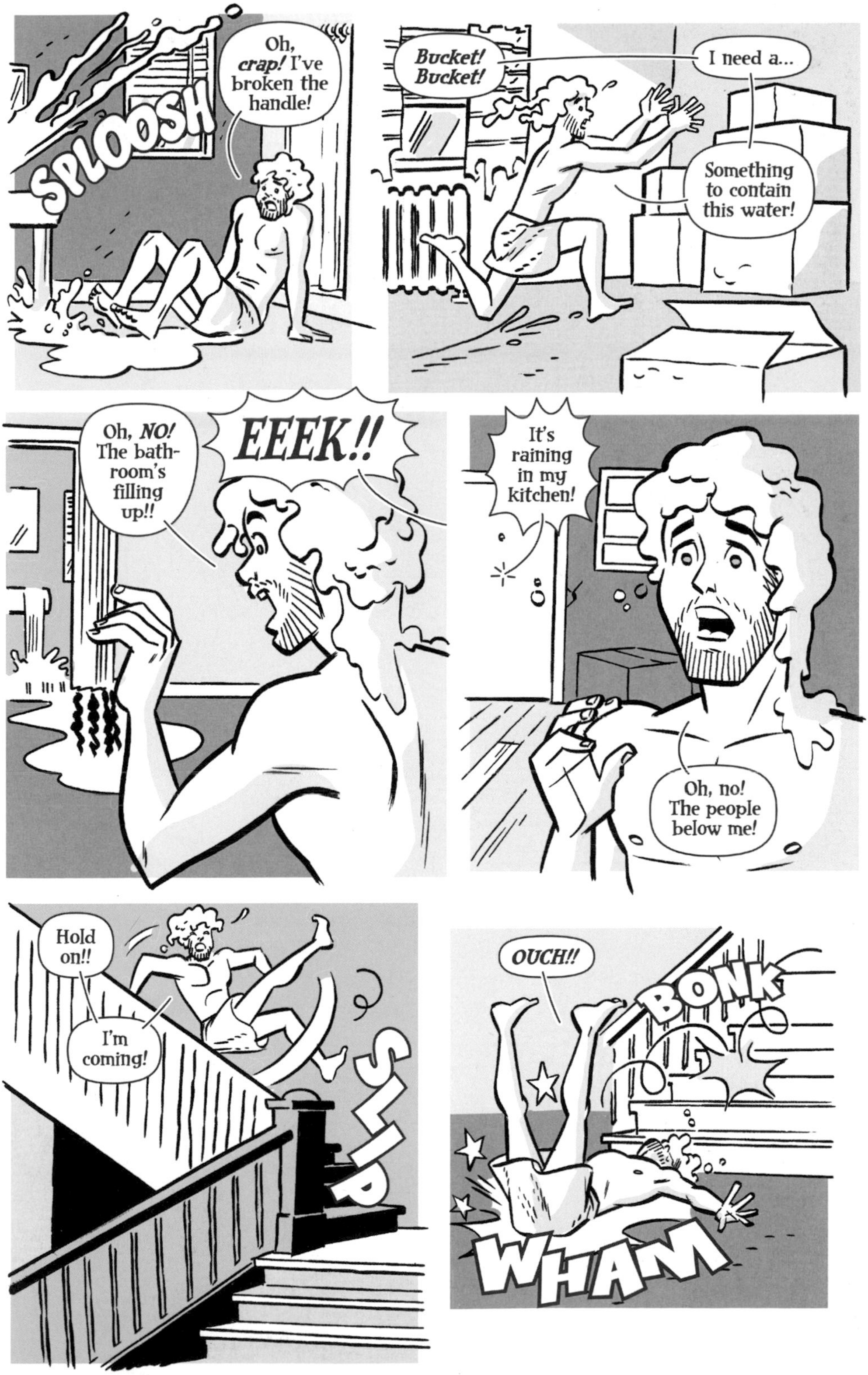
SPLOOSH
Oh, crap! I've broken the handle!
Bucket! Bucket!
I need a...
Something to contain this water!
Oh, NO! The bathroom's filling up!!
EEEK!!
It's raining in my kitchen!
Oh, no! The people below me!
Hold on!!
I'm coming!
SLIP
OUCH!!
BONK
WHAM

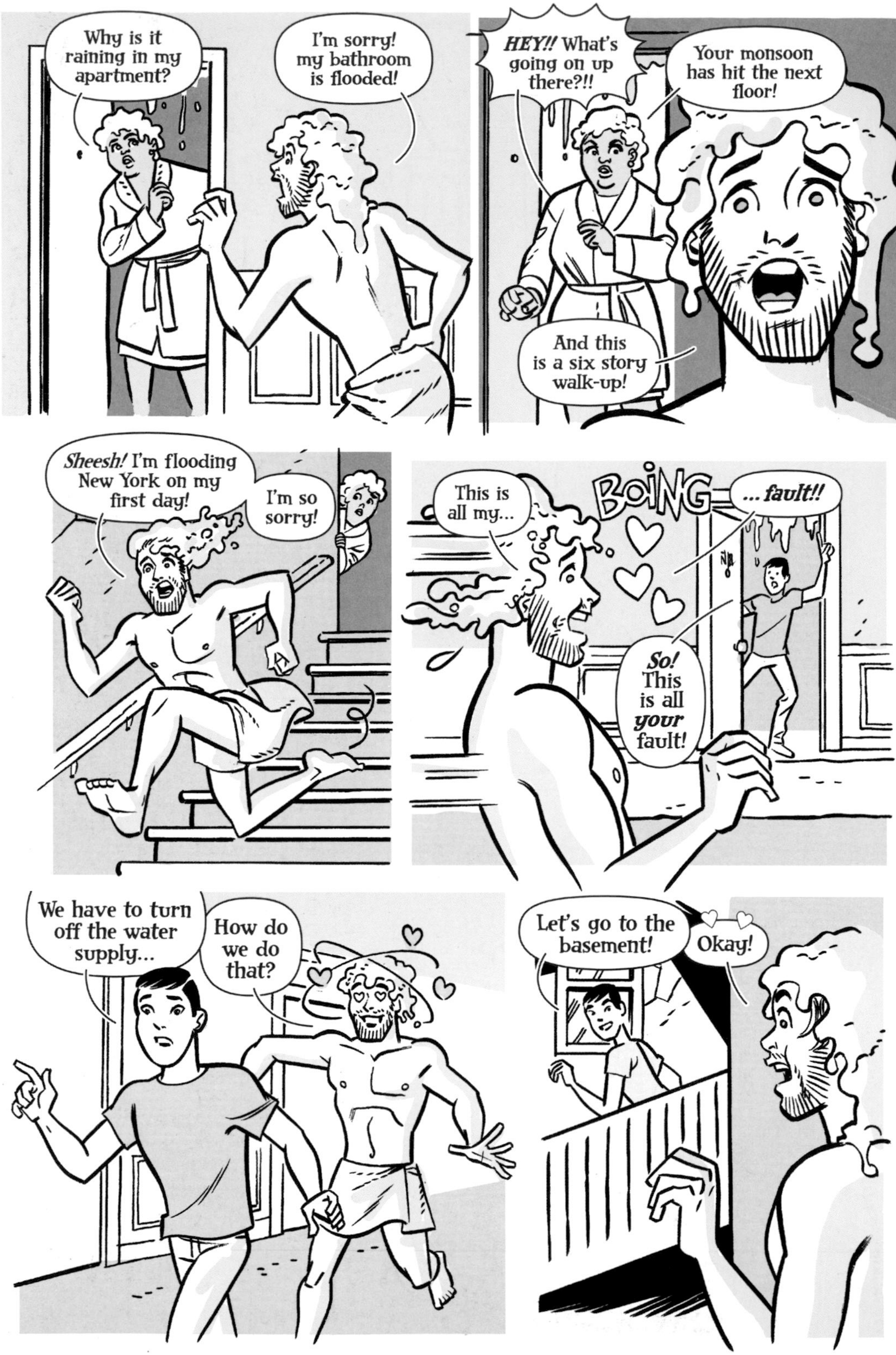
Why is it raining in my apartment?
I'm sorry! my bathroom is flooded!
HEY!! What's going on up there?!!
Your monsoon has hit the next floor!
And this is a six story walk-up!
Sheesh! I'm flooding New York on my first day!
I'm so sorry!
This is all my...
BOING
...fault!!
So! This is all your fault!
We have to turn off the water supply...
How do we do that?
Let's go to the basement!
Okay!

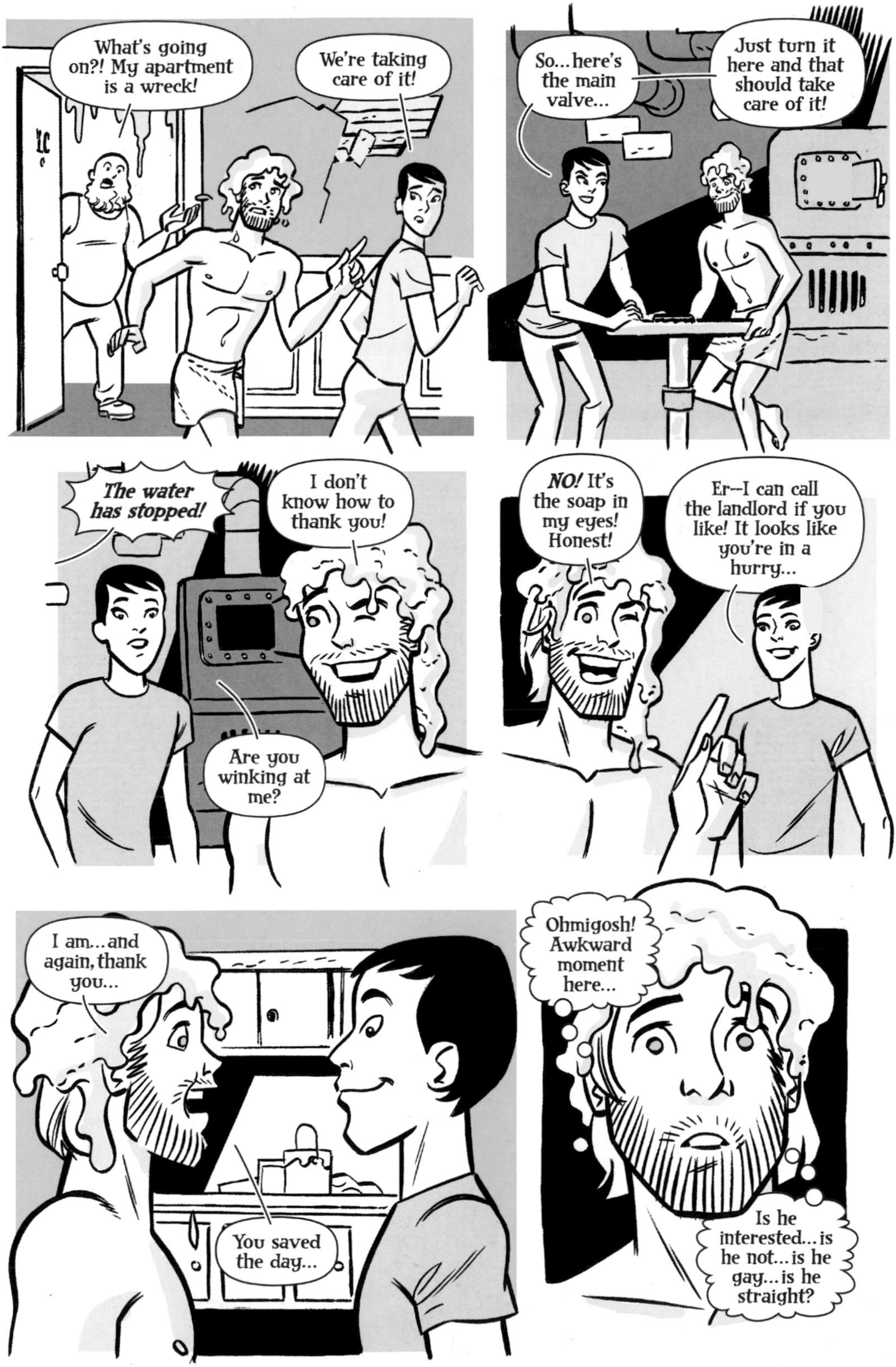
What's going on?! My apartment is a wreck!
We're taking care of it!
So...here's the main valve...
Just turn it here and that should take care of it!
The water has stopped!
I don't know how to thank you!
Are you winking at me?
NO! It's the soap in my eyes! Honest!
Er--I can call the landlord if you like! It looks like you're in a hurry...
I am...and again, thank you...
You saved the day...
Ohmigosh! Awkward moment here...
Is he interested...is he not...is he gay...is he straight?

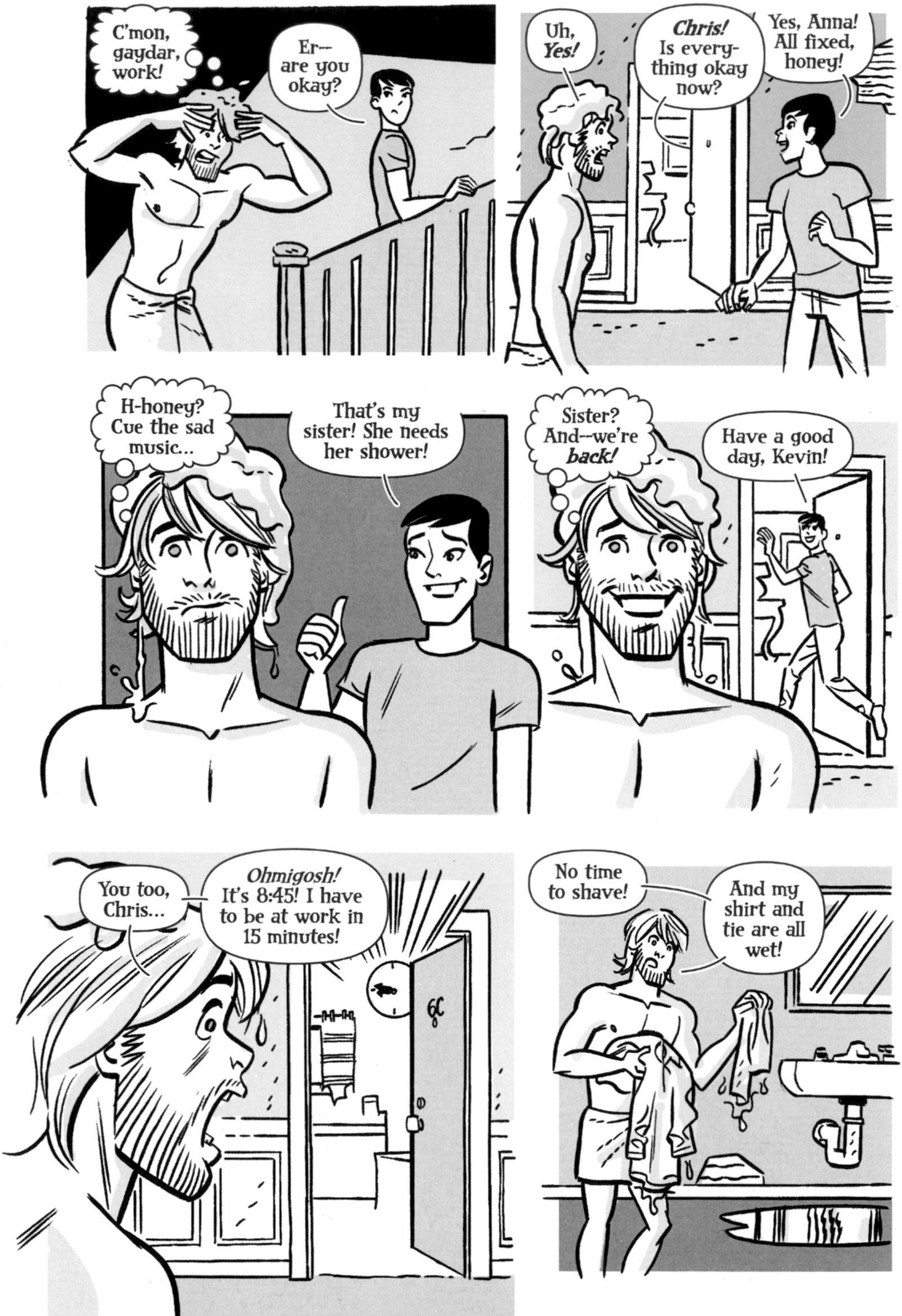
C'mon, gaydar, work!
Er-- are you okay?
Uh, *Yes!*
Chris! Is every-thing okay now?
Yes, Anna! All fixed, honey!
H-honey? Cue the sad music...
That's my sister! She needs her shower!
Sister? And--we're *back!*
Have a good day, Kevin!
You too, Chris...
Ohmigosh! It's 8:45! I have to be at work in 15 minutes!
6C
No time to shave!
And my shirt and tie are all wet!

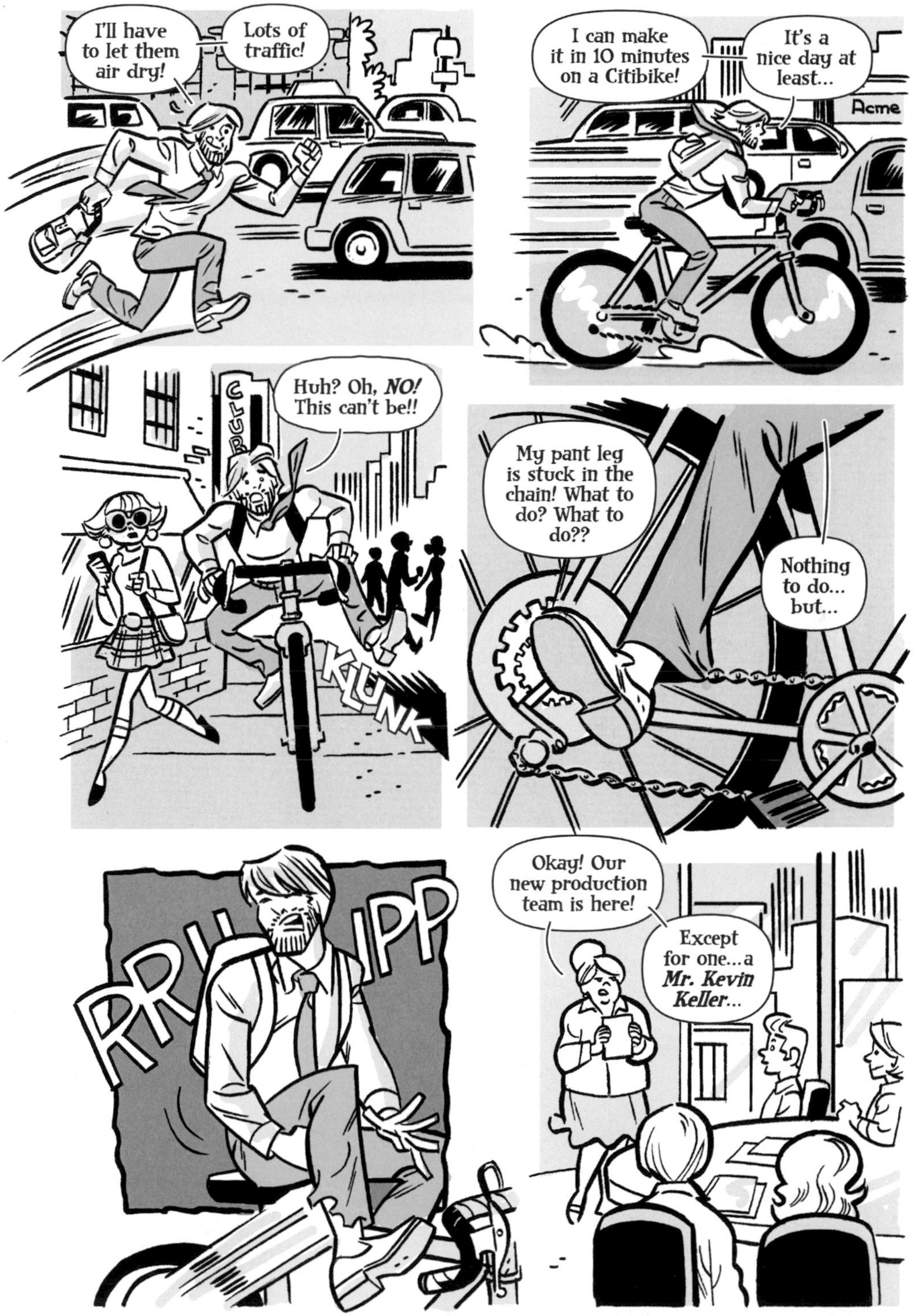
I'll have to let them air dry!
Lots of traffic!
I can make it in 10 minutes on a Citibike!
It's a nice day at least...
Acme
CLUB
Huh? Oh, *NO!* This can't be!!
KLUNK
My pant leg is stuck in the chain! What to do? What to do??
Nothing to do... but...
RRIPP
Okay! Our new production team is here!
Except for one...a *Mr. Kevin Keller*...

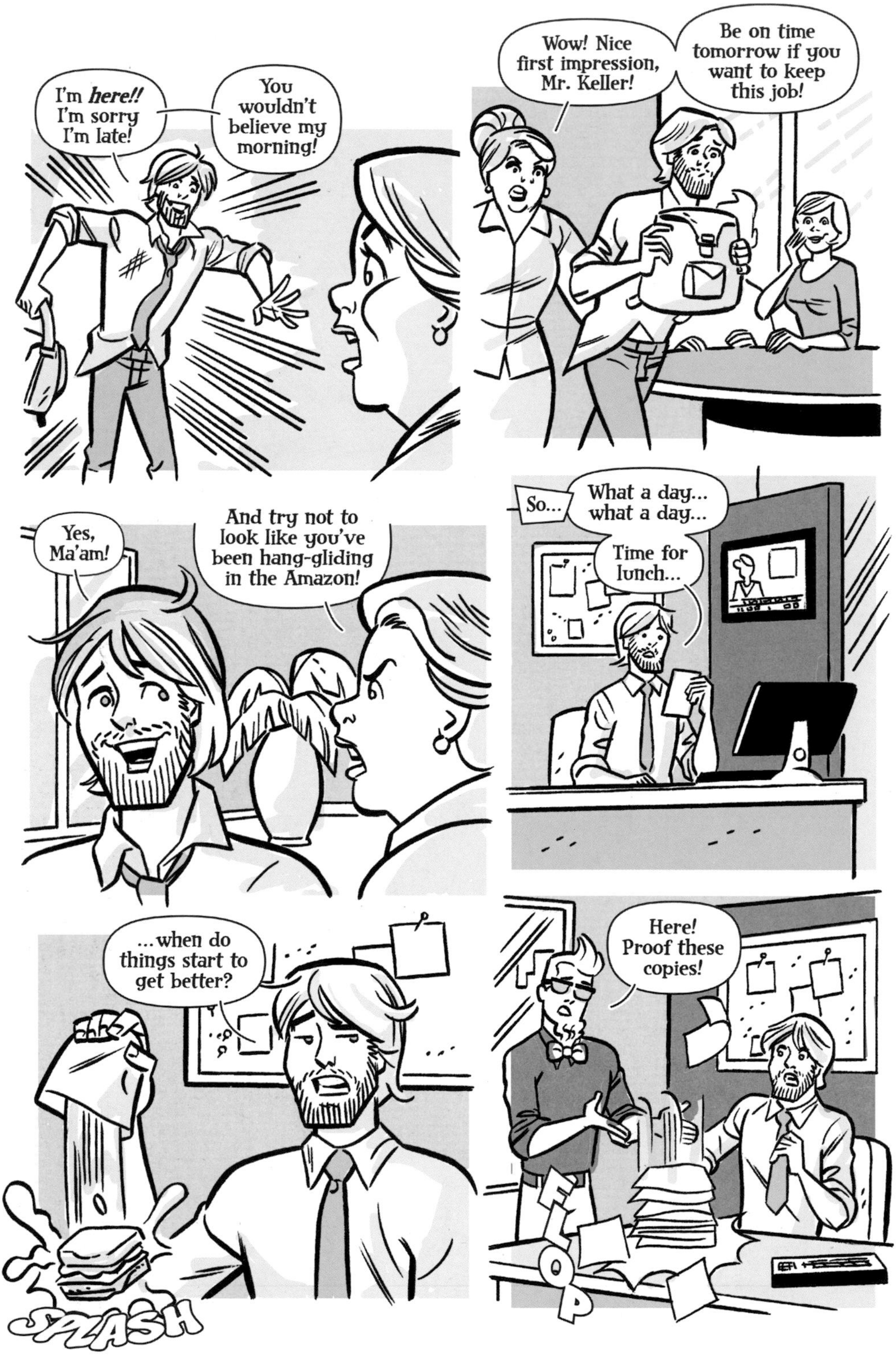

I'm *here!!* I'm sorry I'm late!
You wouldn't believe my morning!
Wow! Nice first impression, Mr. Keller!
Be on time tomorrow if you want to keep this job!
Yes, Ma'am!
And try not to look like you've been hang-gliding in the Amazon!
So...
What a day... what a day...
Time for lunch...
...when do things start to get better?
SPLASH
Here! Proof these copies!
FLOP

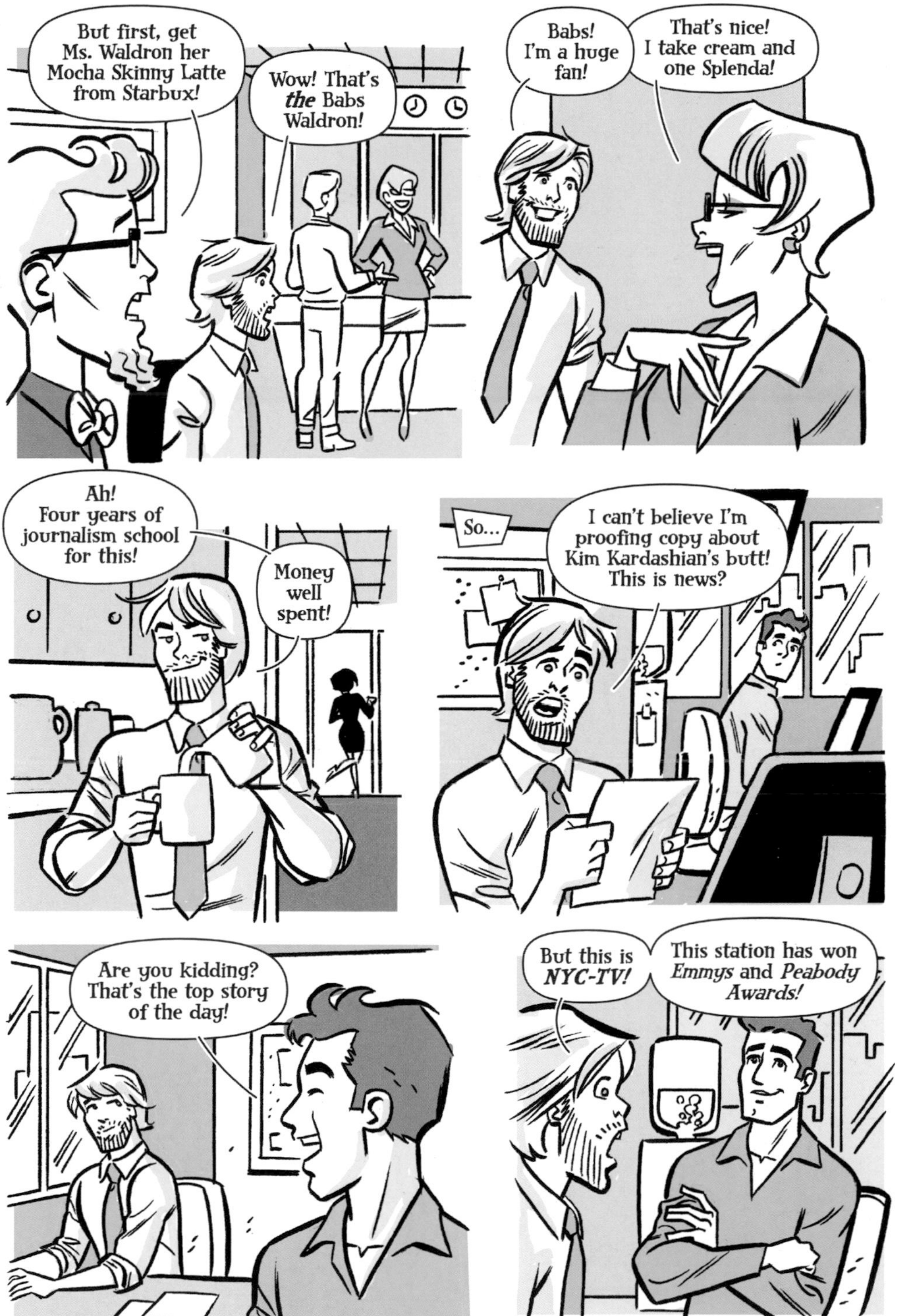
But first, get Ms. Waldron her Mocha Skinny Latte from Starbux!
Wow! That's *the* Babs Waldron!
Babs! I'm a huge fan!
That's nice! I take cream and one Splenda!
Ah! Four years of journalism school for this!
Money well spent!
So...
I can't believe I'm proofing copy about Kim Kardashian's butt! This is news?
Are you kidding? That's the top story of the day!
But this is ***NYC-TV!***
This station has won *Emmys* and *Peabody Awards!*

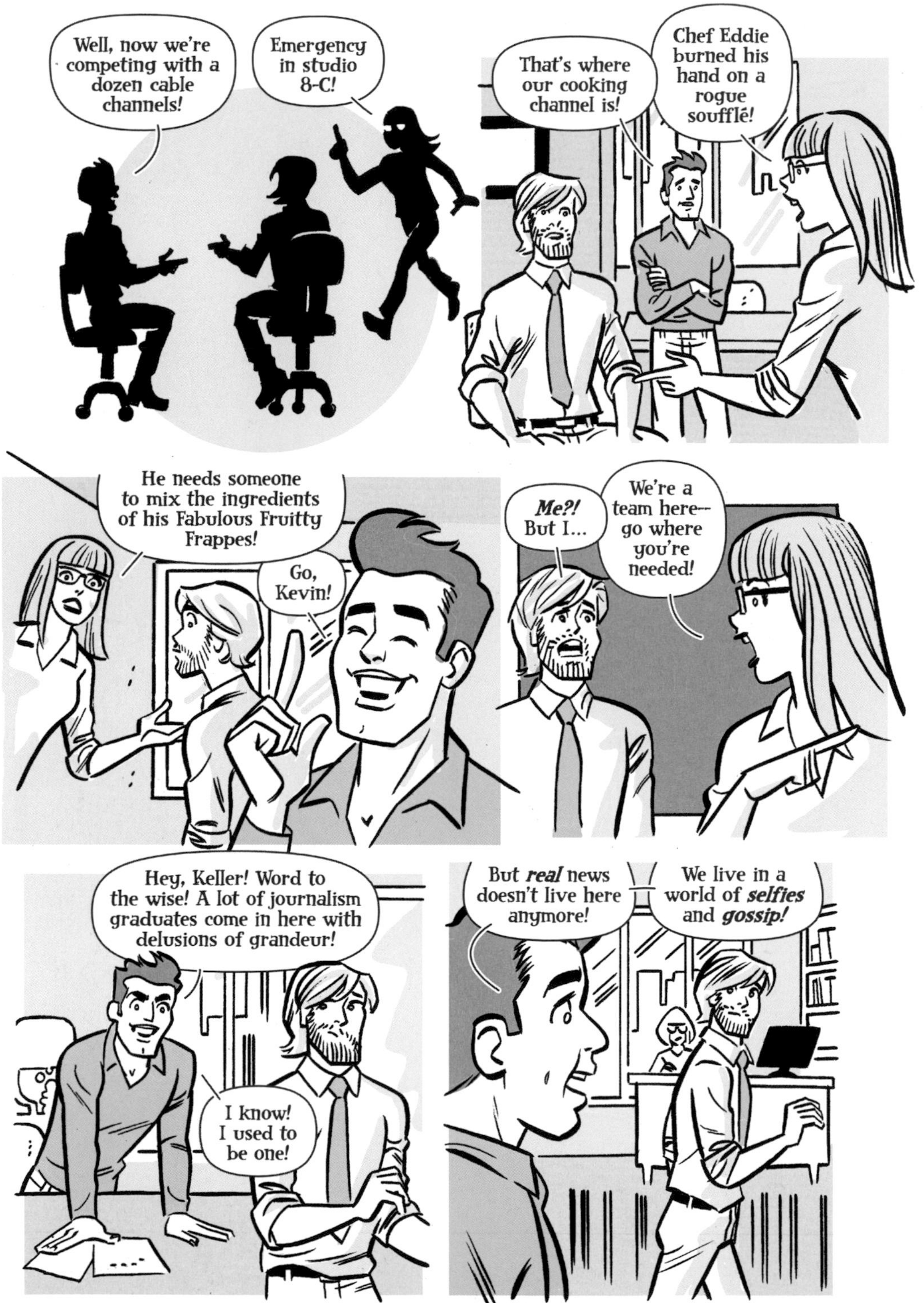
Well, now we're competing with a dozen cable channels!
Emergency in studio 8-C!
That's where our cooking channel is!
Chef Eddie burned his hand on a rogue soufflé!
He needs someone to mix the ingredients of his Fabulous Fruitty Frappes!
Go, Kevin!
Me?! But I...
We're a team here--go where you're needed!
Hey, Keller! Word to the wise! A lot of journalism graduates come in here with delusions of grandeur!
I know! I used to be one!
But real news doesn't live here anymore!
We live in a world of selfies and gossip!

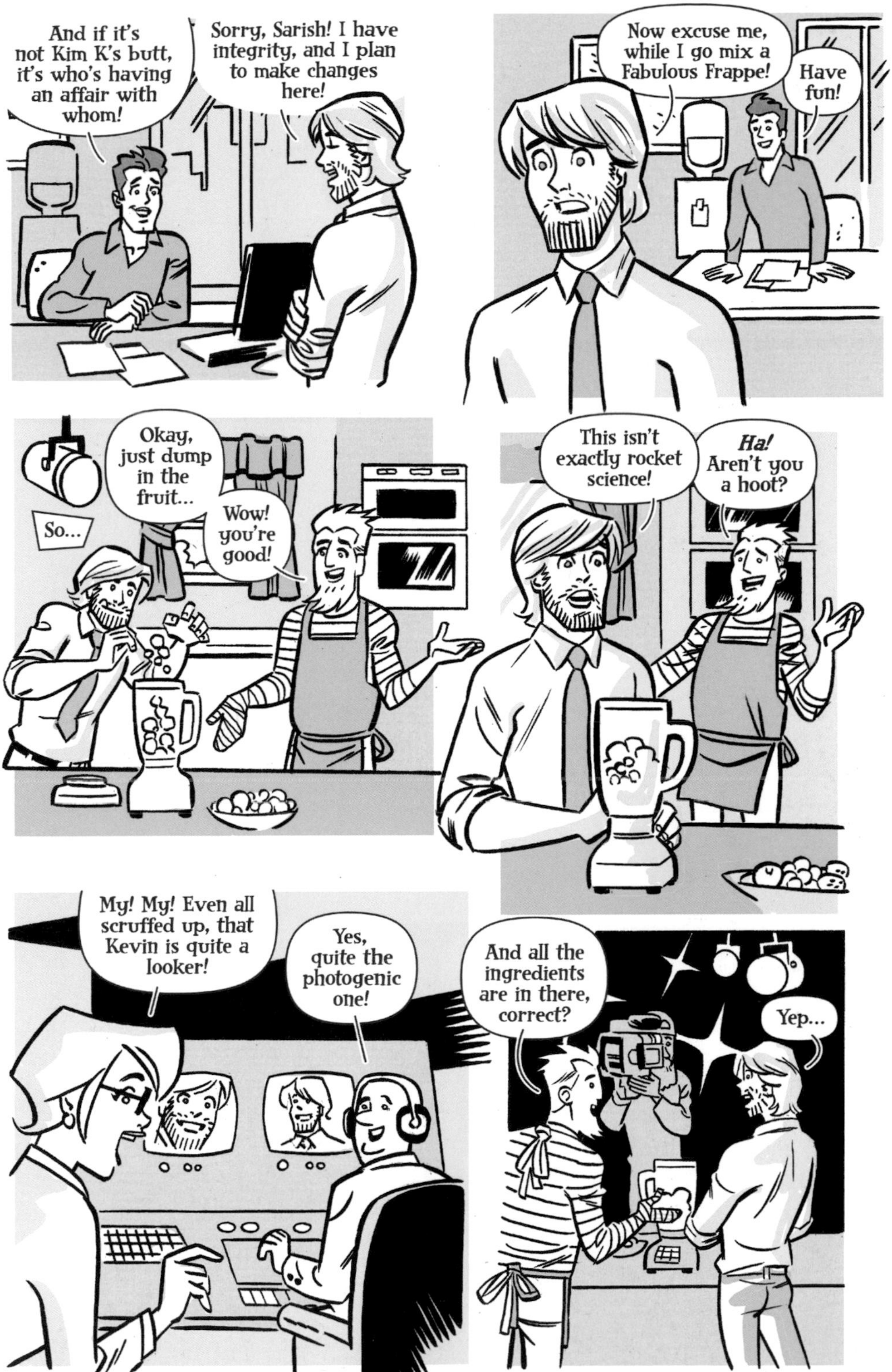
And if it's not Kim K's butt, it's who's having an affair with whom!
Sorry, Sarish! I have integrity, and I plan to make changes here!
Now excuse me, while I go mix a Fabulous Frappe!
Have fun!
So...
Okay, just dump in the fruit...
Wow! you're good!
This isn't exactly rocket science!
Ha! Aren't you a hoot?
My! My! Even all scruffed up, that Kevin is quite a looker!
Yes, quite the photogenic one!
And all the ingredients are in there, correct?
Yep...

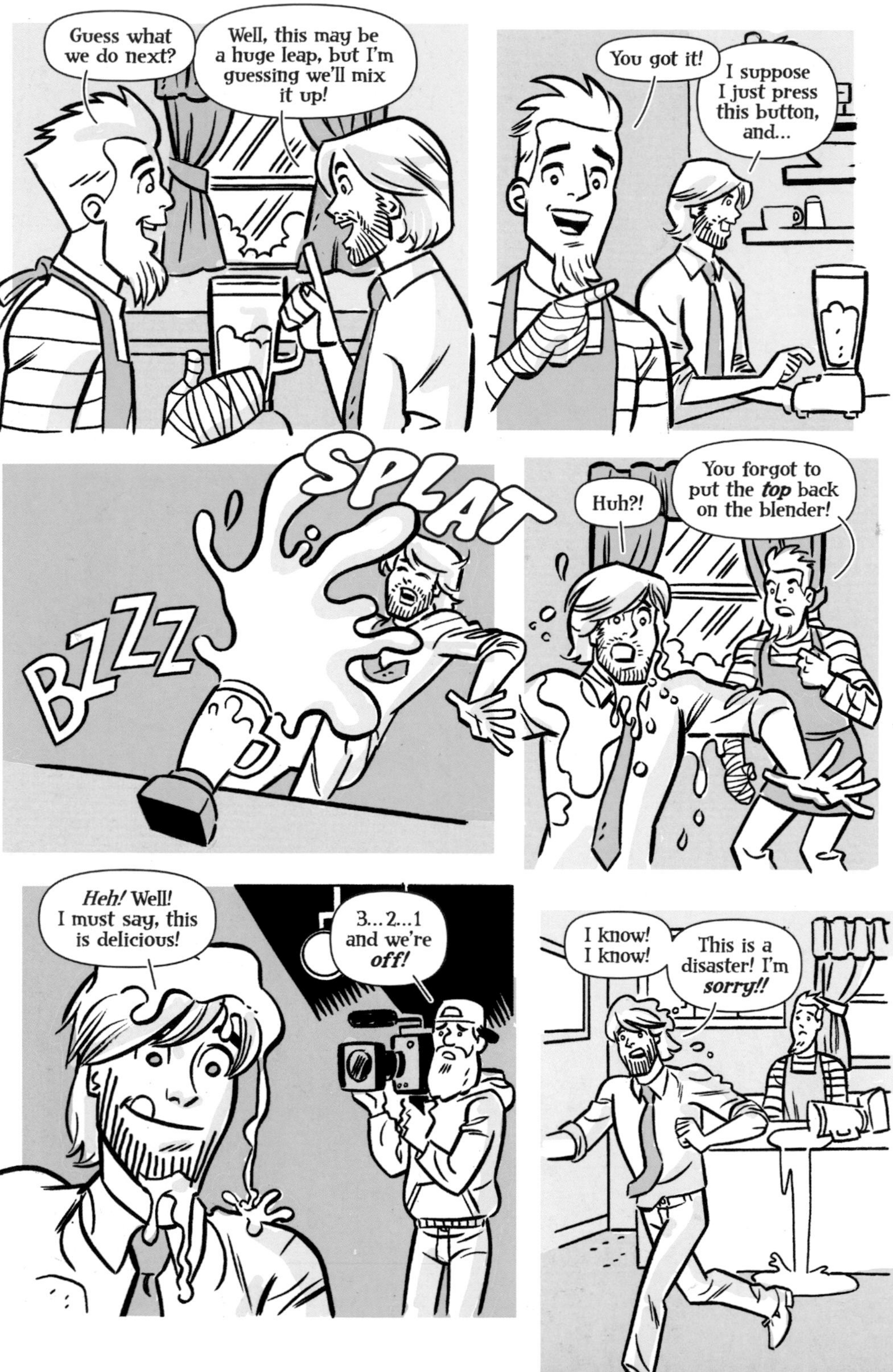
Guess what we do next?
Well, this may be a huge leap, but I'm guessing we'll mix it up!
You got it!
I suppose I just press this button, and...
SPLAT
BZZZ
Huh?!
You forgot to put the *top* back on the blender!
Heh! Well! I must say, this is delicious!
3...2...1 and we're ***off!***
I know! I know!
This is a disaster! I'm ***sorry!!***

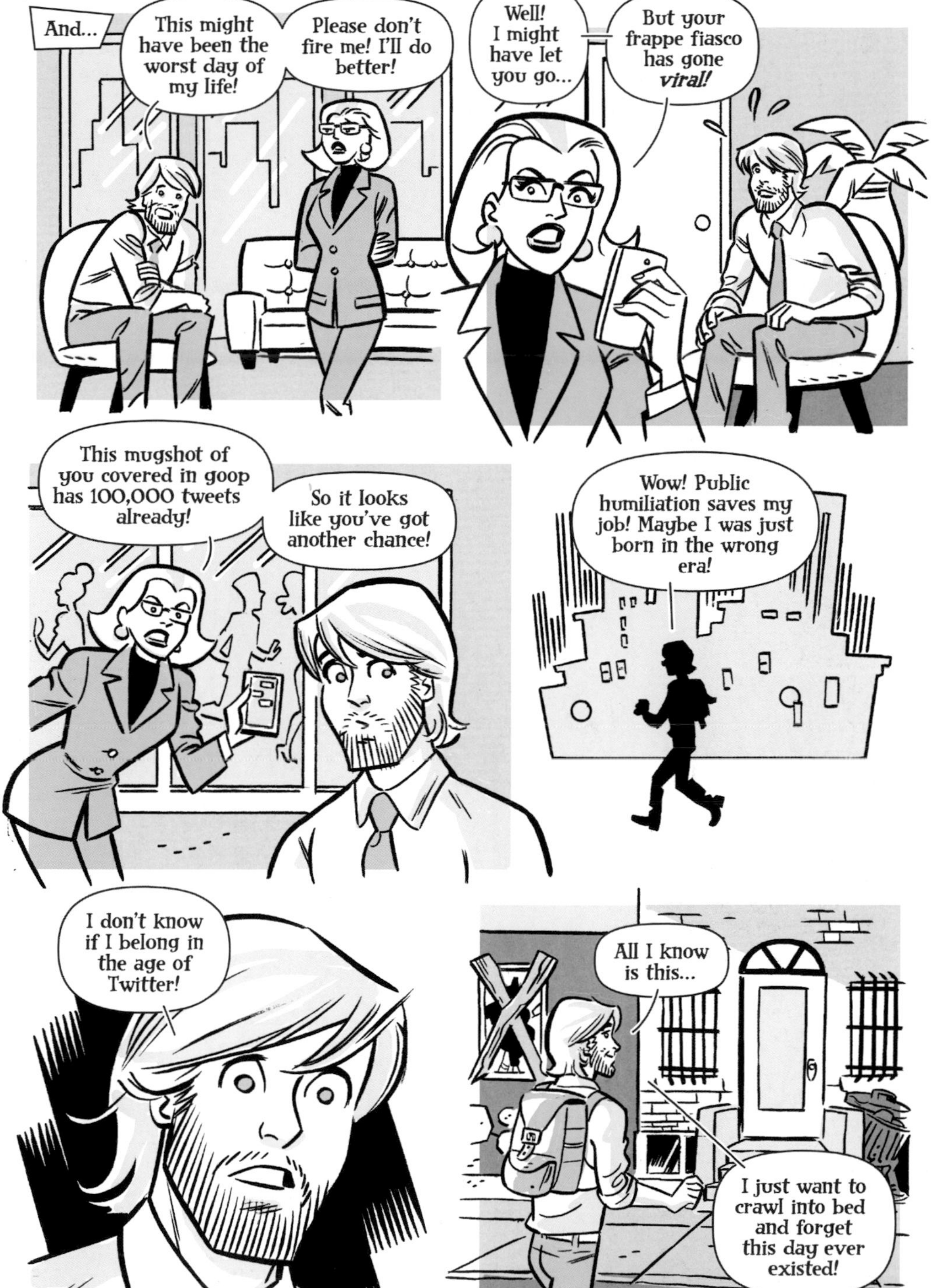
And...
This might have been the worst day of my life!
Please don't fire me! I'll do better!
Well! I might have let you go...
But your frappe fiasco has gone *viral!*
This mugshot of you covered in goop has 100,000 tweets already!
So it looks like you've got another chance!
Wow! Public humiliation saves my job! Maybe I was just born in the wrong era!
I don't know if I belong in the age of Twitter!
All I know is this...
I just want to crawl into bed and forget this day ever existed!

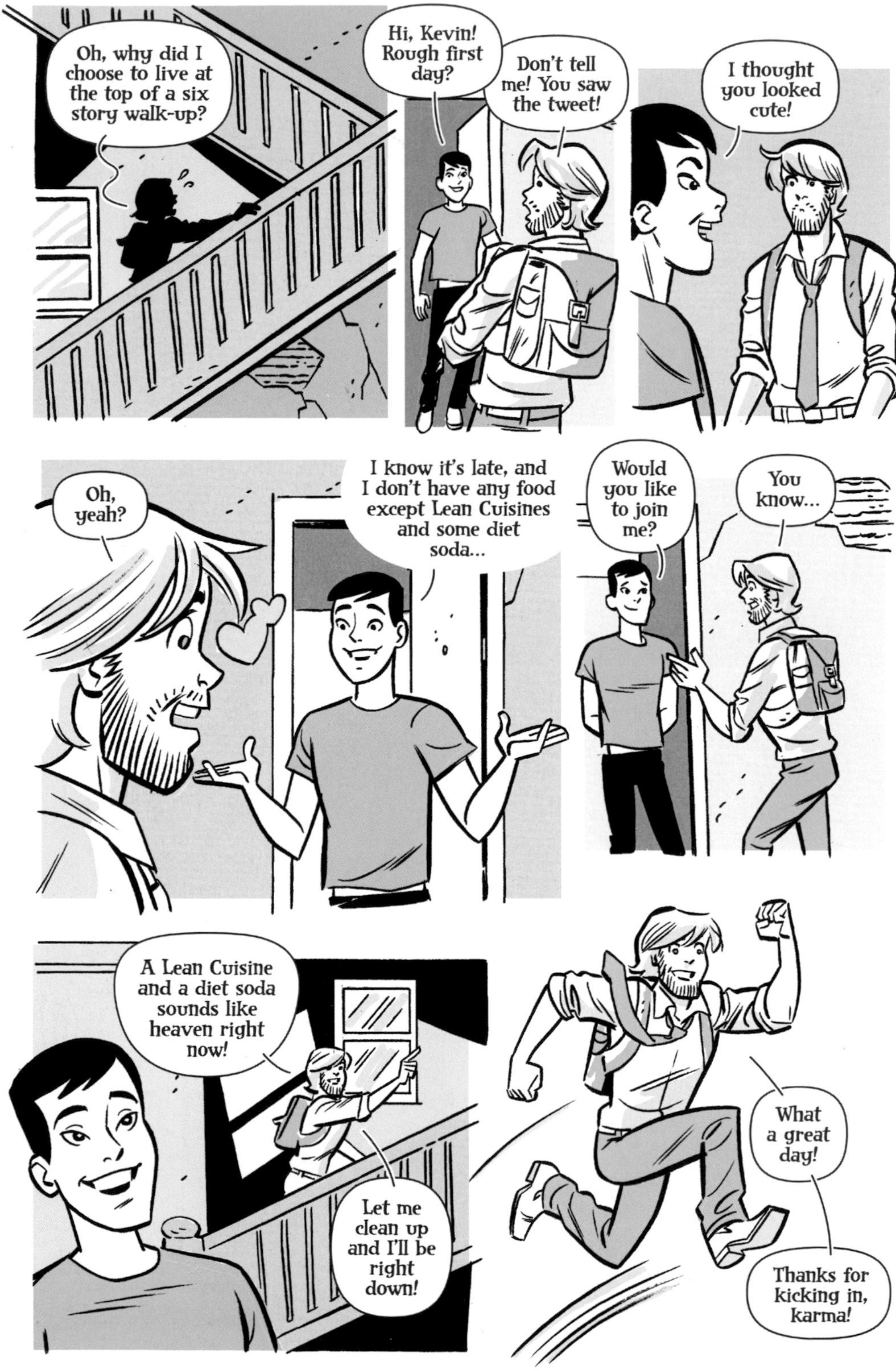

Oh, why did I choose to live at the top of a six story walk-up?
Hi, Kevin! Rough first day?
Don't tell me! You saw the tweet!
I thought you looked cute!
Oh, yeah?
I know it's late, and I don't have any food except Lean Cuisines and some diet soda...
Would you like to join me?
You know...
A Lean Cuisine and a diet soda sounds like heaven right now!
Let me clean up and I'll be right down!
What a great day!
Thanks for kicking in, karma!

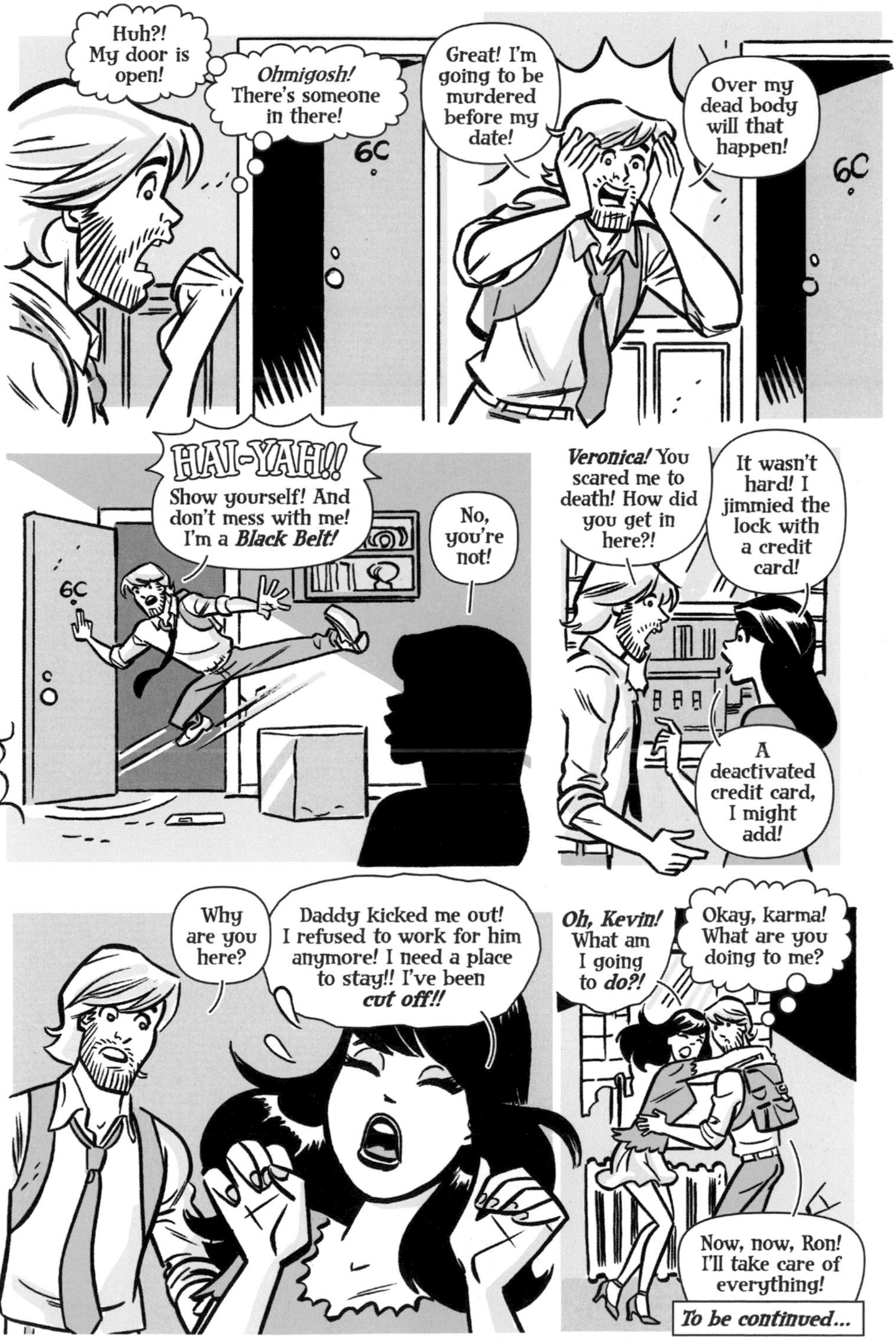
Huh?! My door is open!
Ohmigosh! There's someone in there!
6C
Great! I'm going to be murdered before my date!
Over my dead body will that happen!
6C
HAI-YAH!!
Show yourself! And don't mess with me! I'm a Black Belt!
6C
No, you're not!
Veronica! You scared me to death! How did you get in here?!
It wasn't hard! I jimmied the lock with a credit card!
A deactivated credit card, I might add!
Why are you here?
Daddy kicked me out! I refused to work for him anymore! I need a place to stay!! I've been cut off!!
Oh, Kevin! What am I going to do?!
Okay, karma! What are you doing to me?
Now, now, Ron! I'll take care of everything!
To be continued...

CHAPTER 2

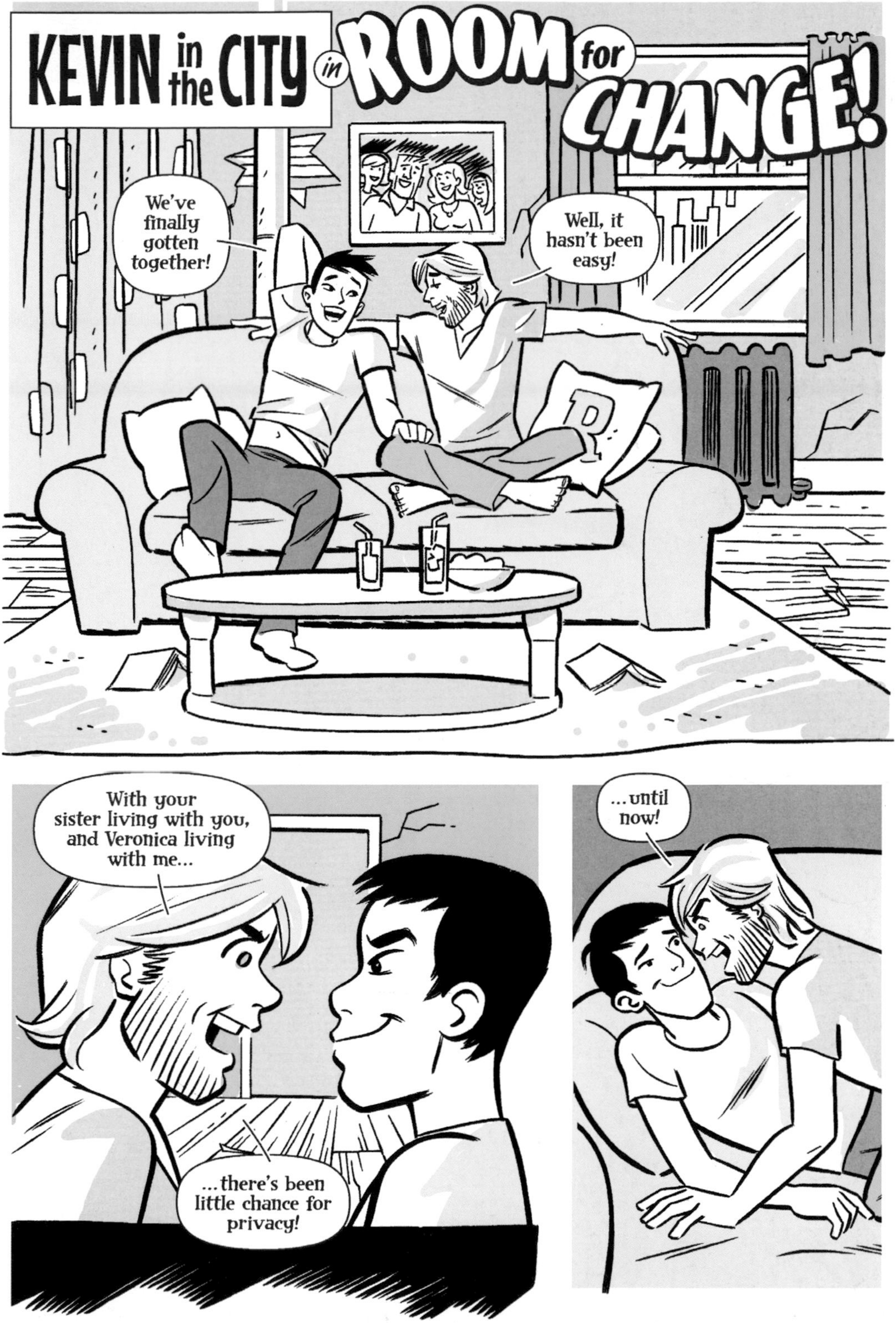

KEVIN in the CITY in ROOM for CHANGE!
We've finally gotten together!
Well, it hasn't been easy!
With your sister living with you, and Veronica living with me...
...there's been little chance for privacy!
...until now!

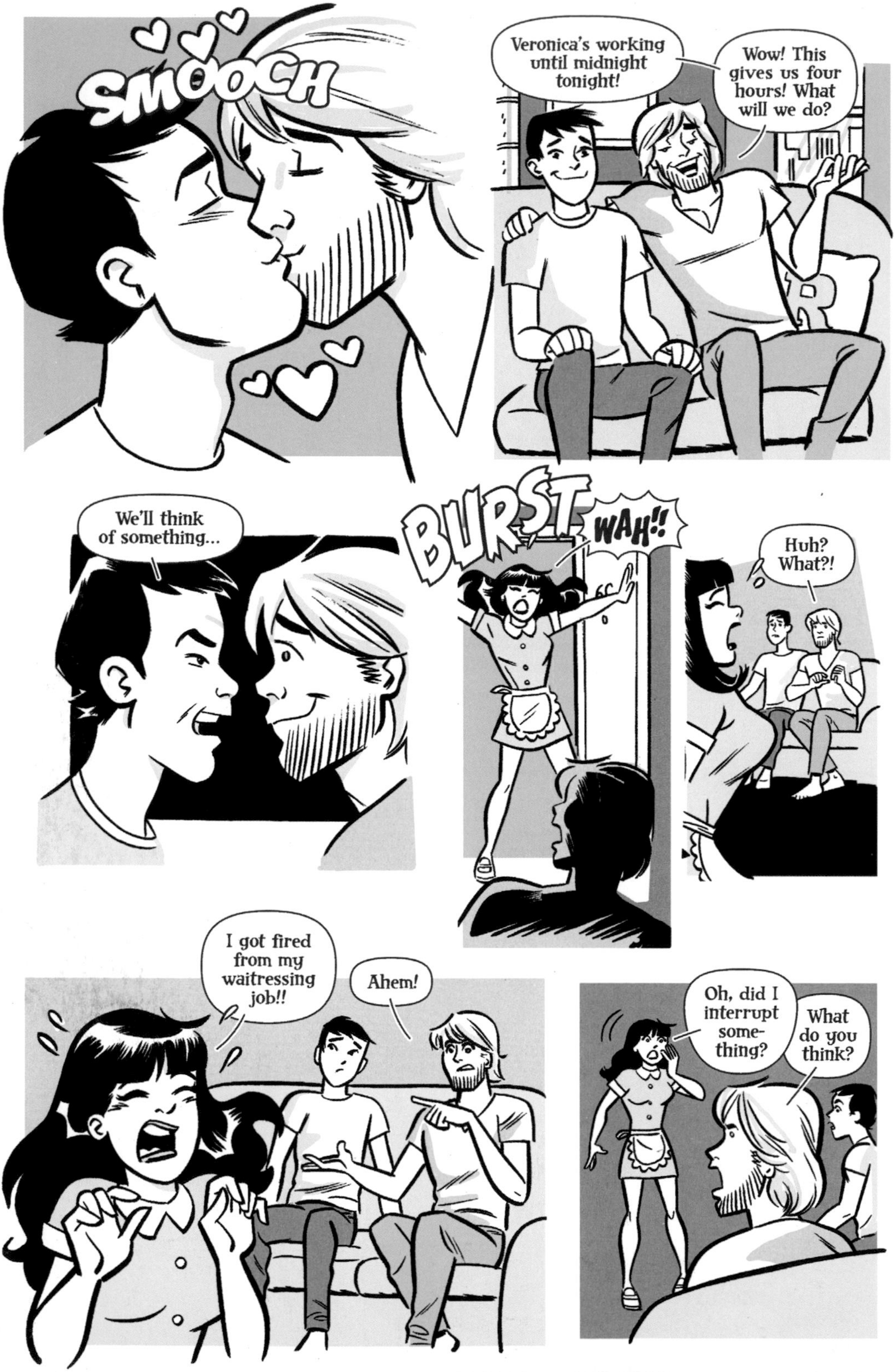
SMOOCH
Veronica's working until midnight tonight!
Wow! This gives us four hours! What will we do?
We'll think of something...
BURST
WAH!!
Huh? What?!
I got fired from my waitressing job!!
Ahem!
Oh, did I interrupt some-thing?
What do you think?

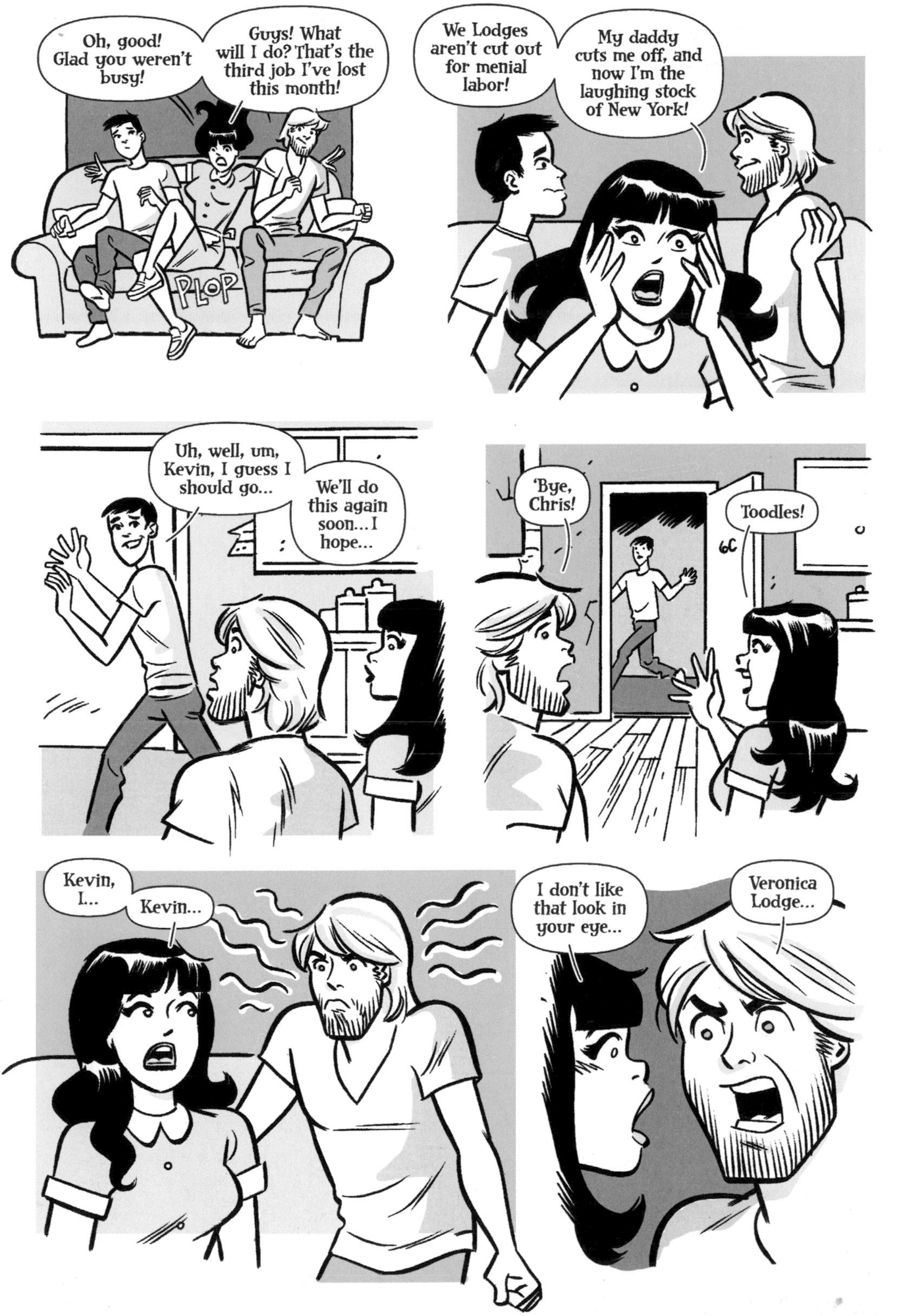
Oh, good! Glad you weren't busy!
Guys! What will I do? That's the third job I've lost this month!
PLOP
We Lodges aren't cut out for menial labor!
My daddy cuts me off, and now I'm the laughing stock of New York!
Uh, well, um, Kevin, I guess I should go...
We'll do this again soon... I hope...
'Bye, Chris!
Toodles!
6C
Kevin, I...
Kevin...
I don't like that look in your eye...
Veronica Lodge...

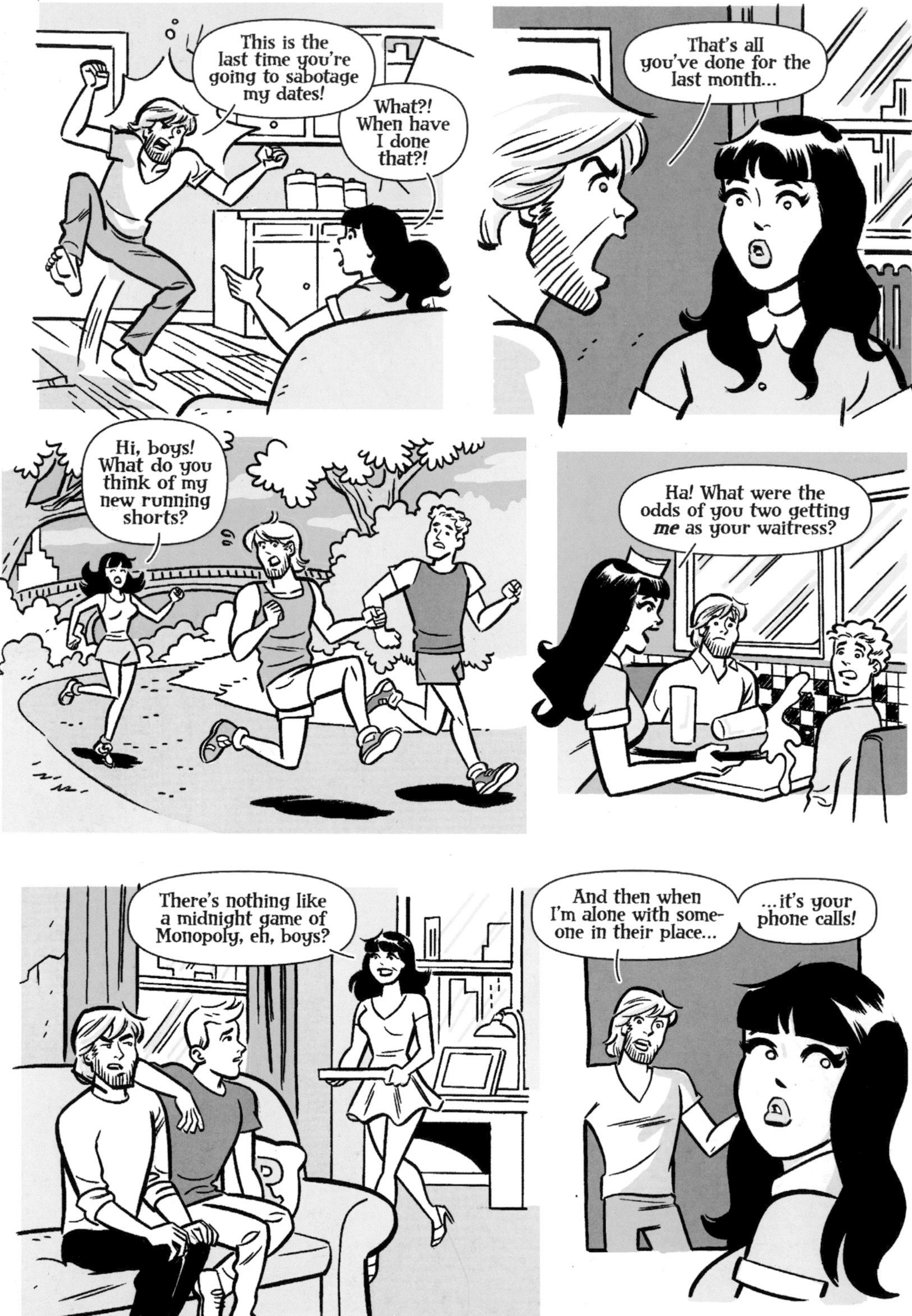
This is the last time you're going to sabotage my dates!
What?! When have I done that?!
That's all you've done for the last month...
Hi, boys! What do you think of my new running shorts?
Ha! What were the odds of you two getting *me* as your waitress?
There's nothing like a midnight game of Monopoly, eh, boys?
And then when I'm alone with some-one in their place...
...it's your phone calls!

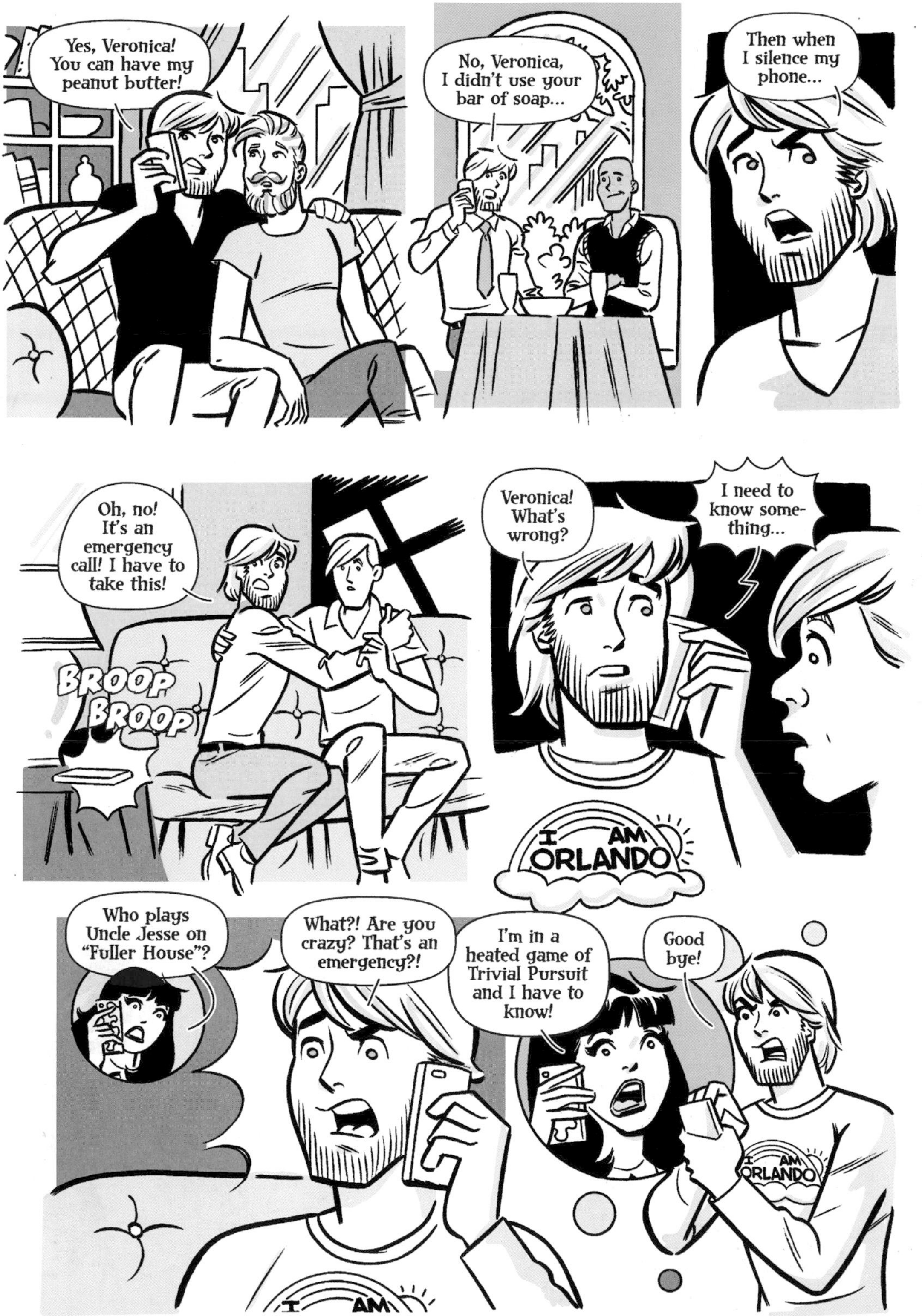
Yes, Veronica! You can have my peanut butter!
No, Veronica, I didn't use your bar of soap...
Then when I silence my phone...
Oh, no! It's an emergency call! I have to take this!
BROOP BROOP
Veronica! What's wrong?
I need to know some-thing...
I AM ORLANDO
Who plays Uncle Jesse on "Fuller House"?
What?! Are you crazy? That's an emergency?!
I'm in a heated game of Trivial Pursuit and I have to know!
Good bye!
I AM ORLANDO
I AM

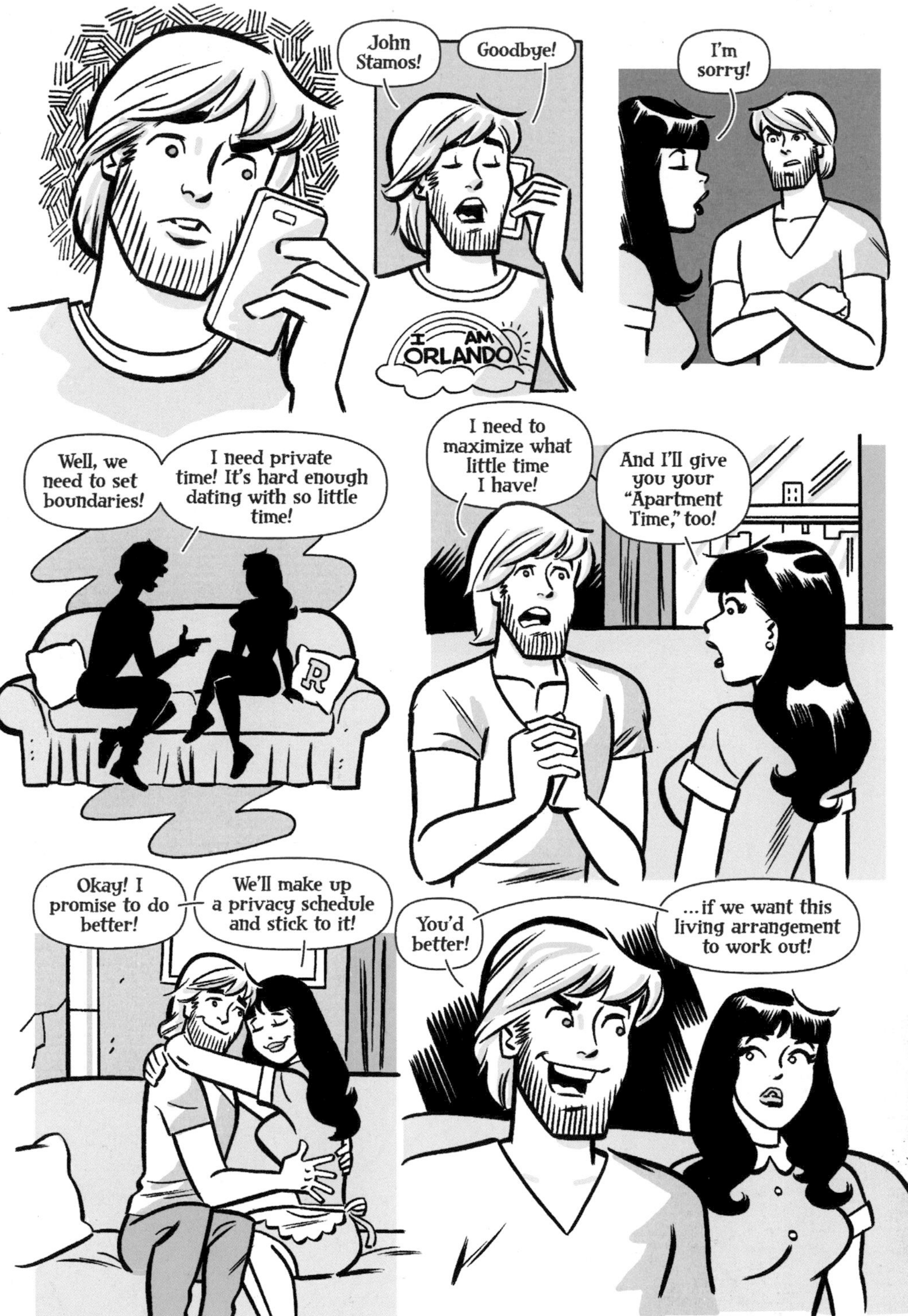
John Stamos!
Goodbye!
I AM ORLANDO
I'm sorry!
Well, we need to set boundaries!
I need private time! It's hard enough dating with so little time!
R
I need to maximize what little time I have!
And I'll give you your "Apartment Time," too!
Okay! I promise to do better!
We'll make up a privacy schedule and stick to it!
You'd better!
...if we want this living arrangement to work out!

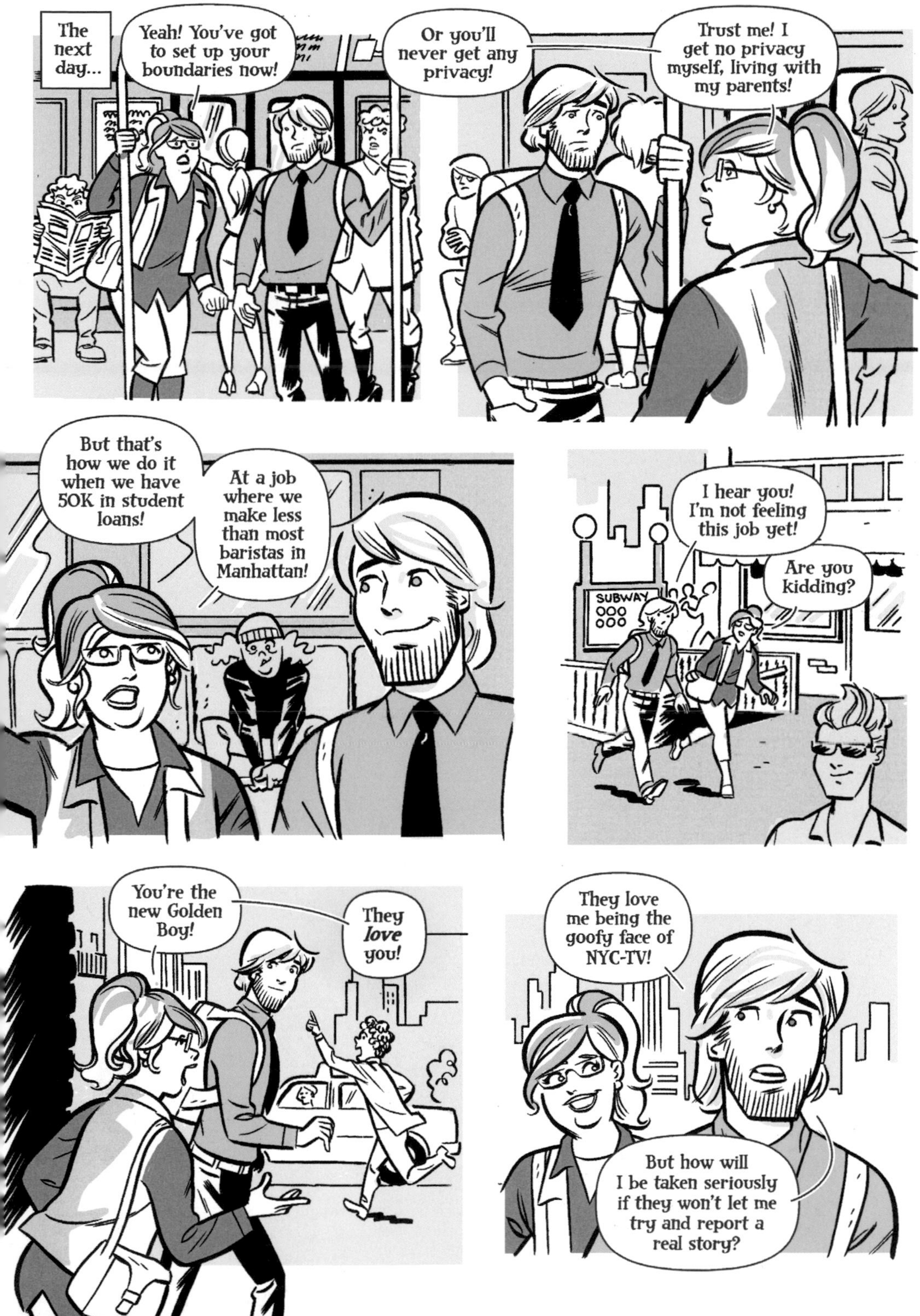
The next day...
Yeah! You've got to set up your boundaries now!
Or you'll never get any privacy!
Trust me! I get no privacy myself, living with my parents!
But that's how we do it when we have 50K in student loans!
At a job where we make less than most baristas in Manhattan!
I hear you! I'm not feeling this job yet!
Are you kidding?
SUBWAY
You're the new Golden Boy!
They *love* you!
They love me being the goofy face of NYC-TV!
But how will I be taken seriously if they won't let me try and report a real story?

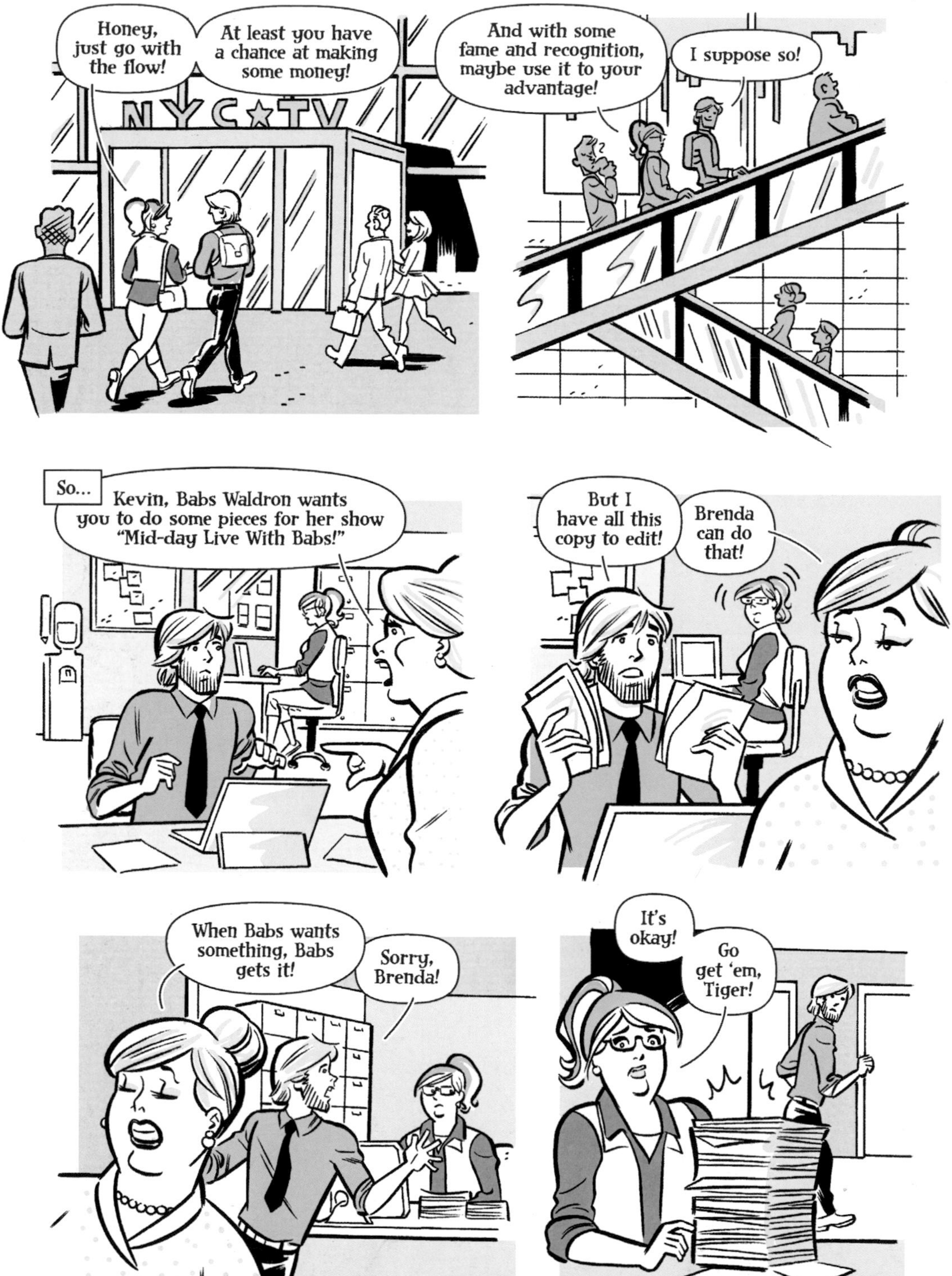
Honey, just go with the flow!
At least you have a chance at making some money!
And with some fame and recognition, maybe use it to your advantage!
I suppose so!
NYC★TV
So...
Kevin, Babs Waldron wants you to do some pieces for her show "Mid-day Live With Babs!"
But I have all this copy to edit!
Brenda can do that!
When Babs wants something, Babs gets it!
Sorry, Brenda!
It's okay!
Go get 'em, Tiger!

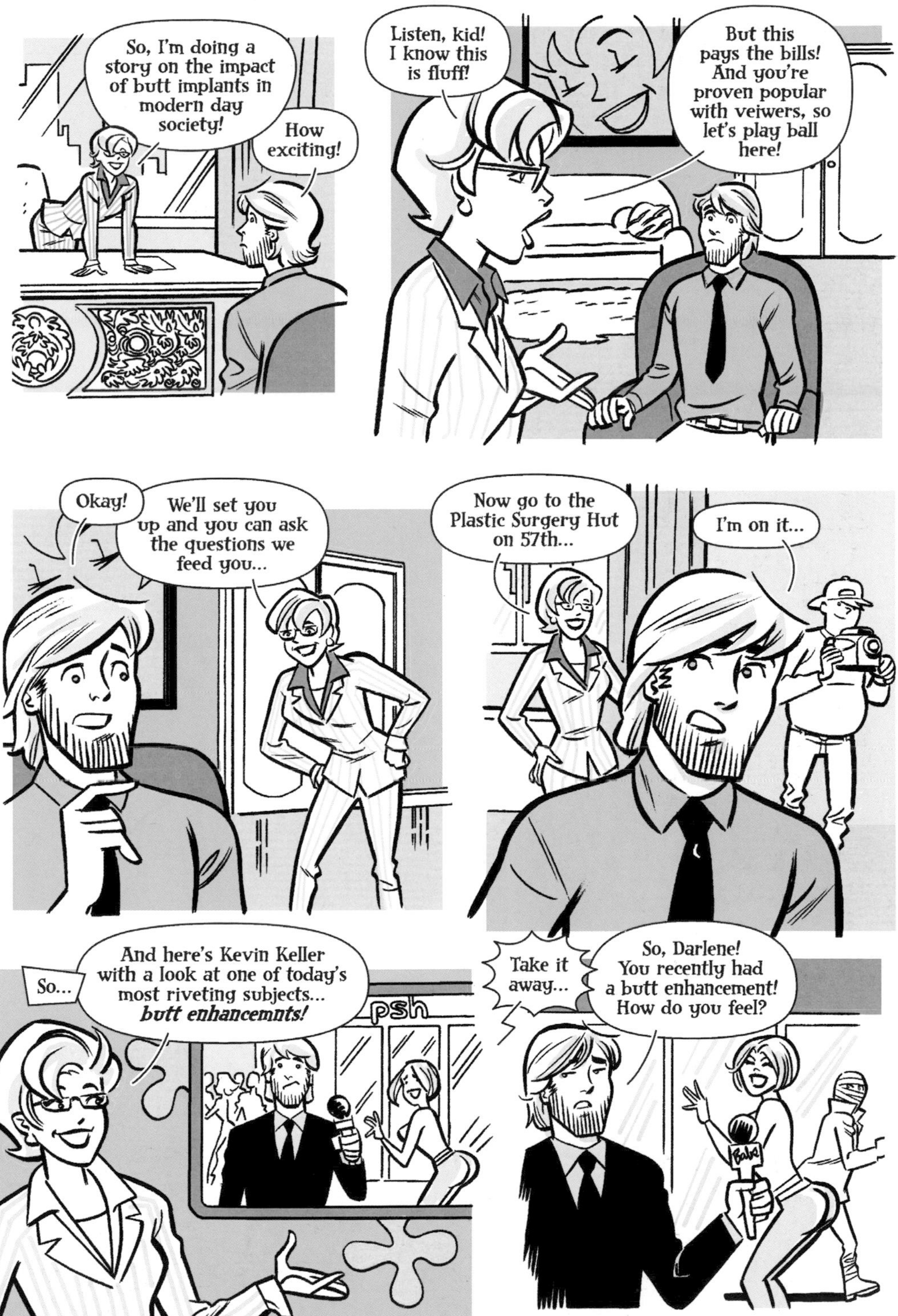

So, I'm doing a story on the impact of butt implants in modern day society!
How exciting!
Listen, kid! I know this is fluff!
But this pays the bills! And you're proven popular with veiwers, so let's play ball here!
Okay!
We'll set you up and you can ask the questions we feed you...
Now go to the Plastic Surgery Hut on 57th...
I'm on it...
So...
And here's Kevin Keller with a look at one of today's most riveting subjects... *butt enhancemnts!*
psh
Take it away...
So, Darlene! You recently had a butt enhancement! How do you feel?

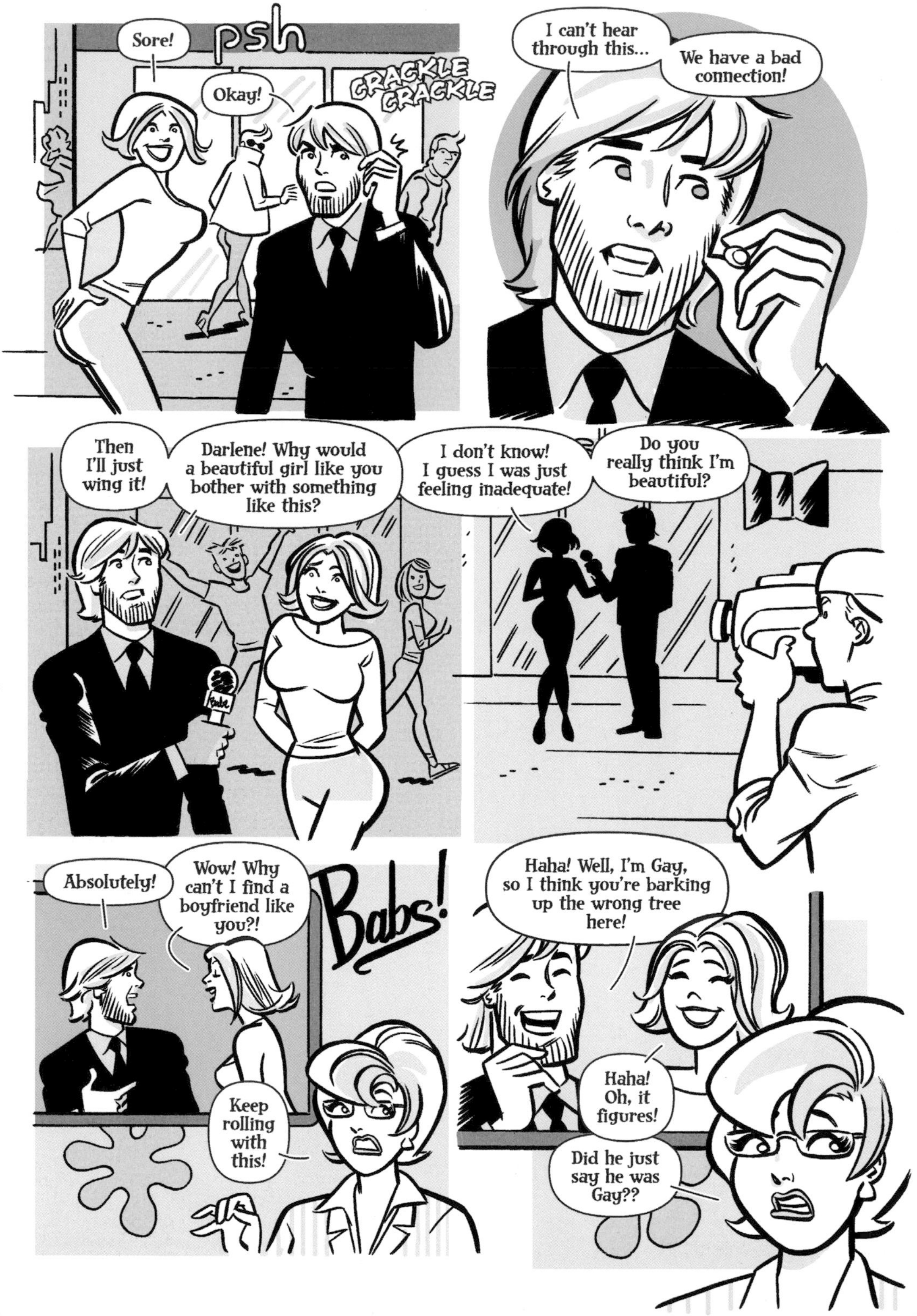
psh
Sore!
Okay!
CRACKLE CRACKLE
I can't hear through this...
We have a bad connection!
Then I'll just wing it!
Darlene! Why would a beautiful girl like you bother with something like this?
I don't know! I guess I was just feeling inadequate!
Do you really think I'm beautiful?
Babs
Absolutely!
Wow! Why can't I find a boyfriend like you?!
Babs!
Keep rolling with this!
Haha! Well, I'm Gay, so I think you're barking up the wrong tree here!
Haha! Oh, it figures!
Did he just say he was Gay??

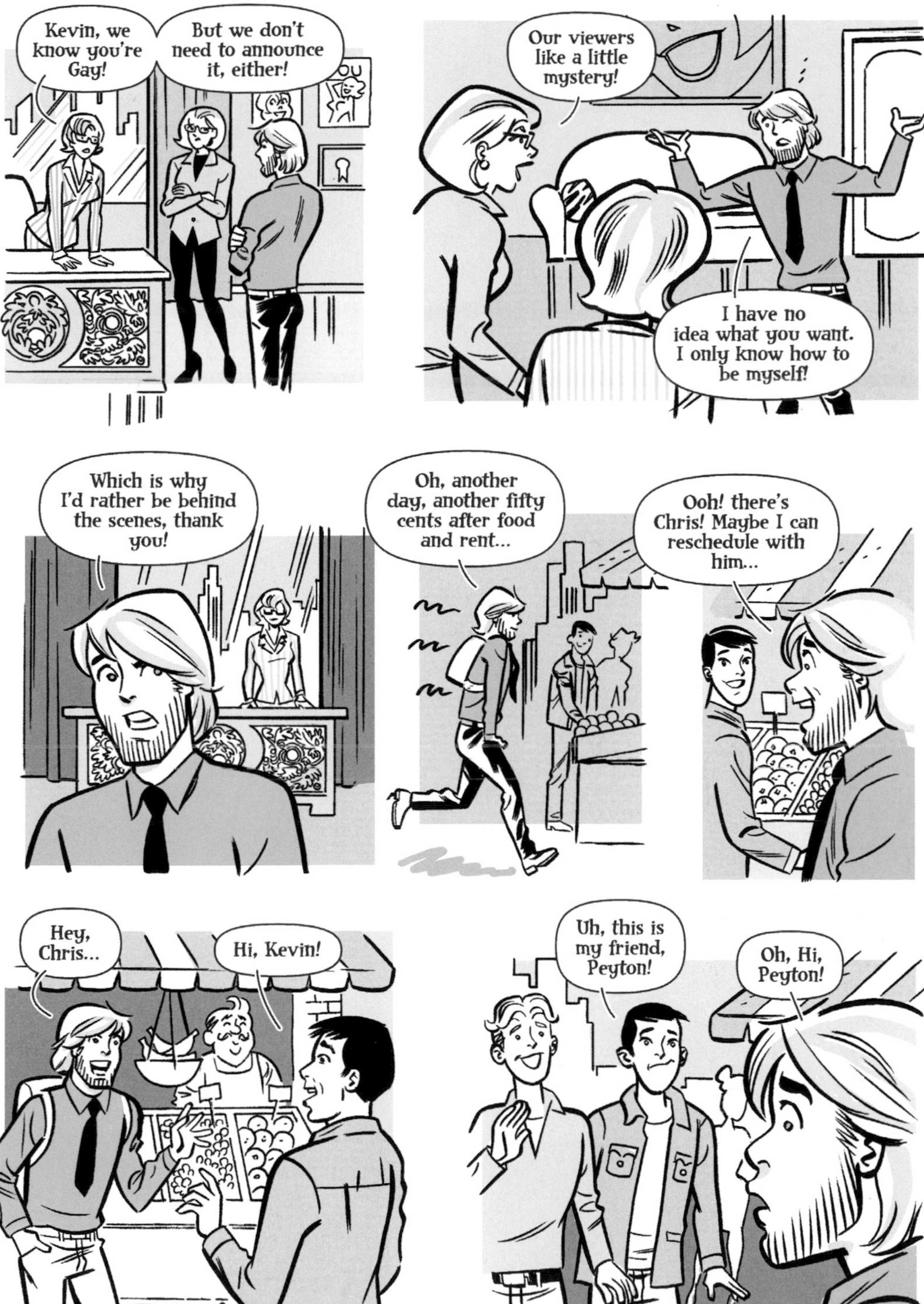
Kevin, we know you're Gay!
But we don't need to announce it, either!
Our viewers like a little mystery!
I have no idea what you want. I only know how to be myself!
Which is why I'd rather be behind the scenes, thank you!
Oh, another day, another fifty cents after food and rent...
Ooh! there's Chris! Maybe I can reschedule with him...
Hey, Chris...
Hi, Kevin!
Uh, this is my friend, Peyton!
Oh, Hi, Peyton!

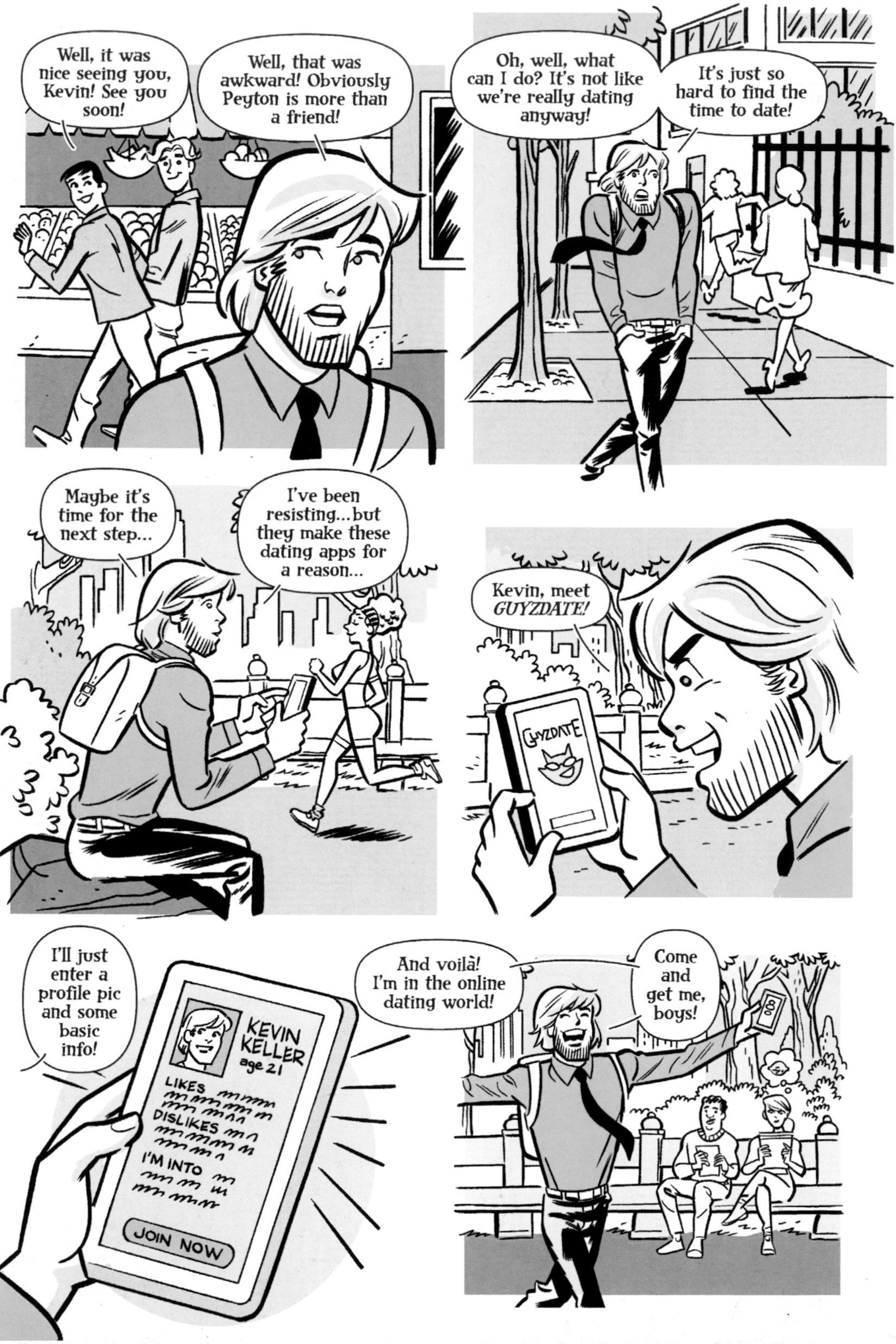
Well, it was nice seeing you, Kevin! See you soon!
Well, that was awkward! Obviously Peyton is more than a friend!
Oh, well, what can I do? It's not like we're really dating anyway!
It's just so hard to find the time to date!
Maybe it's time for the next step...
I've been resisting...but they make these dating apps for a reason...
Kevin, meet *GUYZDATE!*
GUYZDATE
I'll just enter a profile pic and some basic info!
KEVIN KELLER
age 21
LIKES
DISLIKES
I'M INTO
JOIN NOW
And voilà! I'm in the online dating world!
Come and get me, boys!

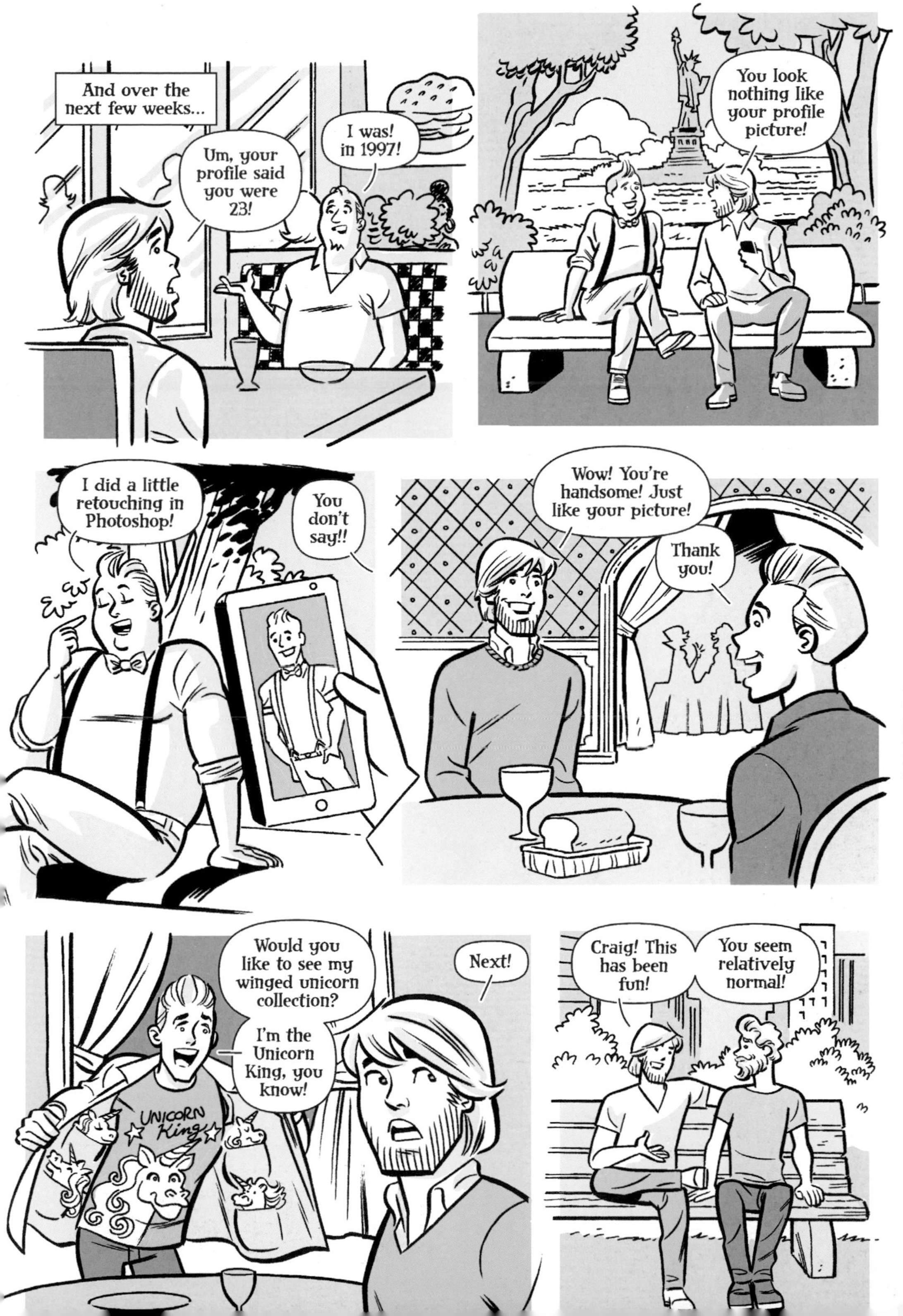
And over the next few weeks...
Um, your profile said you were 23!
I was! in 1997!
You look nothing like your profile picture!
I did a little retouching in Photoshop!
You don't say!!
Wow! You're handsome! Just like your picture!
Thank you!
Would you like to see my winged unicorn collection?
I'm the Unicorn King, you know!
UNICORN King
Next!
Craig! This has been fun!
You seem relatively normal!

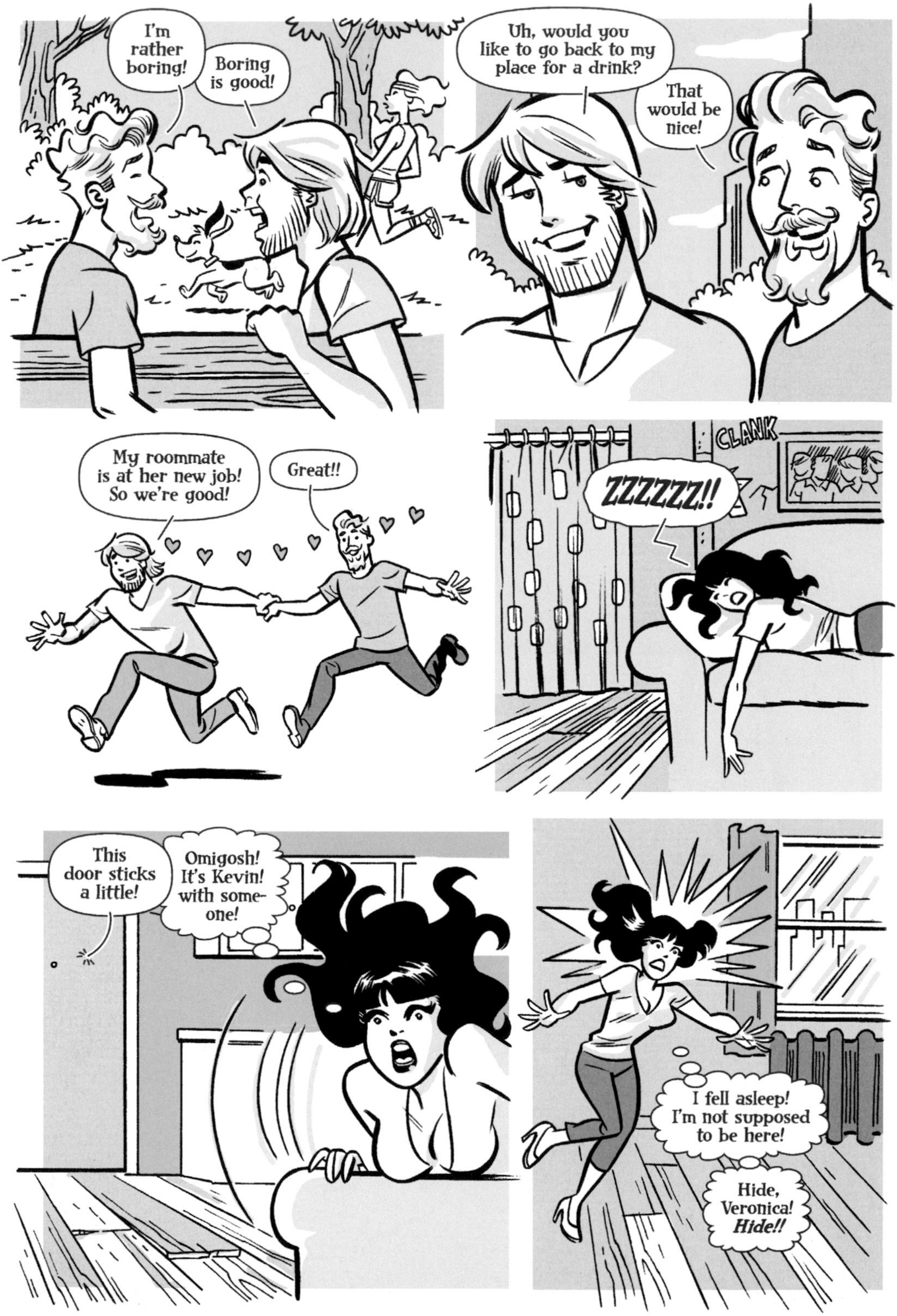
I'm rather boring!
Boring is good!
Uh, would you like to go back to my place for a drink?
That would be nice!
My roommate is at her new job! So we're good!
Great!!
CLANK
ZZZZZZ!!
This door sticks a little!
Omigosh! It's Kevin! with some-one!
I fell asleep! I'm not supposed to be here!
Hide, Veronica! *Hide!!*

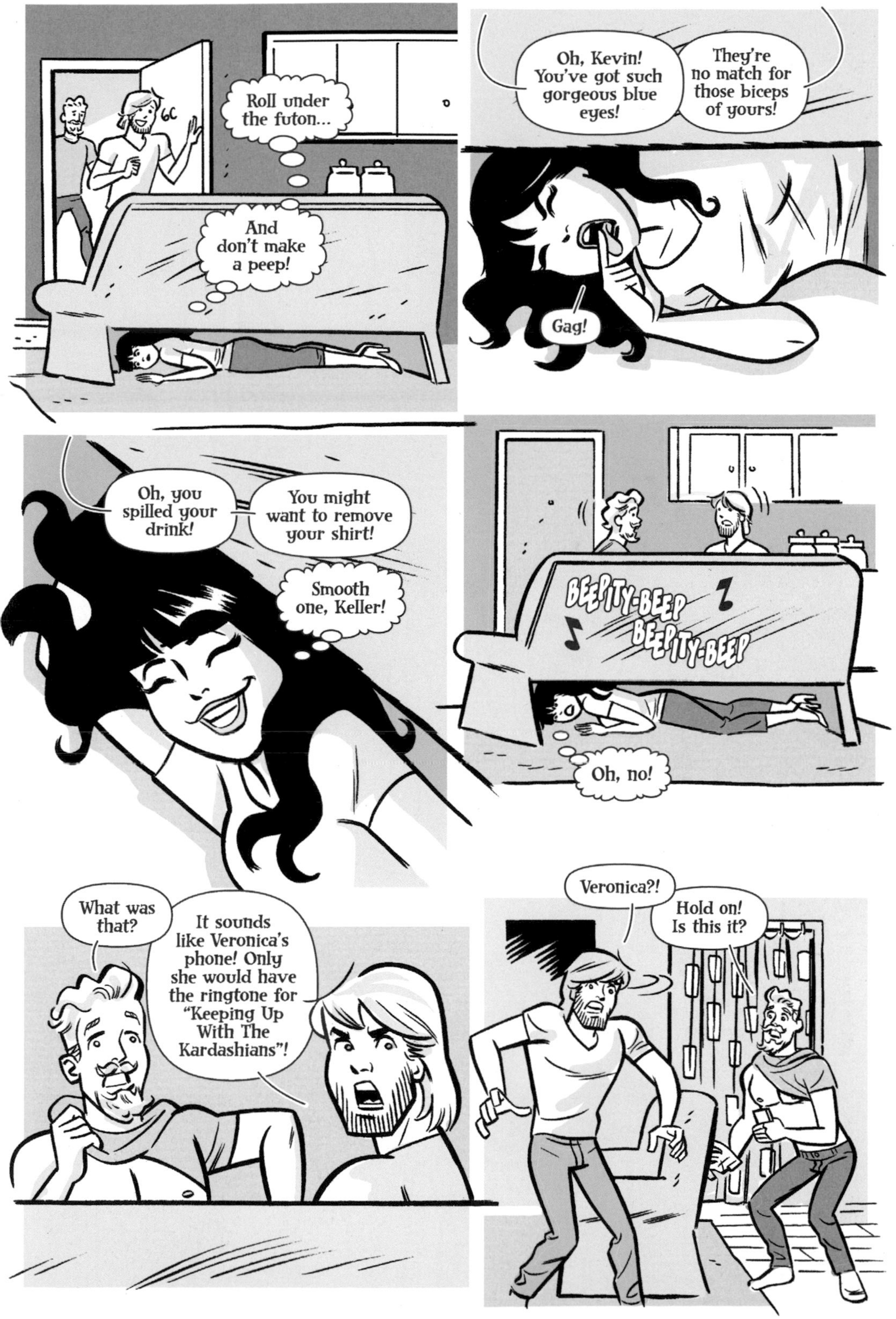
6C
Roll under the futon...
And don't make a peep!
Oh, Kevin! You've got such gorgeous blue eyes!
They're no match for those biceps of yours!
Gag!
Oh, you spilled your drink!
You might want to remove your shirt!
Smooth one, Keller!
BEEPITY-BEEP BEEPITY-BEEP
Oh, no!
What was that?
It sounds like Veronica's phone! Only she would have the ringtone for "Keeping Up With The Kardashians"!
Veronica?!
Hold on! Is this it?

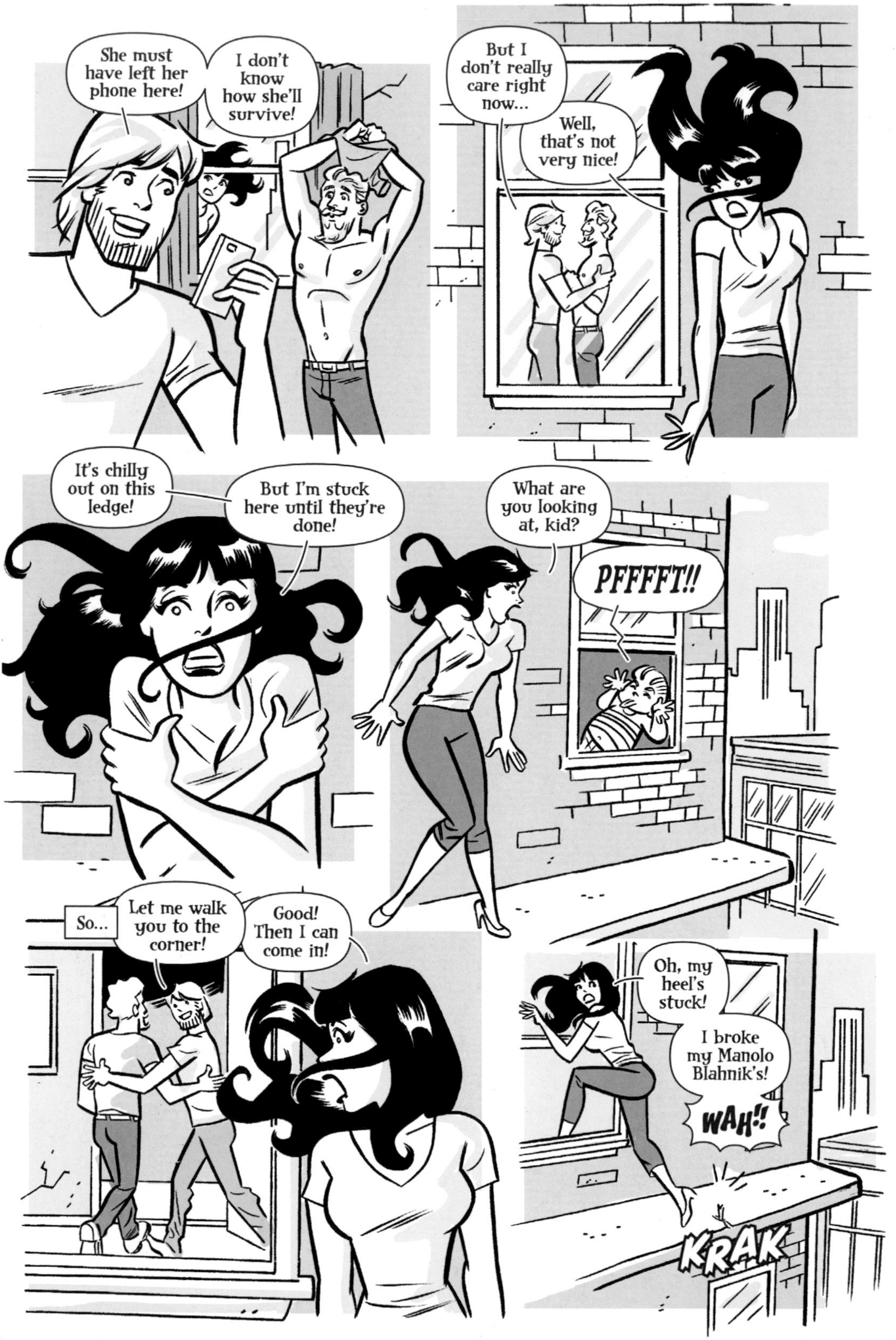
She must have left her phone here!
I don't know how she'll survive!
But I don't really care right now...
Well, that's not very nice!
It's chilly out on this ledge!
But I'm stuck here until they're done!
What are you looking at, kid?
PFFFFT!!
So...
Let me walk you to the corner!
Good! Then I can come in!
Oh, my heel's stuck!
I broke my Manolo Blahnik's!
WAH!!
KRAK

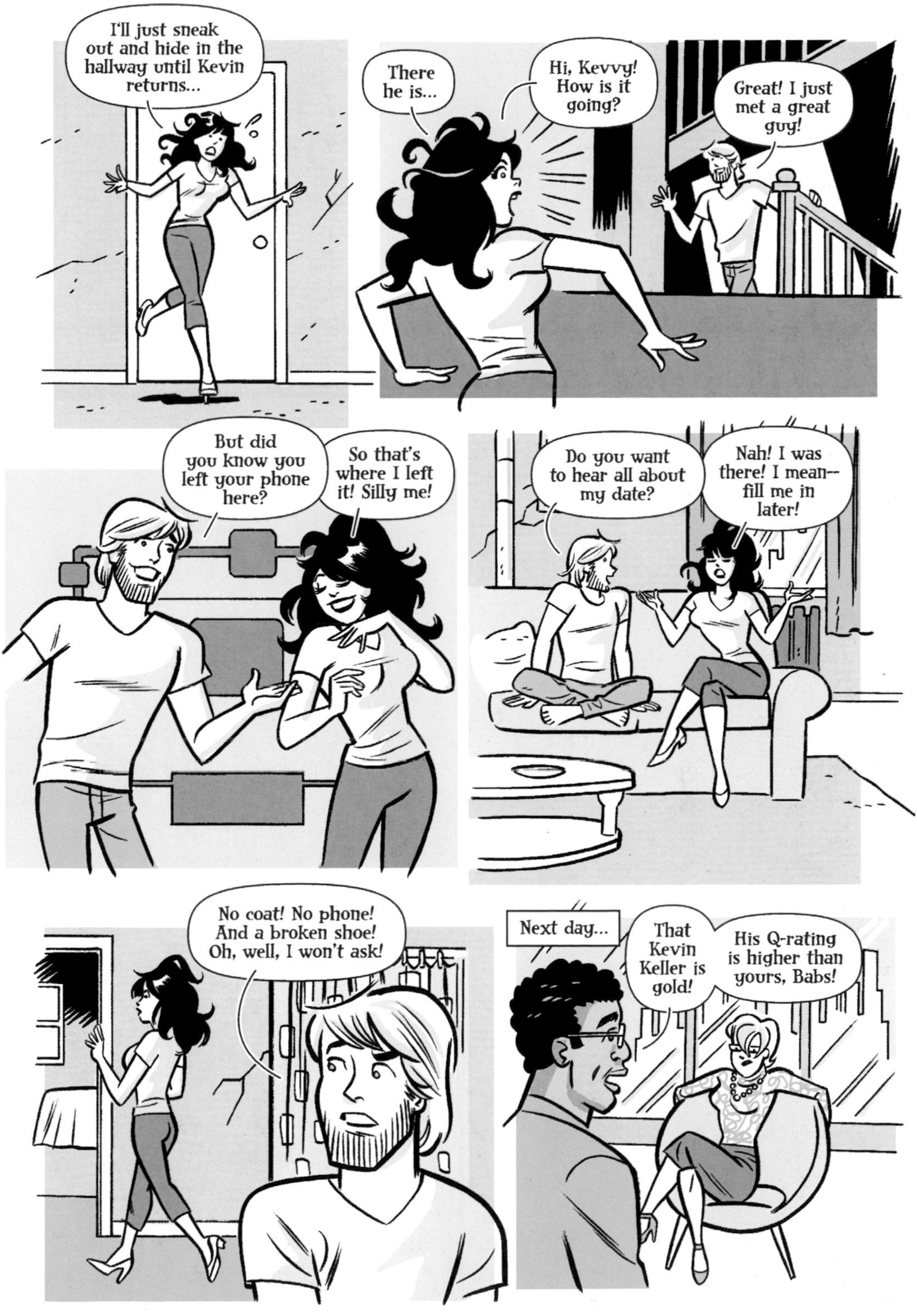

I'll just sneak out and hide in the hallway until Kevin returns...
There he is...
Hi, Kevvy! How is it going?
Great! I just met a great guy!
But did you know you left your phone here?
So that's where I left it! Silly me!
Do you want to hear all about my date?
Nah! I was there! I mean-- fill me in later!
No coat! No phone! And a broken shoe! Oh, well, I won't ask!
Next day...
That Kevin Keller is gold!
His Q-rating is higher than yours, Babs!

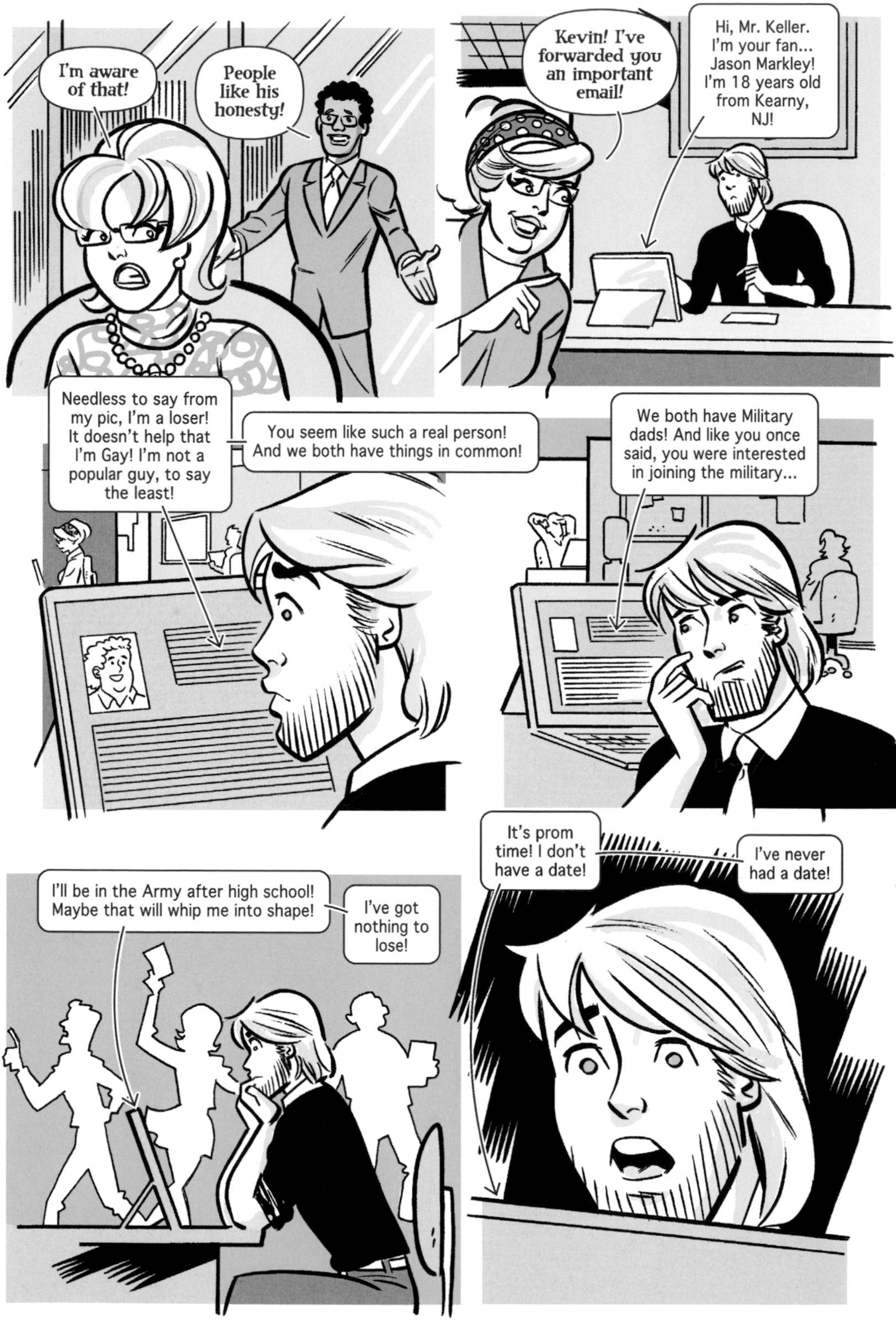
I'm aware of that!
People like his honesty!
Kevin! I've forwarded you an important email!
Hi, Mr. Keller. I'm your fan... Jason Markley! I'm 18 years old from Kearny, NJ!
Needless to say from my pic, I'm a loser! It doesn't help that I'm Gay! I'm not a popular guy, to say the least!
You seem like such a real person! And we both have things in common!
We both have Military dads! And like you once said, you were interested in joining the military...
I'll be in the Army after high school! Maybe that will whip me into shape!
I've got nothing to lose!
It's prom time! I don't have a date!
I've never had a date!

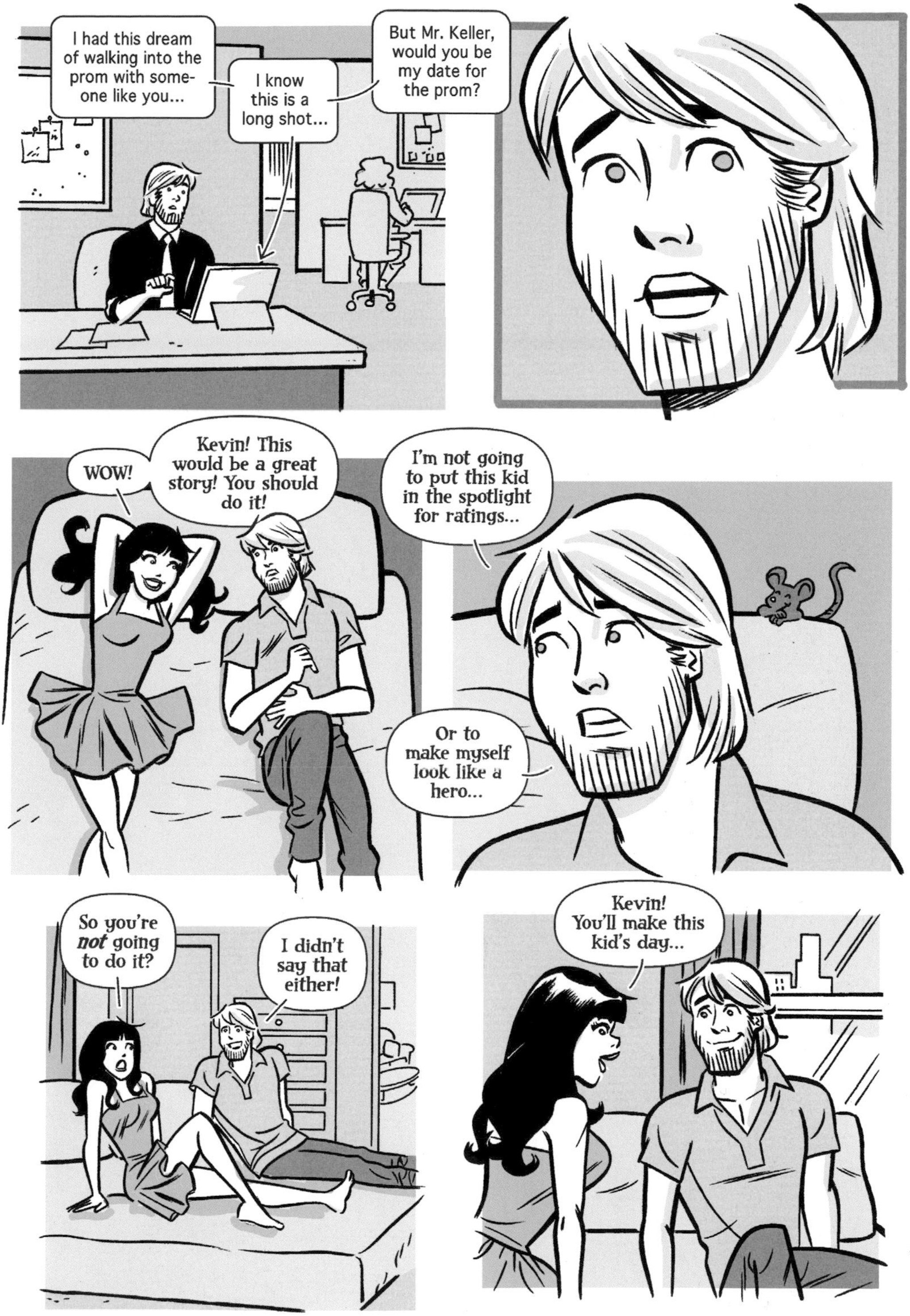

I had this dream of walking into the prom with some-one like you...
I know this is a long shot...
But Mr. Keller, would you be my date for the prom?
WOW!
Kevin! This would be a great story! You should do it!
I'm not going to put this kid in the spotlight for ratings...
Or to make myself look like a hero...
So you're *not* going to do it?
I didn't say that either!
Kevin! You'll make this kid's day...

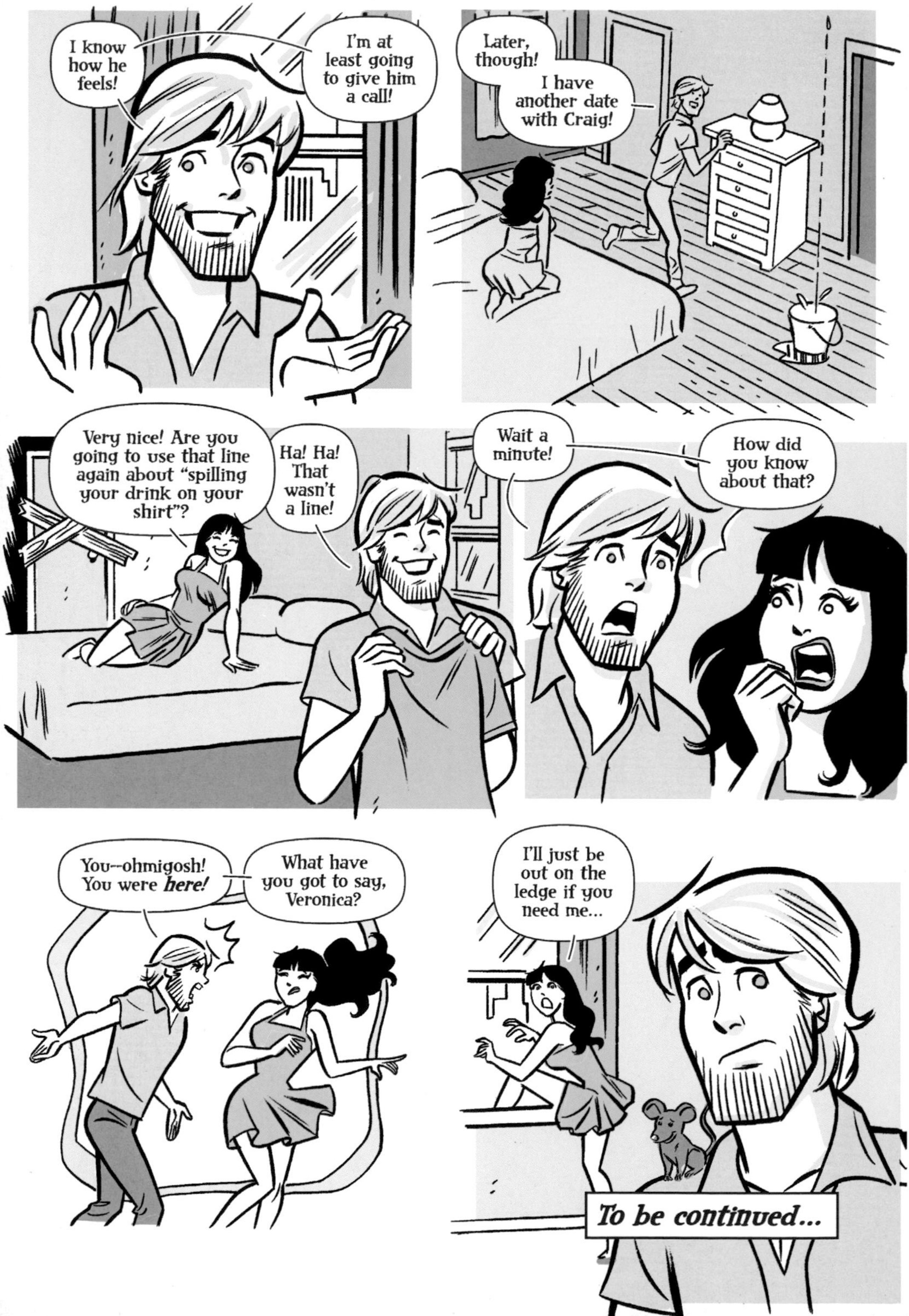

I know how he feels!
I'm at least going to give him a call!
Later, though!
I have another date with Craig!
Very nice! Are you going to use that line again about "spilling your drink on your shirt"?
Ha! Ha! That wasn't a line!
Wait a minute!
How did you know about that?
You--ohmigosh! You were *here!*
What have you got to say, Veronica?
I'll just be out on the ledge if you need me...
To be continued...

CHAPTER 3

KEVIN in the CITY in I'M DANCING AS FAST AS I CAN!

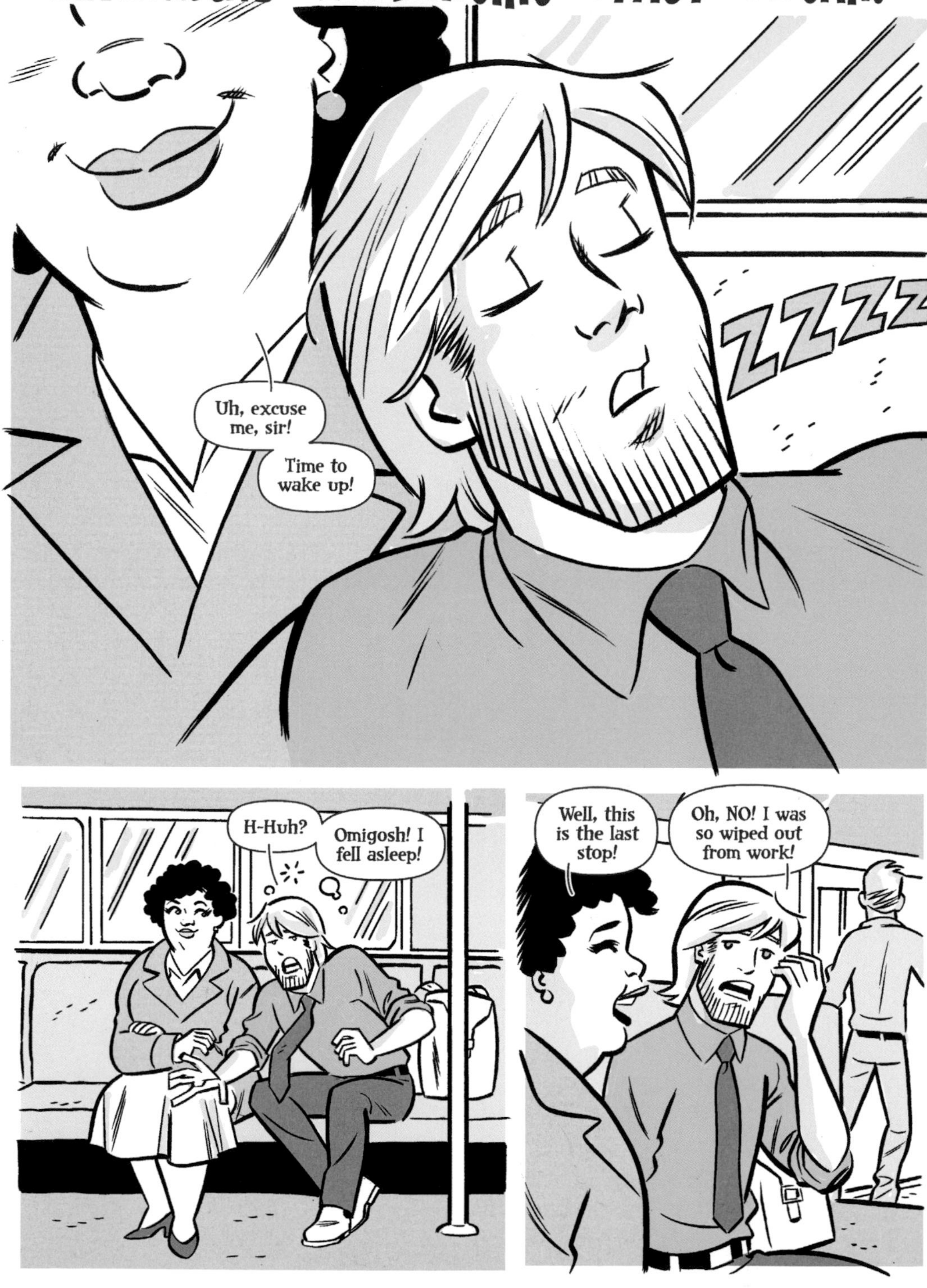

ZZZZ
Uh, excuse me, sir!
Time to wake up!
H-Huh?
Omigosh! I fell asleep!
Well, this is the last stop!
Oh, NO! I was so wiped out from work!

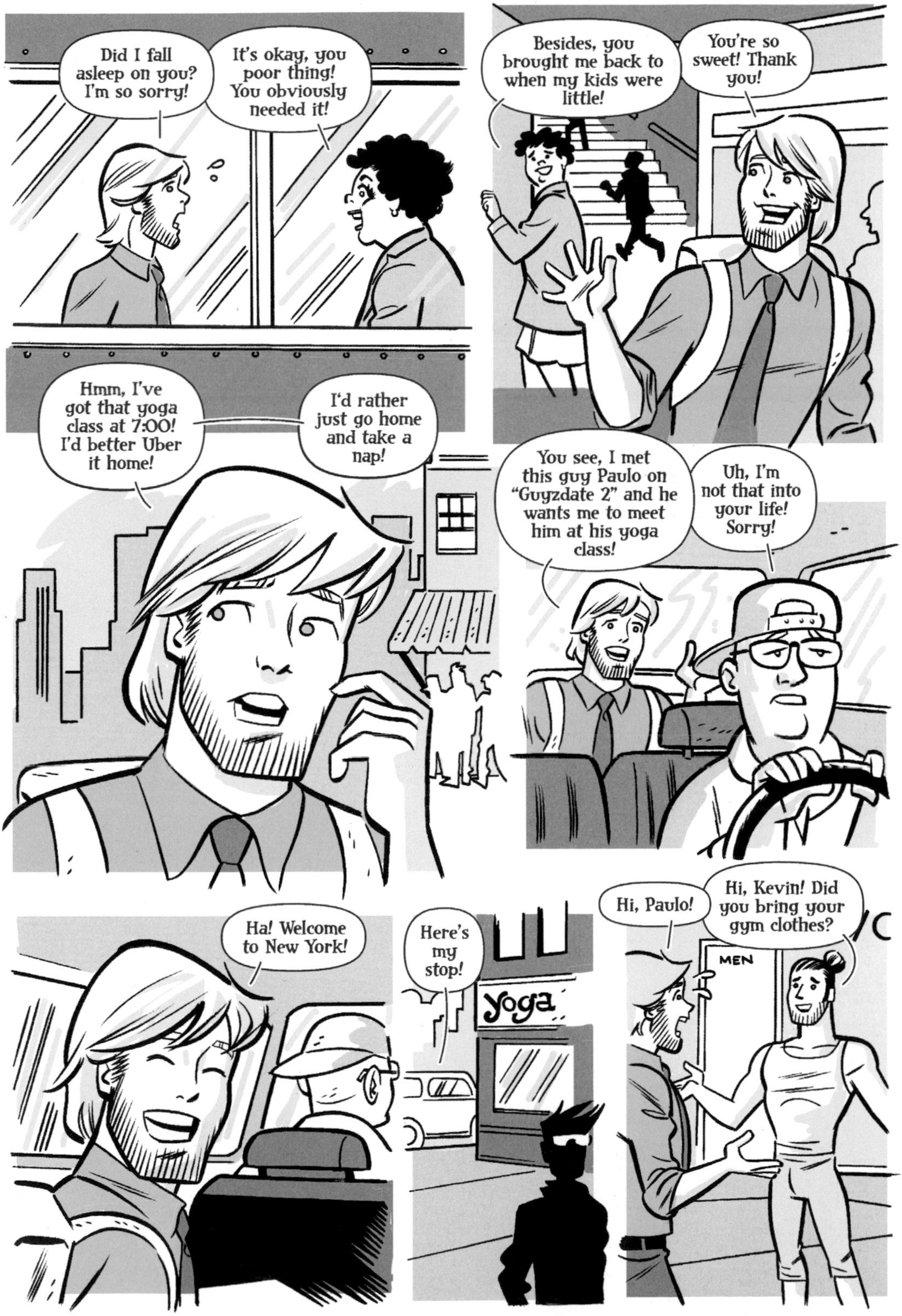

Did I fall asleep on you? I'm so sorry!
It's okay, you poor thing! You obviously needed it!
Besides, you brought me back to when my kids were little!
You're so sweet! Thank you!
Hmm, I've got that yoga class at 7:00! I'd better Uber it home!
I'd rather just go home and take a nap!
You see, I met this guy Paulo on "Guyzdate 2" and he wants me to meet him at his yoga class!
Uh, I'm not that into your life! Sorry!
Ha! Welcome to New York!
Here's my stop!
Yoga
Hi, Paulo!
MEN
Hi, Kevin! Did you bring your gym clothes?

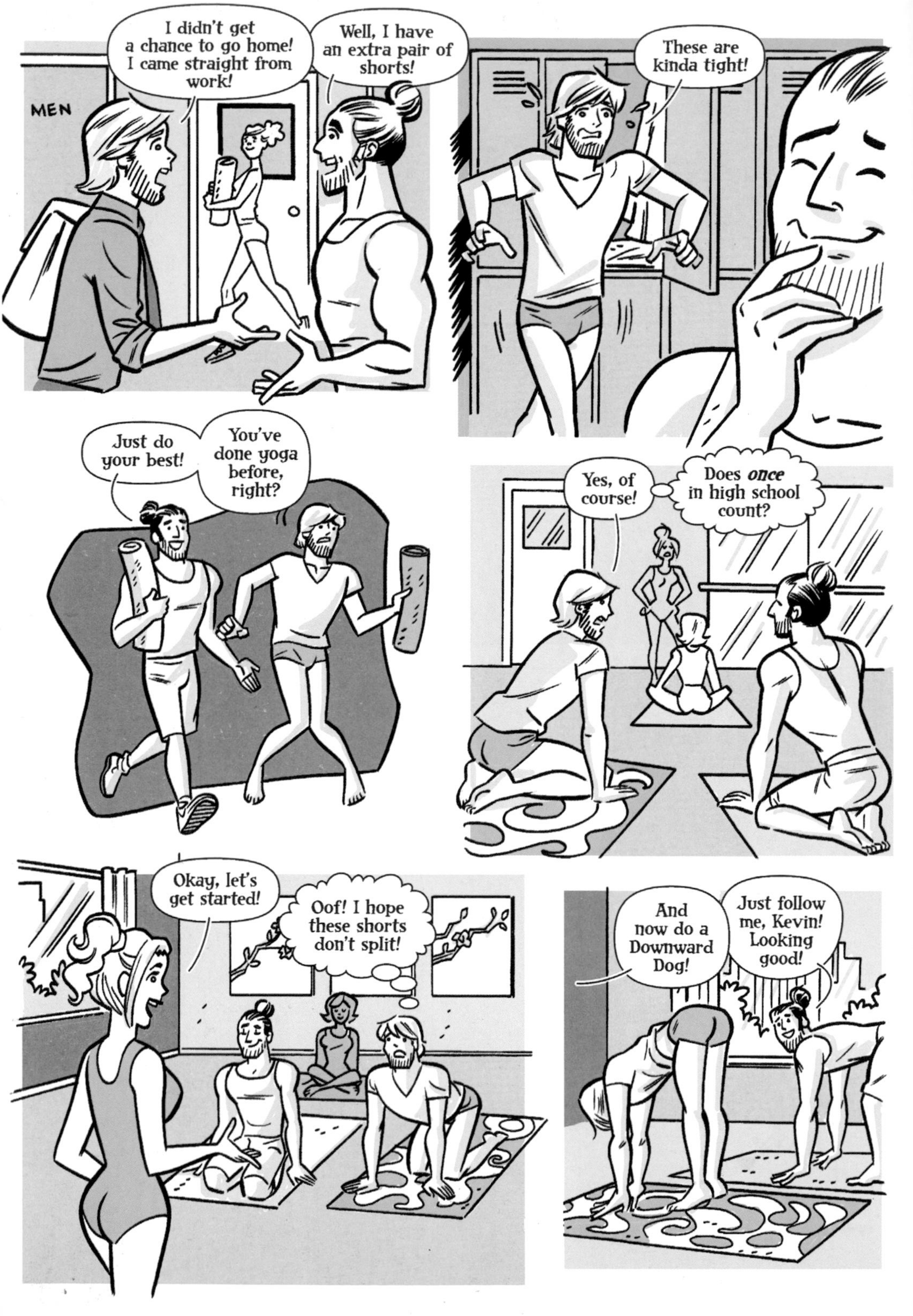

MEN
I didn't get a chance to go home! I came straight from work!
Well, I have an extra pair of shorts!
These are kinda tight!
Just do your best!
You've done yoga before, right?
Yes, of course!
Does *once* in high school count?
Okay, let's get started!
Oof! I hope these shorts don't split!
And now do a Downward Dog!
Just follow me, Kevin! Looking good!

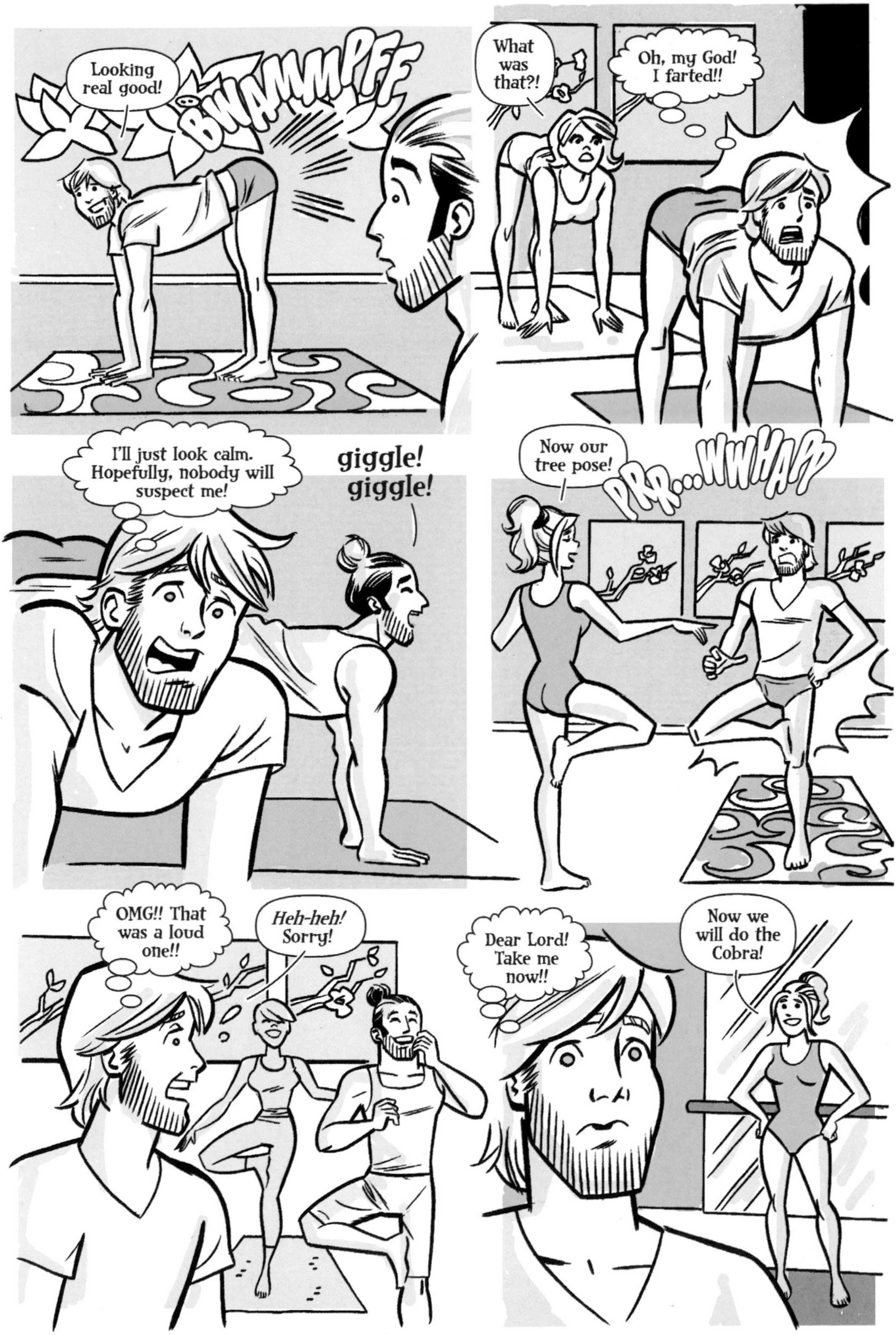

Looking real good!
BWAMMMPFF
What was that?!
Oh, my God! I farted!!
I'll just look calm. Hopefully, nobody will suspect me!
giggle! giggle!
Now our tree pose!
PRR...WWHAP
OMG!! That was a loud one!!
Heh-heh! Sorry!
Dear Lord! Take me now!!
Now we will do the Cobra!

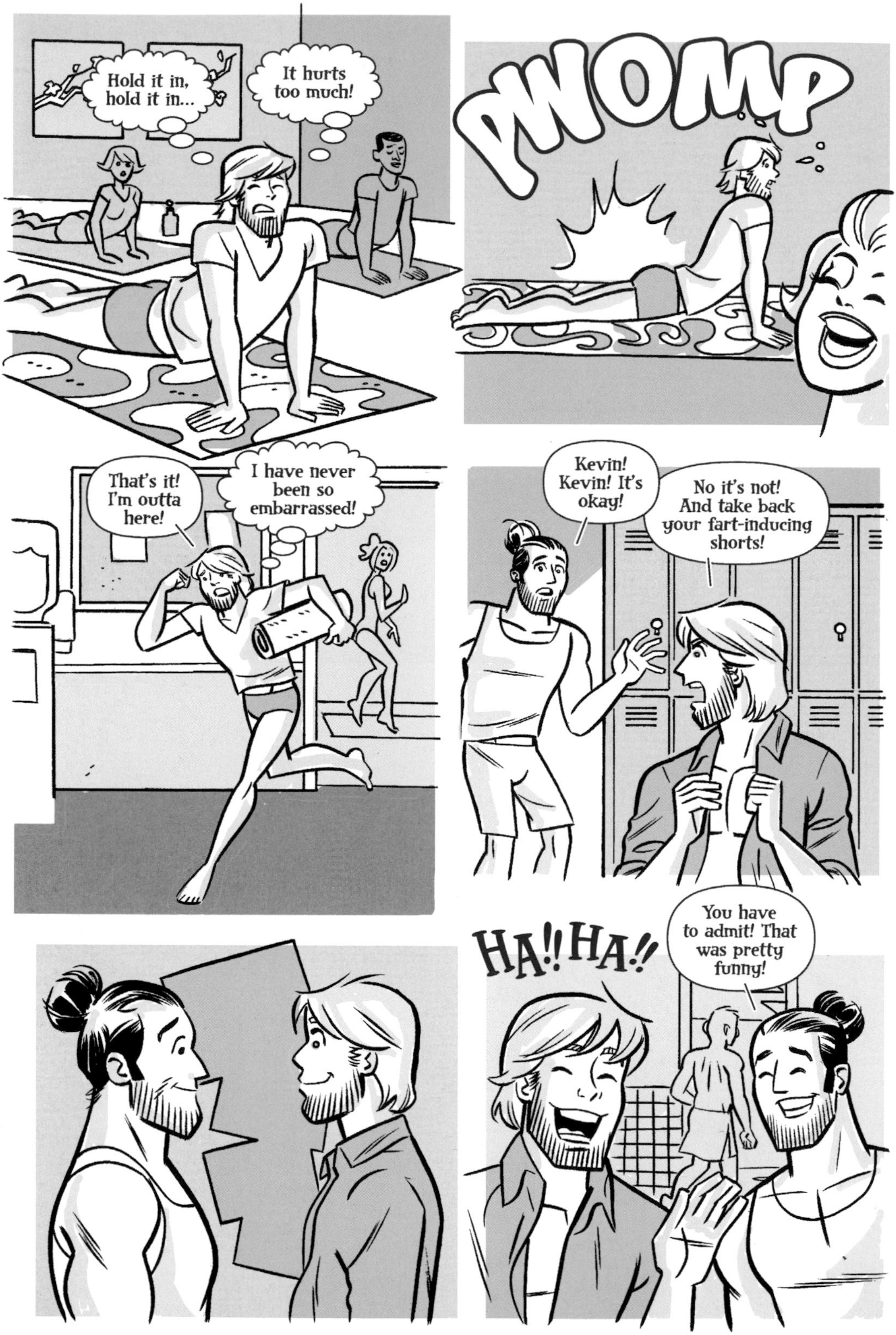
Hold it in, hold it in...
It hurts too much!
PWOMP
That's it! I'm outta here!
I have never been so embarrassed!
Kevin! Kevin! It's okay!
No it's not! And take back your fart-inducing shorts!
HA!! HA!!
You have to admit! That was pretty funny!

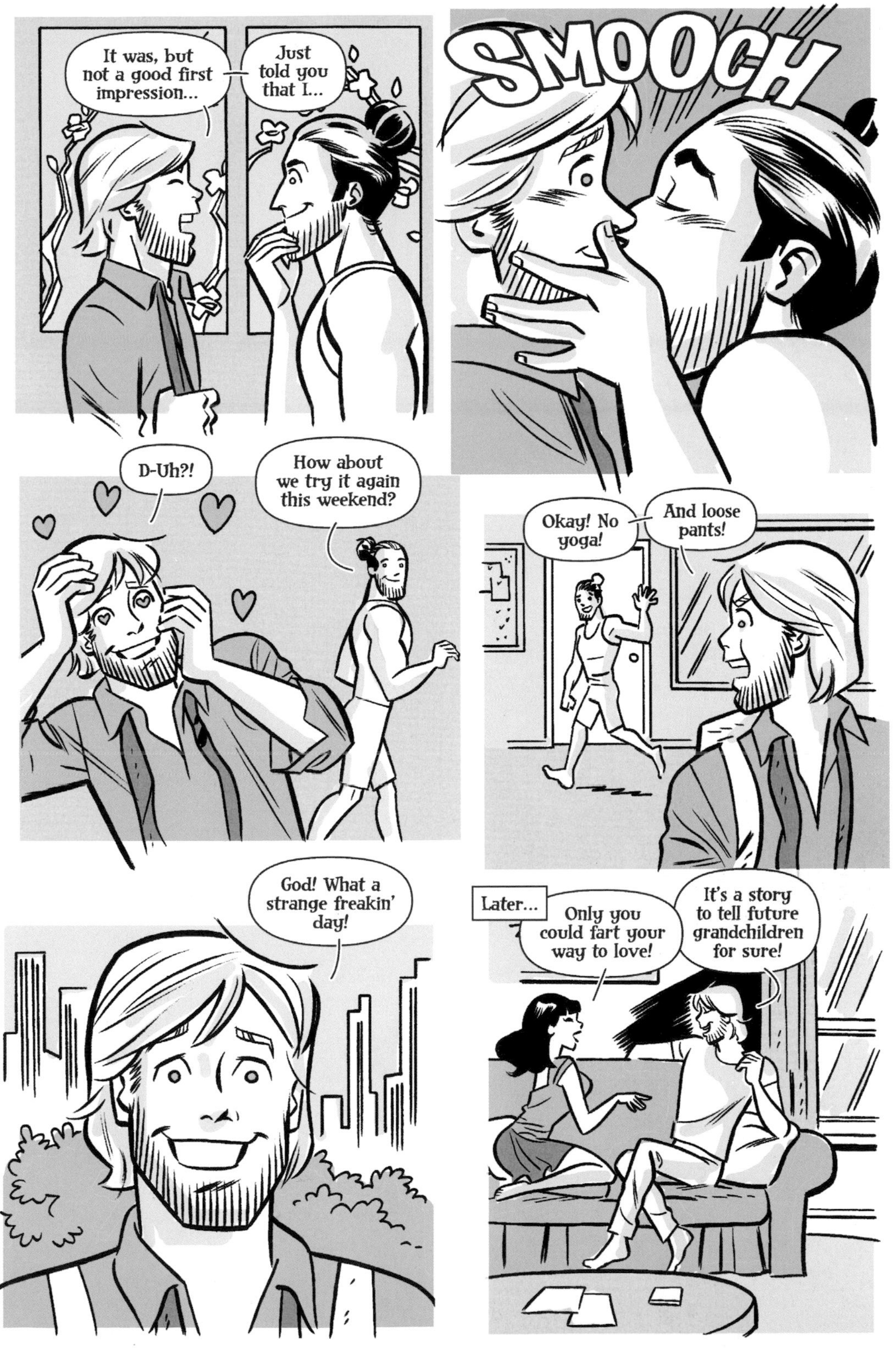

It was, but not a good first impression...
Just told you that I...
SMOOCH
D-Uh?!
How about we try it again this weekend?
Okay! No yoga!
And loose pants!
God! What a strange freakin' day!
Later...
Only you could fart your way to love!
It's a story to tell future grandchildren for sure!

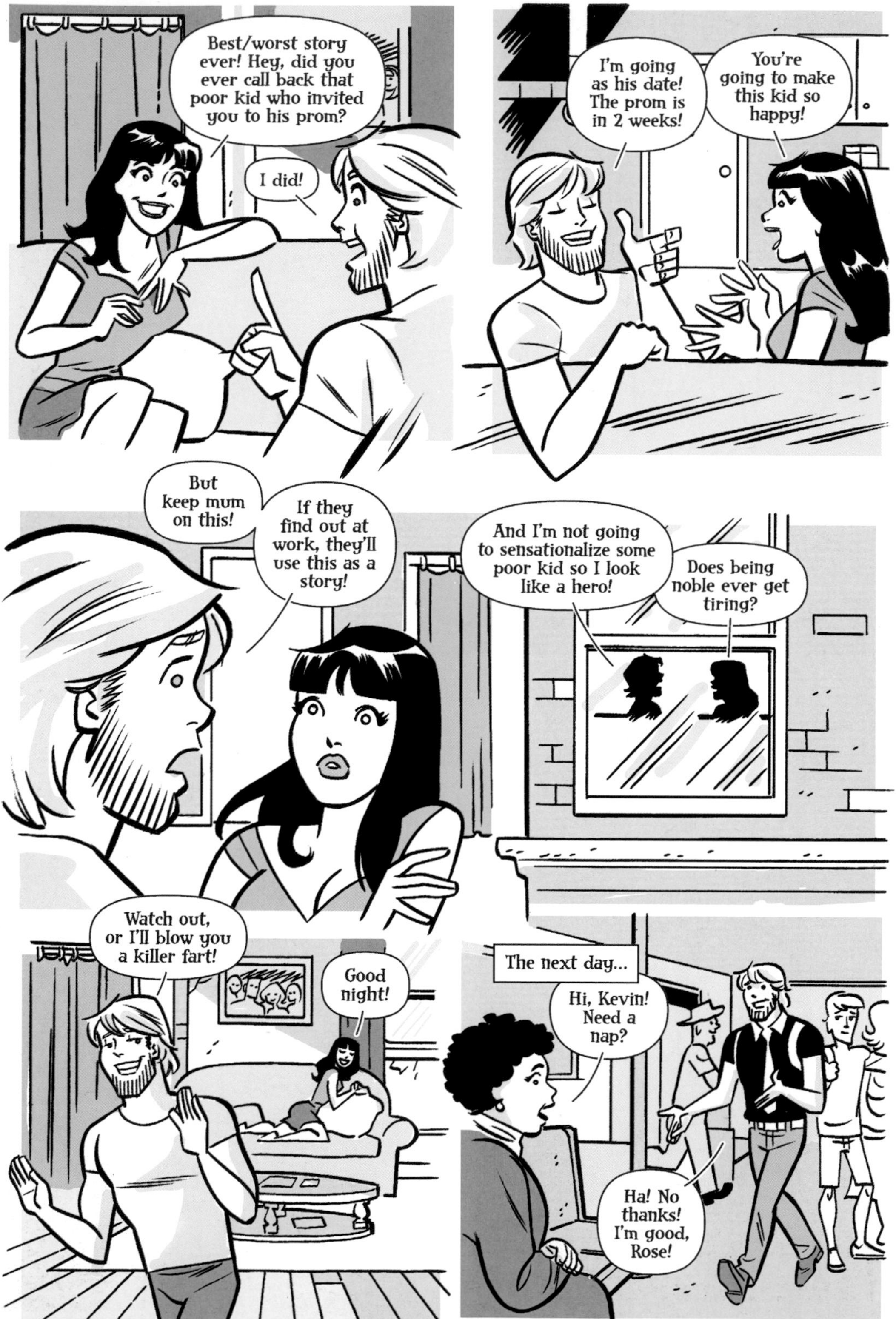

Best/worst story ever! Hey, did you ever call back that poor kid who invited you to his prom?
I did!
I'm going as his date! The prom is in 2 weeks!
You're going to make this kid so happy!
But keep mum on this!
If they find out at work, they'll use this as a story!
And I'm not going to sensationalize some poor kid so I look like a hero!
Does being noble ever get tiring?
Watch out, or I'll blow you a killer fart!
Good night!
The next day...
Hi, Kevin! Need a nap?
Ha! No thanks! I'm good, Rose!

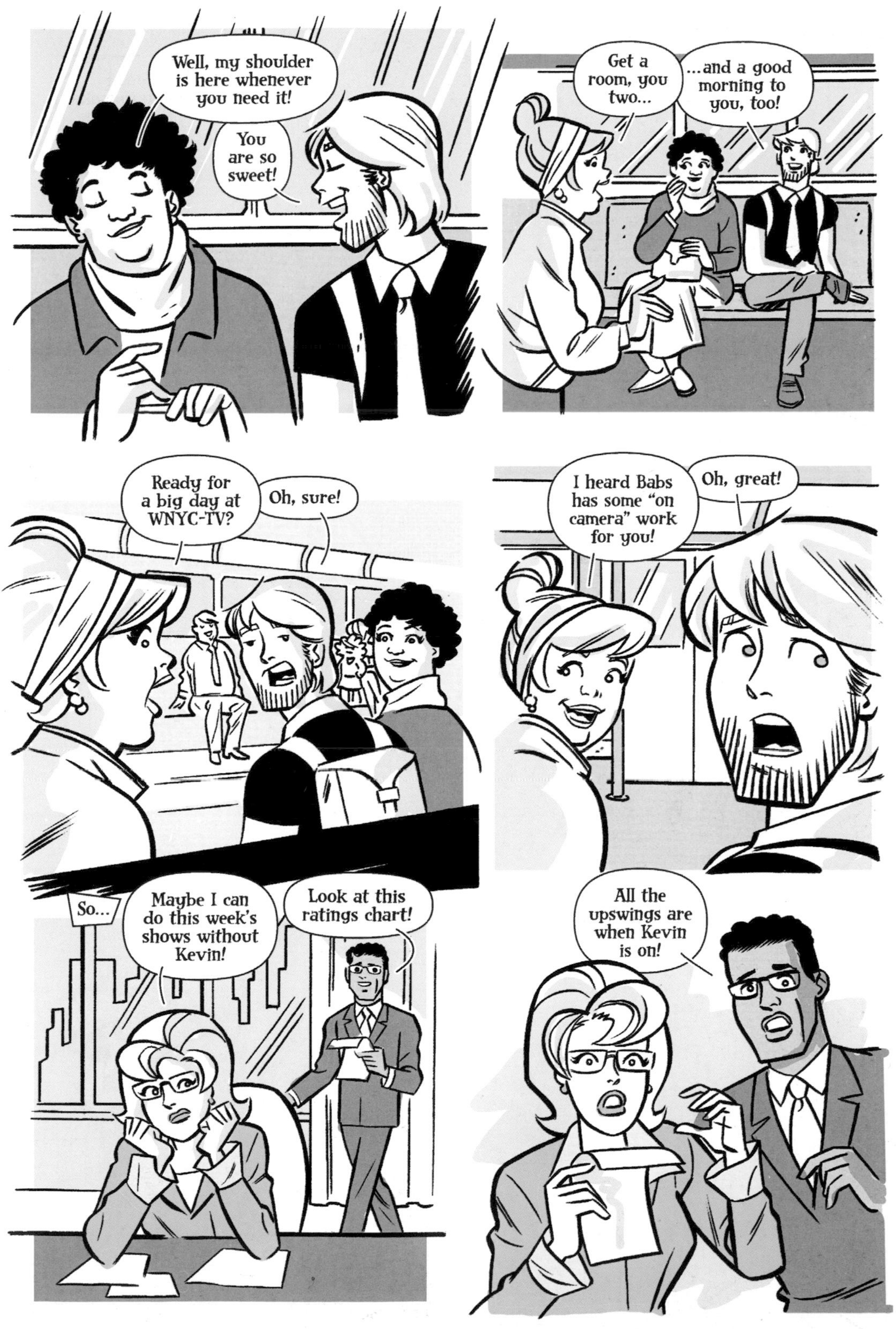
Well, my shoulder is here whenever you need it!
You are so sweet!
Get a room, you two...
...and a good morning to you, too!
Ready for a big day at WNYC-TV?
Oh, sure!
I heard Babs has some "on camera" work for you!
Oh, great!
So...
Maybe I can do this week's shows without Kevin!
Look at this ratings chart!
All the upswings are when Kevin is on!

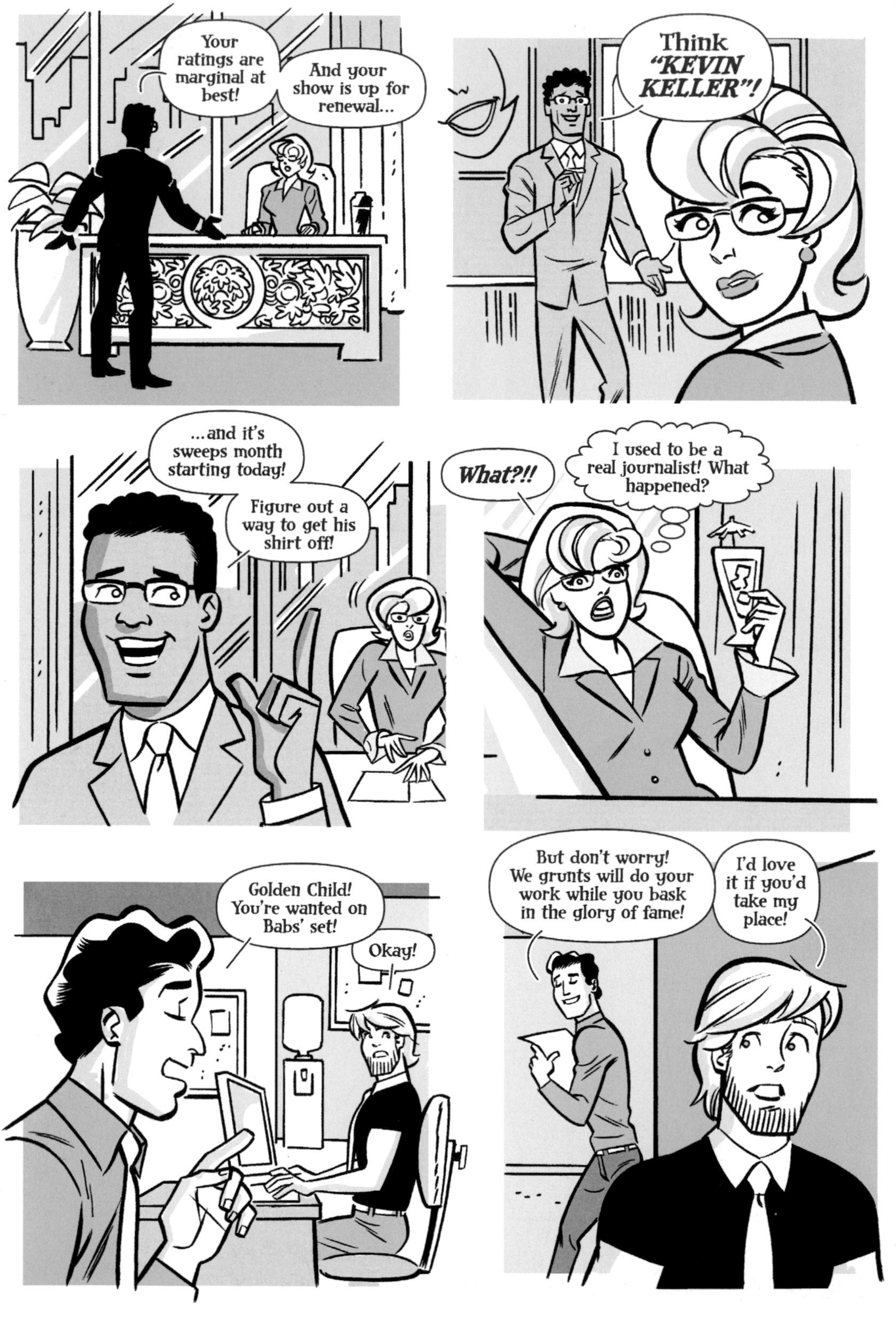
Your ratings are marginal at best!
And your show is up for renewal...
Think "KEVIN KELLER"!
...and it's sweeps month starting today!
Figure out a way to get his shirt off!
What?!!
I used to be a real journalist! What happened?
Golden Child! You're wanted on Babs' set!
Okay!
But don't worry! We grunts will do your work while you bask in the glory of fame!
I'd love it if you'd take my place!

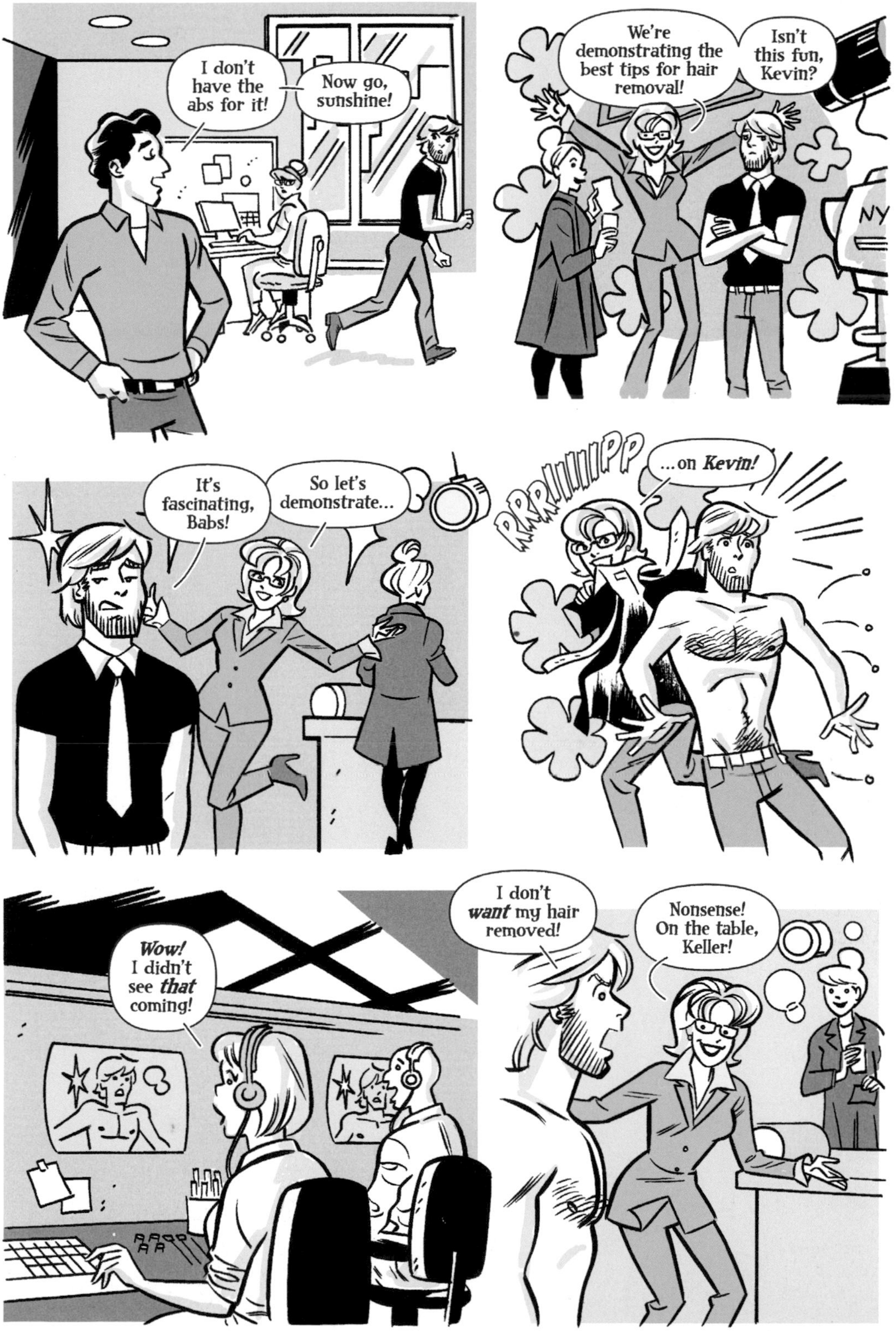
I don't have the abs for it!
Now go, sunshine!
We're demonstrating the best tips for hair removal!
Isn't this fun, Kevin?
It's fascinating, Babs!
So let's demonstrate...
RRRIIIIIIPP
...on *Kevin!*
Wow! I didn't see *that* coming!
I don't *want* my hair removed!
Nonsense! On the table, Keller!

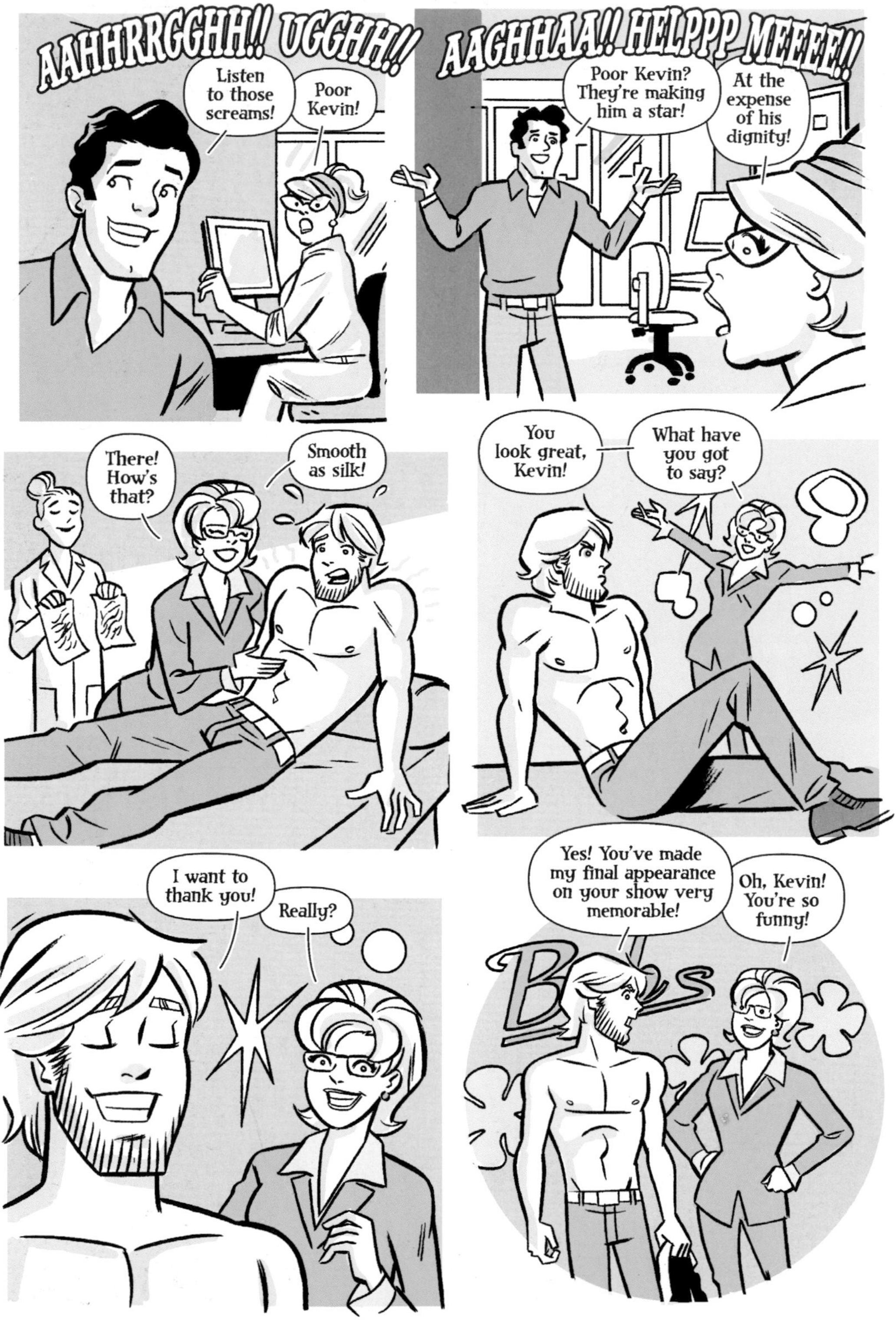
AAHHRRGGHH!! UGGHH!!
Listen to those screams!
Poor Kevin!
AAGHHAA!! HELPPP MEEEE!!
Poor Kevin? They're making him a star!
At the expense of his dignity!
There! How's that?
Smooth as silk!
You look great, Kevin!
What have you got to say?
I want to thank you!
Really?
Yes! You've made my final appearance on your show very memorable!
Oh, Kevin! You're so funny!

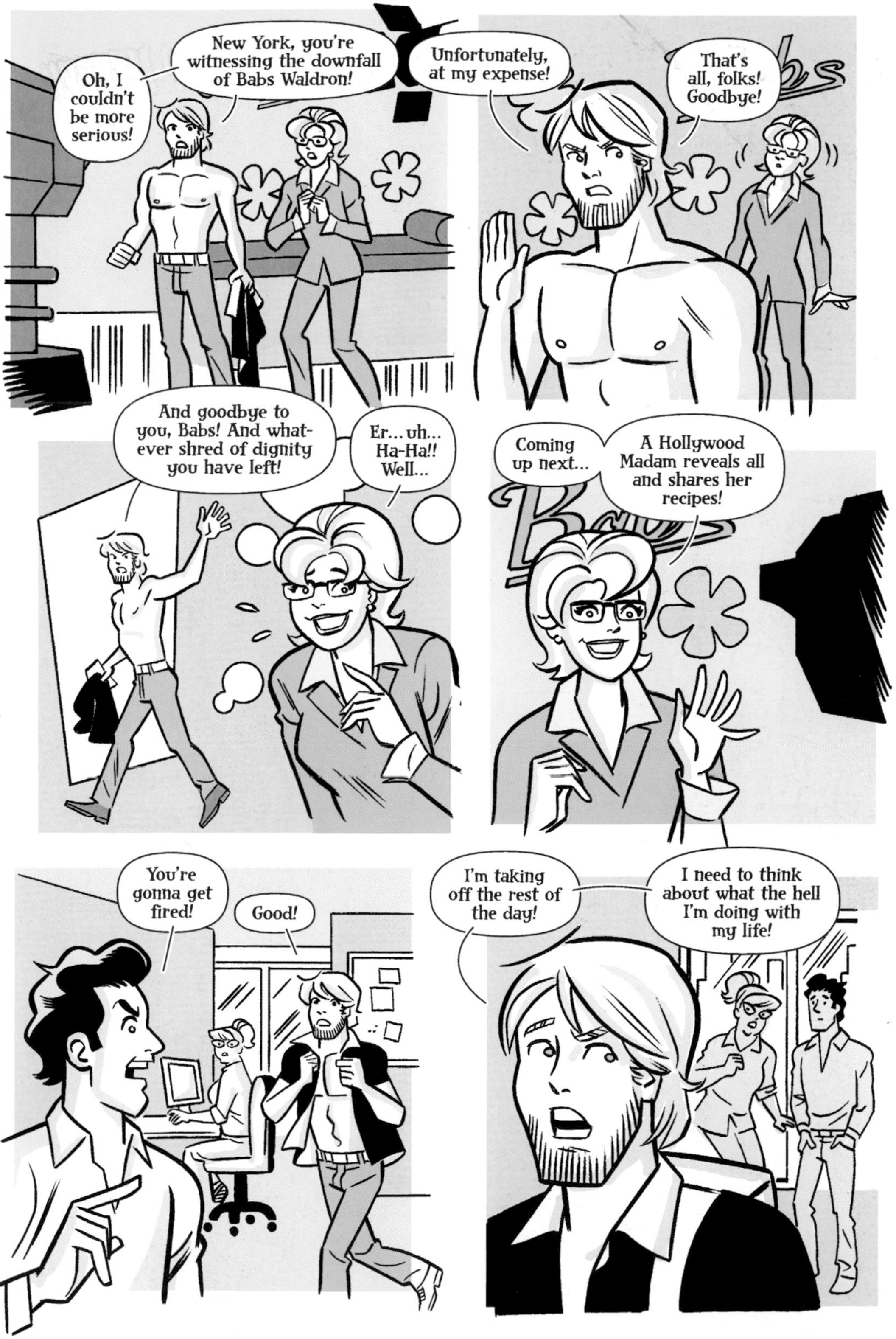
Oh, I couldn't be more serious!
New York, you're witnessing the downfall of Babs Waldron!
Unfortunately, at my expense!
That's all, folks! Goodbye!
And goodbye to you, Babs! And whatever shred of dignity you have left!
Er... uh... Ha-Ha!! Well...
Coming up next...
A Hollywood Madam reveals all and shares her recipes!
You're gonna get fired!
Good!
I'm taking off the rest of the day!
I need to think about what the hell I'm doing with my life!

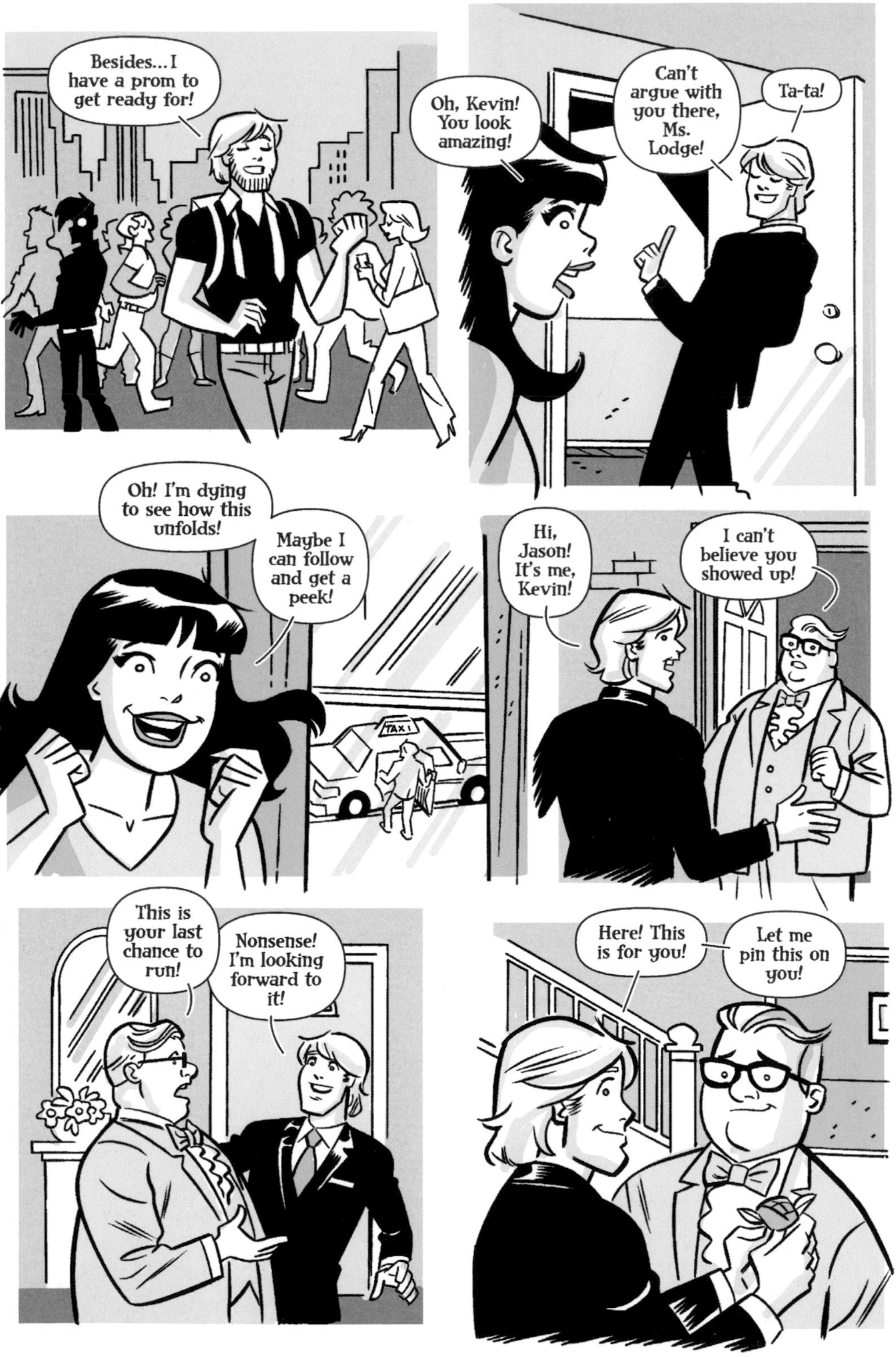
Besides...I have a prom to get ready for!
Oh, Kevin! You look amazing!
Can't argue with you there, Ms. Lodge!
Ta-ta!
Oh! I'm dying to see how this unfolds!
Maybe I can follow and get a peek!
TAXI
Hi, Jason! It's me, Kevin!
I can't believe you showed up!
This is your last chance to run!
Nonsense! I'm looking forward to it!
Here! This is for you!
Let me pin this on you!

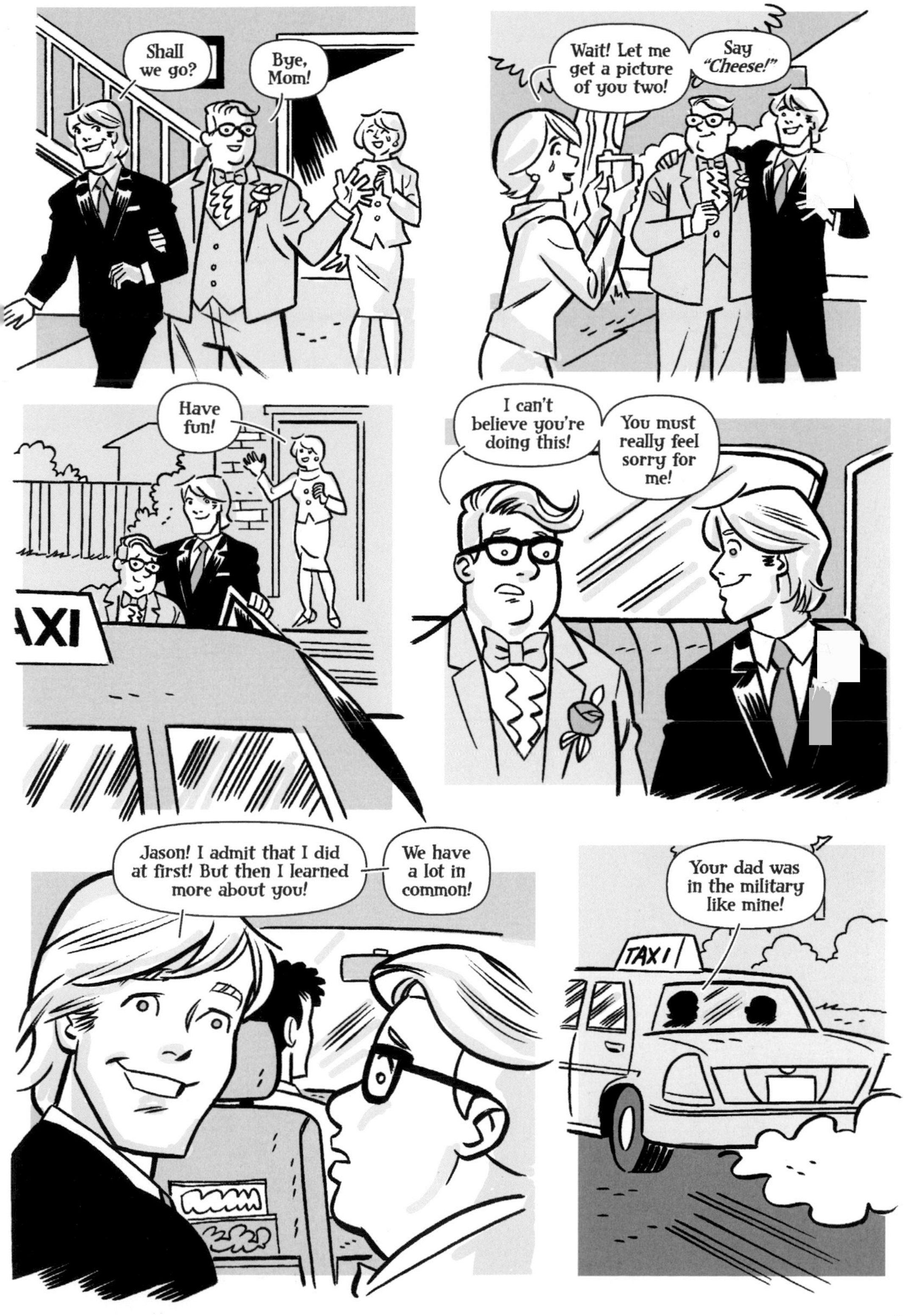
Shall we go?
Bye, Mom!
Wait! Let me get a picture of you two!
Say "Cheese!"
Have fun!
I can't believe you're doing this!
You must really feel sorry for me!
TAXI
Jason! I admit that I did at first! But then I learned more about you!
We have a lot in common!
Your dad was in the military like mine!
TAXI

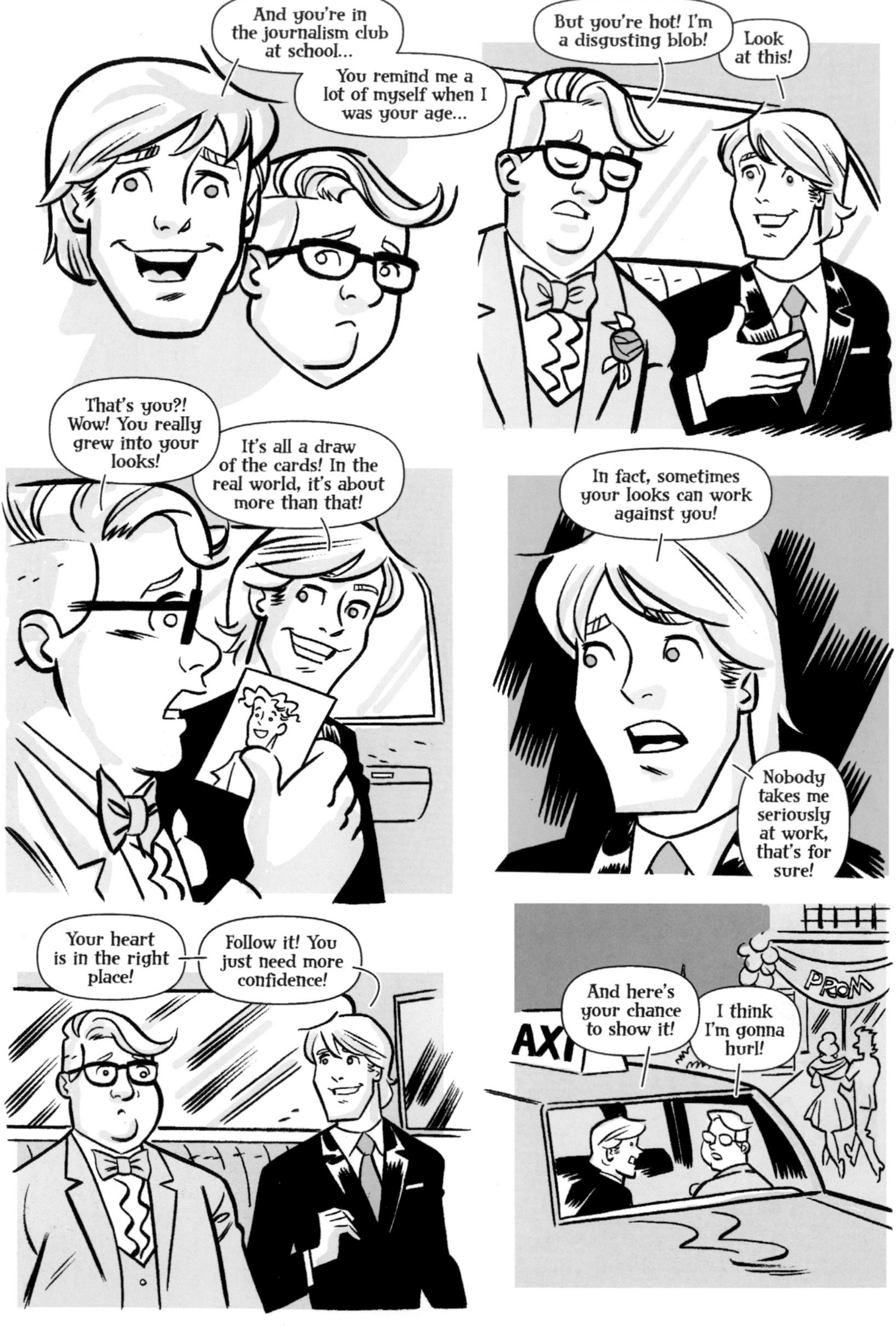

And you're in the journalism club at school...
You remind me a lot of myself when I was your age...
But you're hot! I'm a disgusting blob!
Look at this!
That's you?! Wow! You really grew into your looks!
It's all a draw of the cards! In the real world, it's about more than that!
In fact, sometimes your looks can work against you!
Nobody takes me seriously at work, that's for sure!
Your heart is in the right place!
Follow it! You just need more confidence!
PROM
AXI
And here's your chance to show it!
I think I'm gonna hurl!

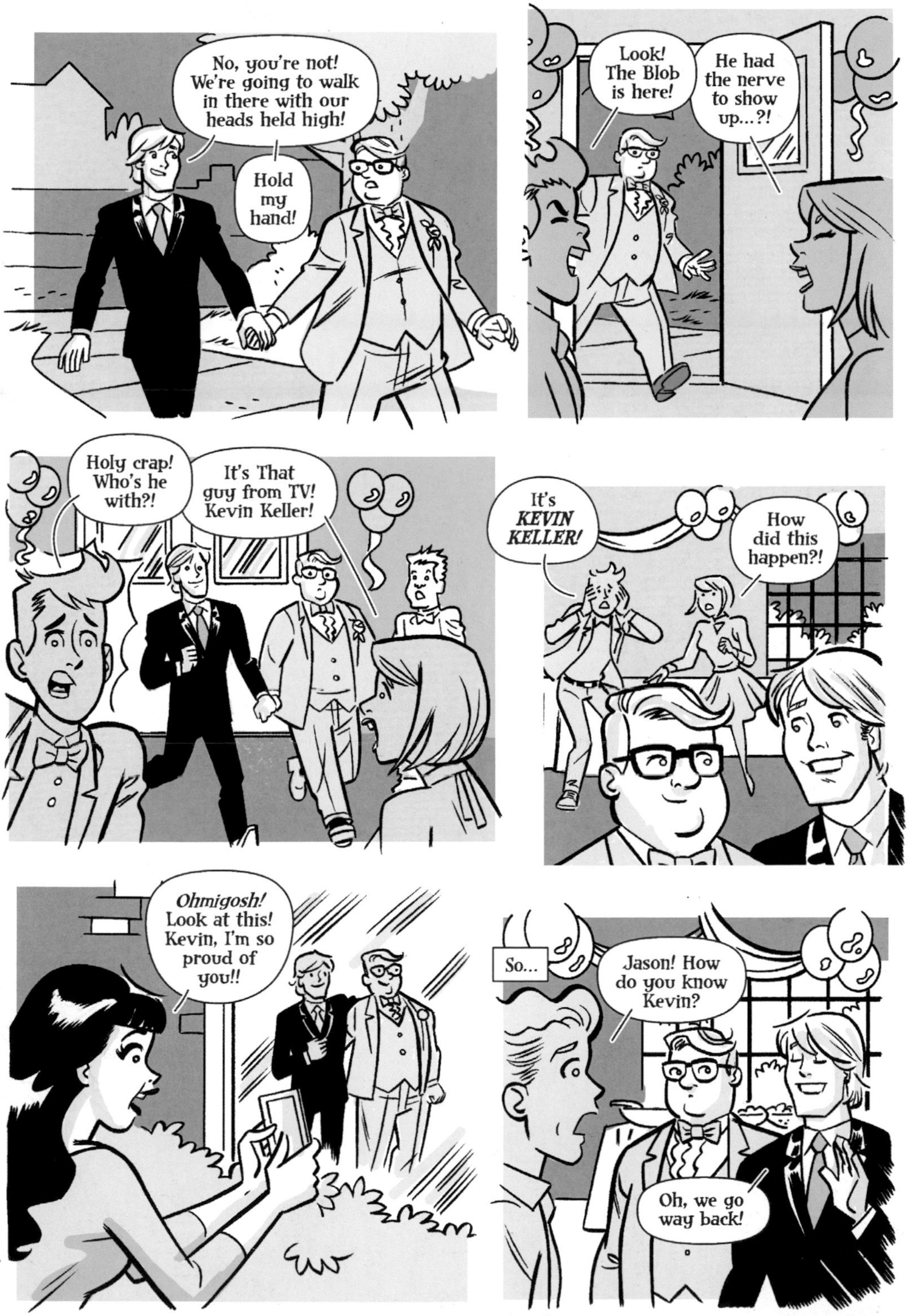
No, you're not! We're going to walk in there with our heads held high!
Hold my hand!
Look! The Blob is here!
He had the nerve to show up...?!
Holy crap! Who's he with?!
It's That guy from TV! Kevin Keller!
It's *KEVIN KELLER!*
How did this happen?!
Ohmigosh! Look at this! Kevin, I'm so proud of you!!
So...
Jason! How do you know Kevin?
Oh, we go way back!

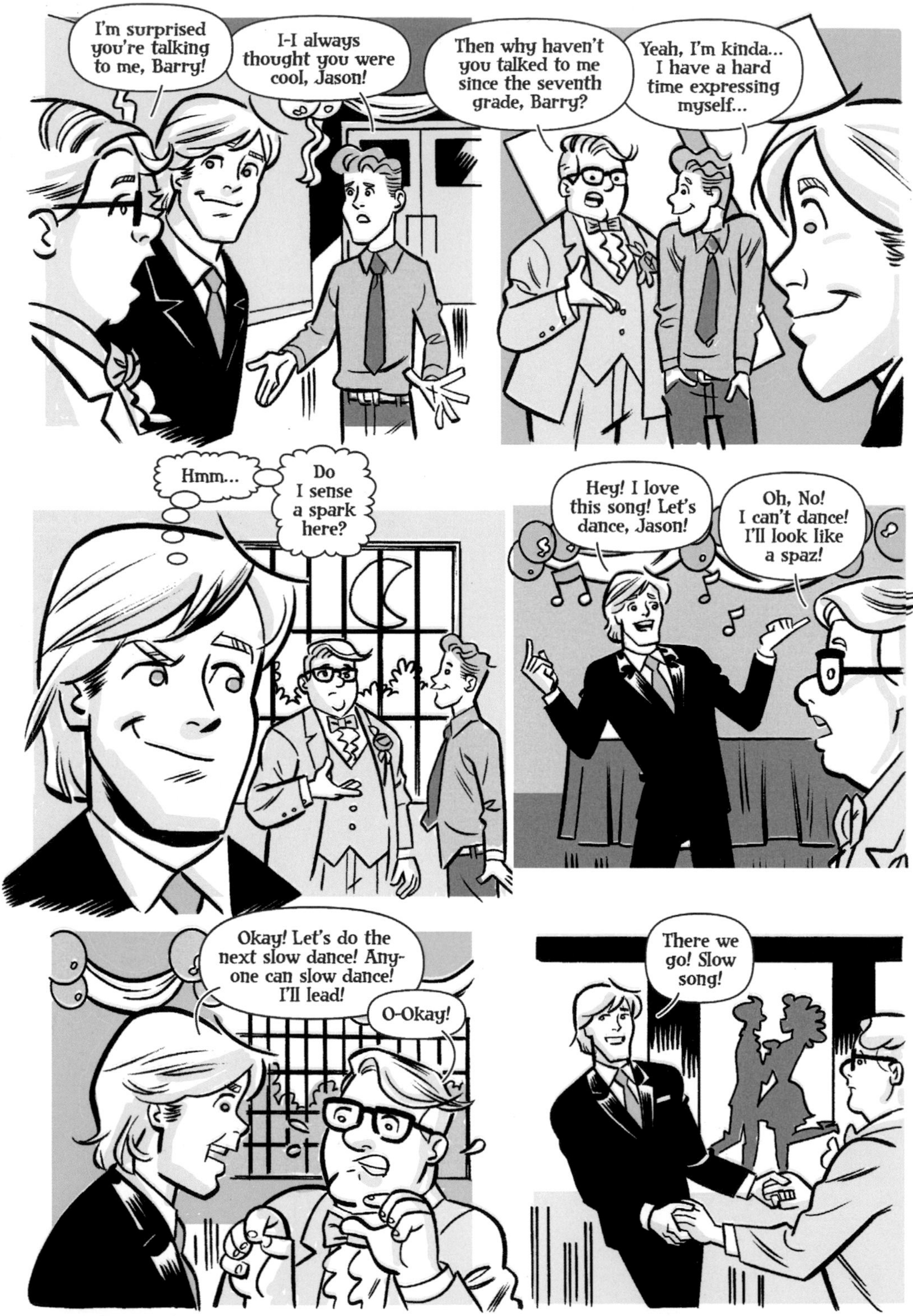
I'm surprised you're talking to me, Barry!
I-I always thought you were cool, Jason!
Then why haven't you talked to me since the seventh grade, Barry?
Yeah, I'm kinda... I have a hard time expressing myself...
Hmm...
Do I sense a spark here?
Hey! I love this song! Let's dance, Jason!
Oh, No! I can't dance! I'll look like a spaz!
Okay! Let's do the next slow dance! Anyone can slow dance! I'll lead!
O-Okay!
There we go! Slow song!

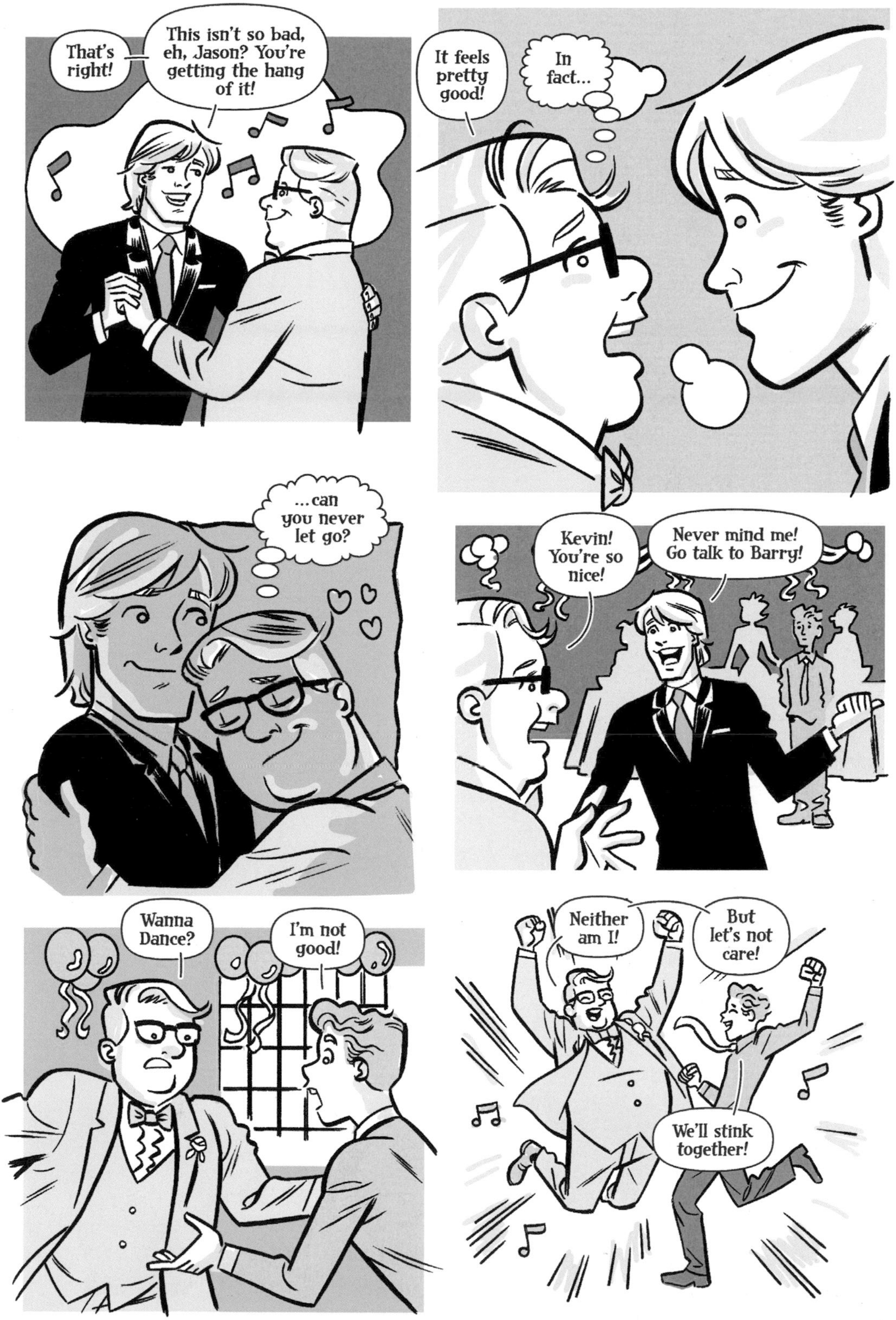
That's right!
This isn't so bad, eh, Jason? You're getting the hang of it!
It feels pretty good!
In fact...
...can you never let go?
Kevin! You're so nice!
Never mind me! Go talk to Barry!
Wanna Dance?
I'm not good!
Neither am I!
But let's not care!
We'll stink together!

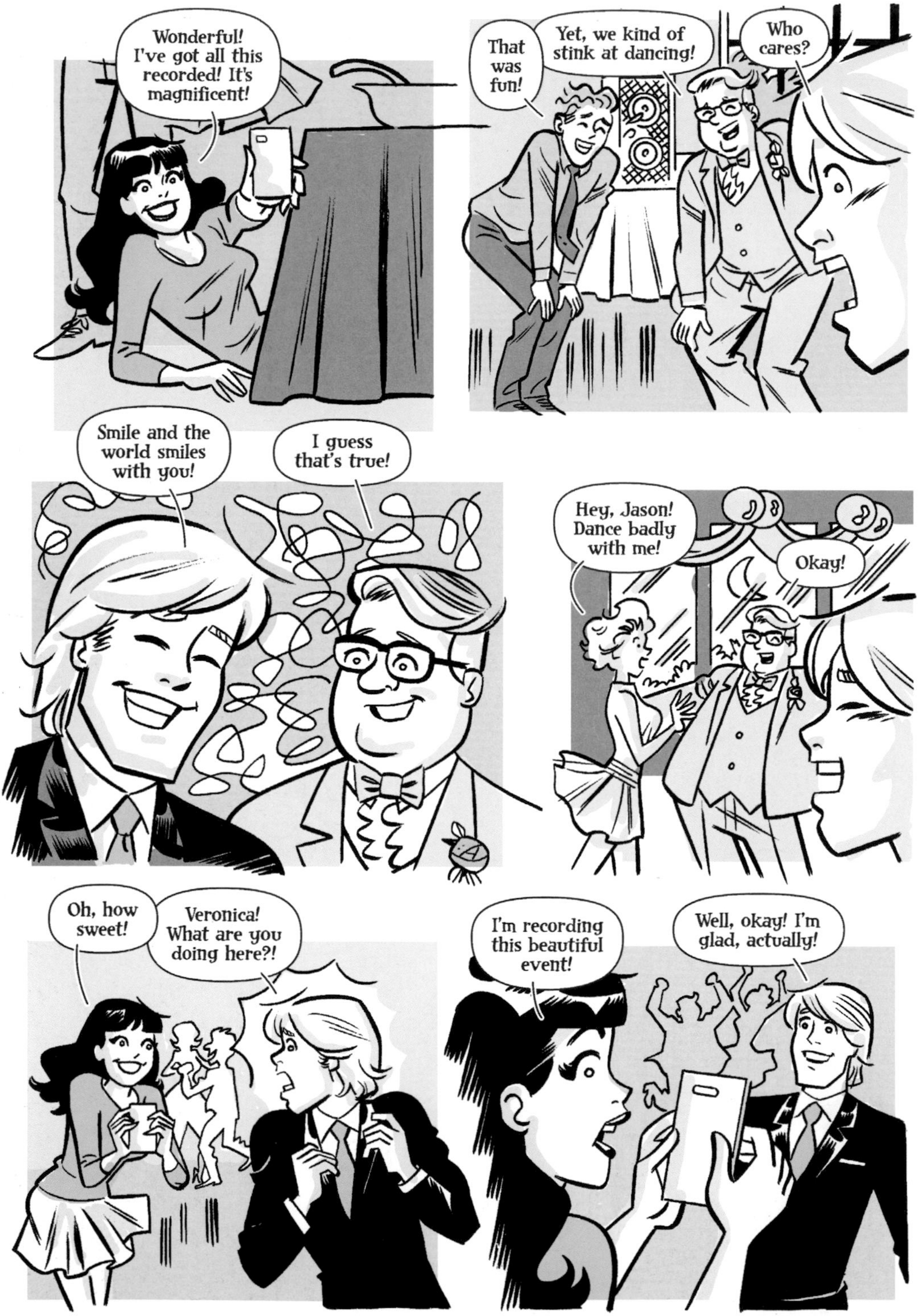
Wonderful! I've got all this recorded! It's magnificent!
That was fun!
Yet, we kind of stink at dancing!
Who cares?
Smile and the world smiles with you!
I guess that's true!
Hey, Jason! Dance badly with me!
Okay!
Oh, how sweet!
Veronica! What are you doing here?!
I'm recording this beautiful event!
Well, okay! I'm glad, actually!

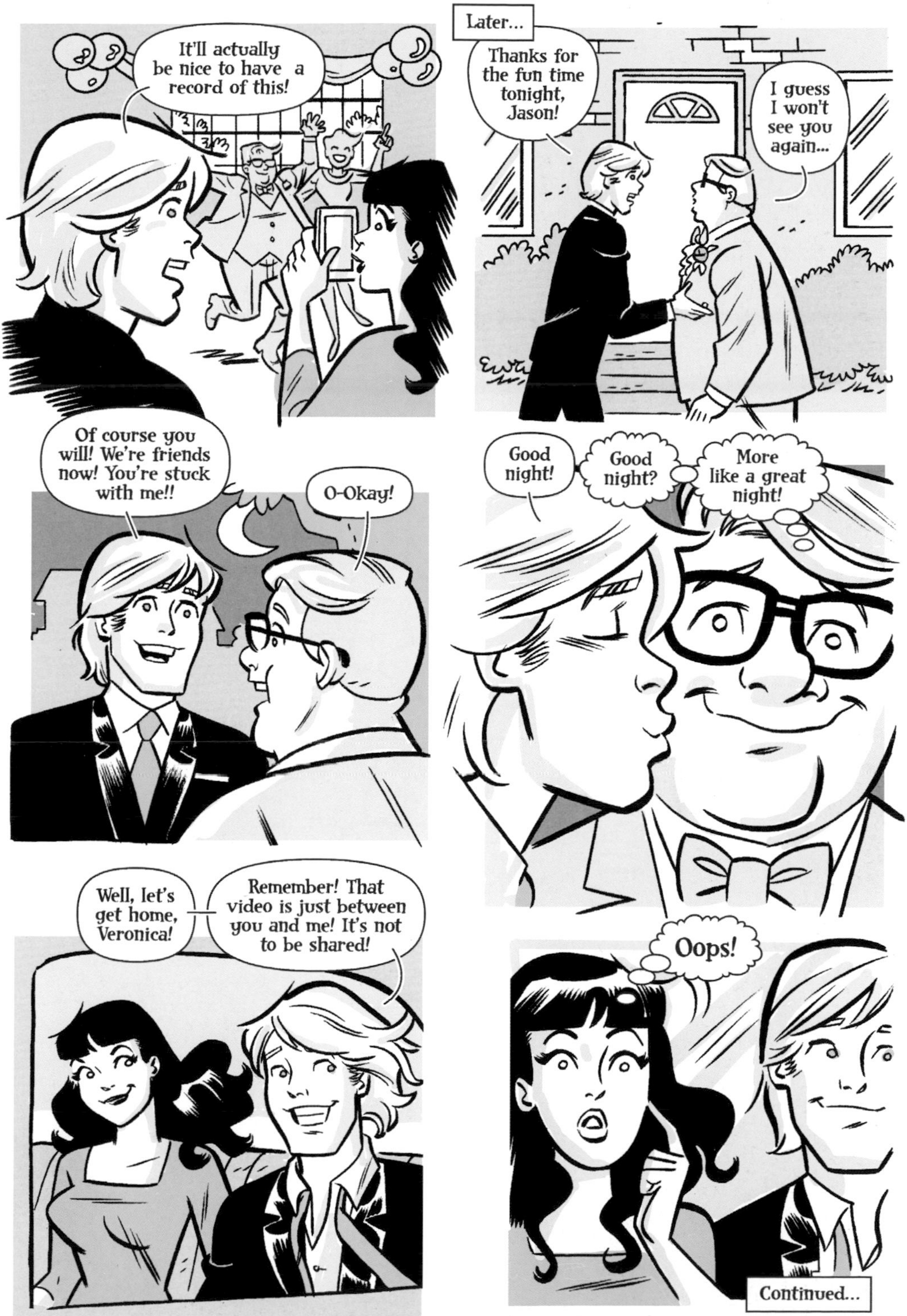
It'll actually be nice to have a record of this!
Later...
Thanks for the fun time tonight, Jason!
I guess I won't see you again...
Of course you will! We're friends now! You're stuck with me!!
O-Okay!
Good night!
Good night?
More like a great night!
Well, let's get home, Veronica!
Remember! That video is just between you and me! It's not to be shared!
Oops!
Continued...

CHAPTER 4

KEVIN in the CITY in PAST TENSE!

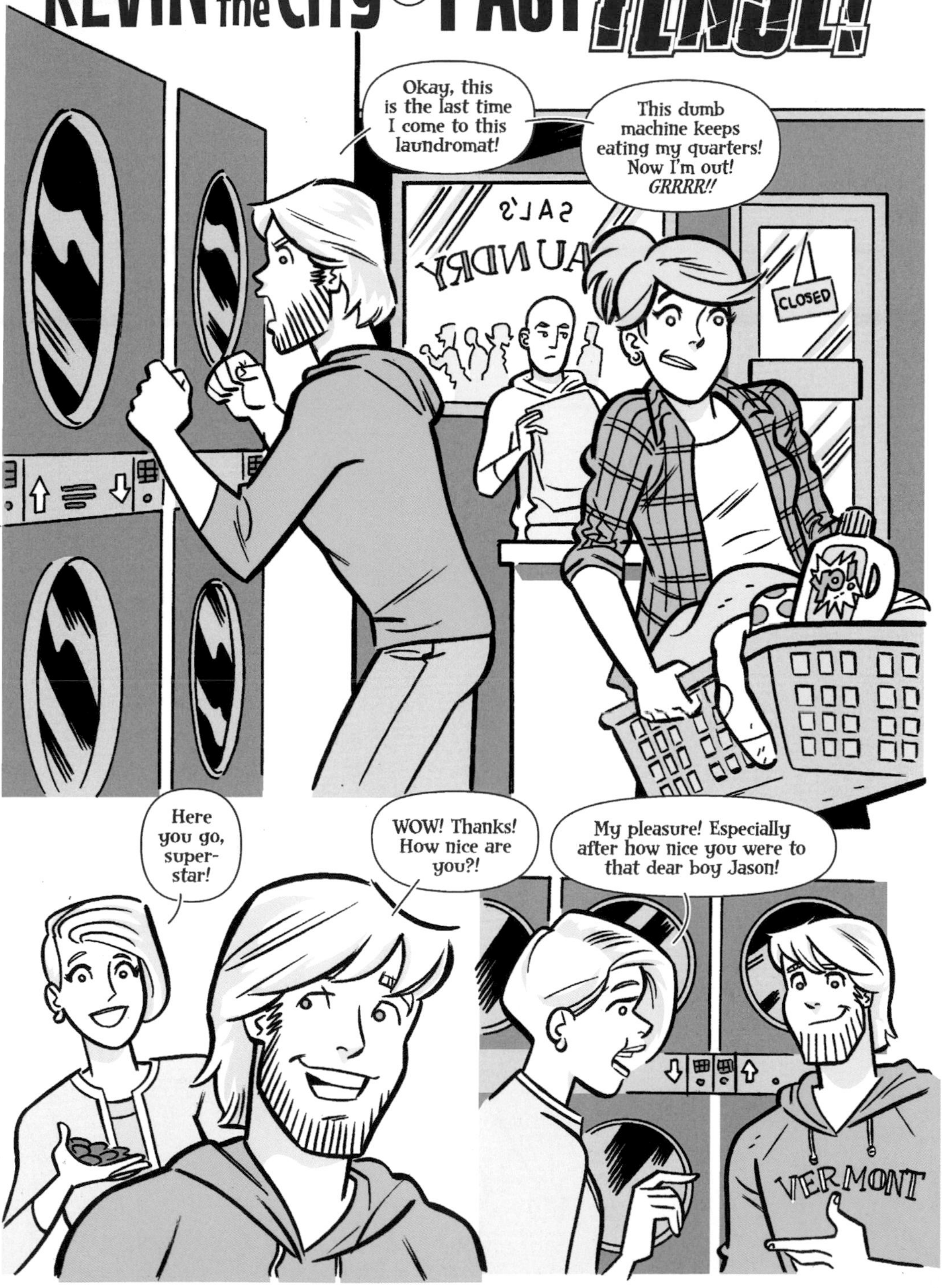

Okay, this is the last time I come to this laundromat!
This dumb machine keeps eating my quarters! Now I'm out! *GRRRR!!*
CLOSED
Here you go, super-star!
WOW! Thanks! How nice are you?!
My pleasure! Especially after how nice you were to that dear boy Jason!
VERMONT

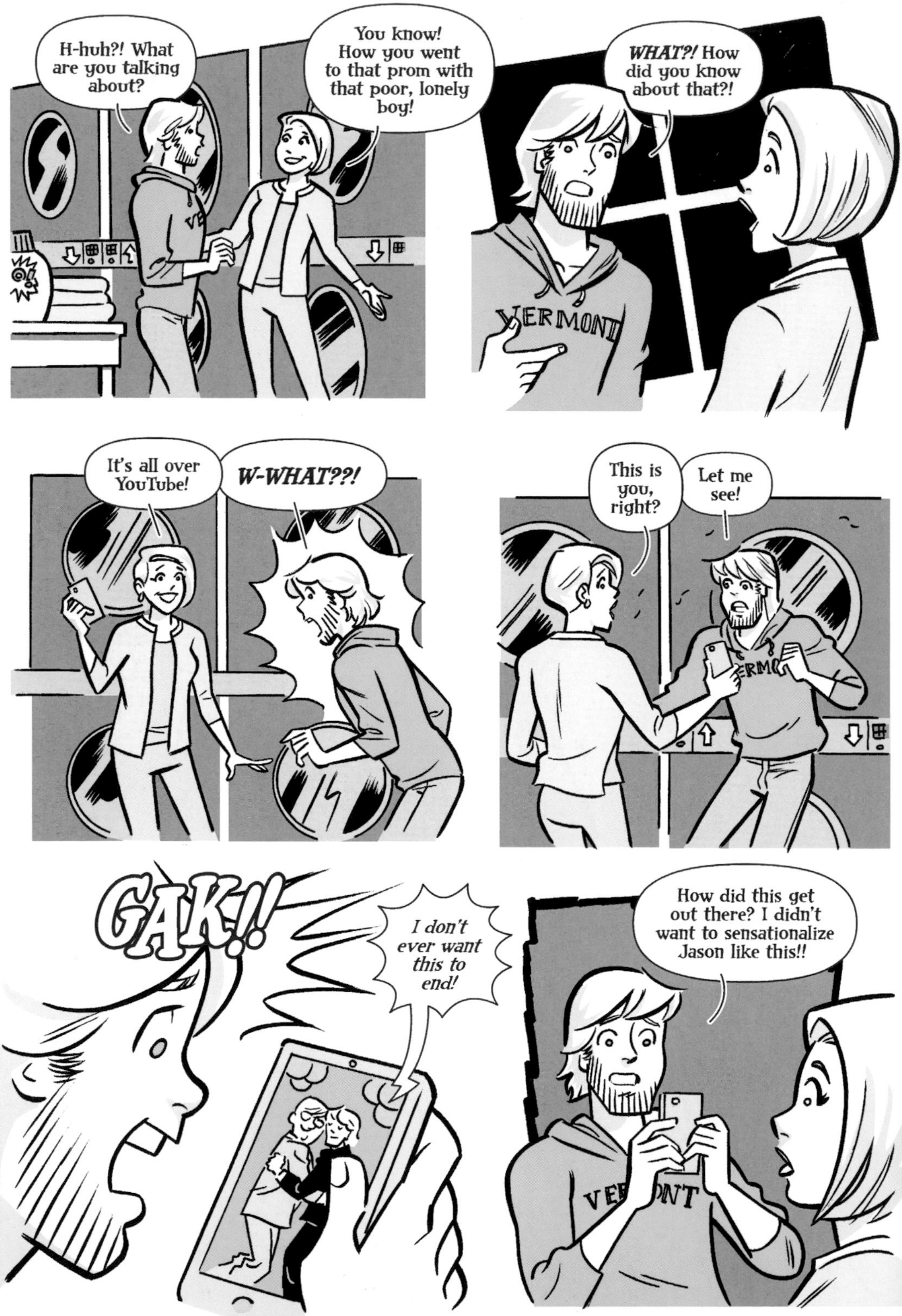
H-huh?! What are you talking about?
You know! How you went to that prom with that poor, lonely boy!
WHAT?! How did you know about that?!
VERMONT
It's all over YouTube!
W-WHAT??!
This is you, right?
Let me see!
GAK!!
I don't ever want this to end!
How did this get out there? I didn't want to sensationalize Jason like this!!

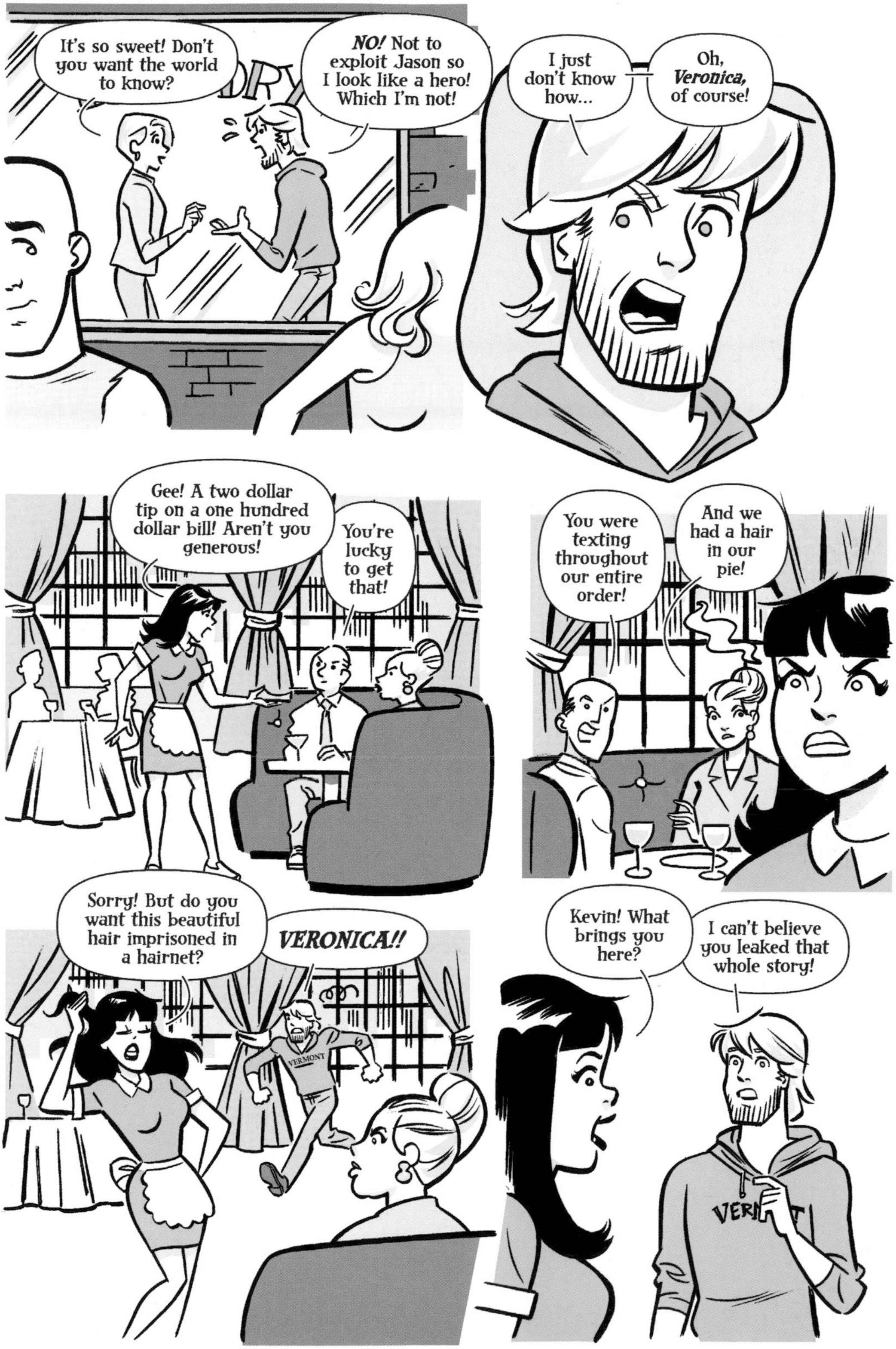
It's so sweet! Don't you want the world to know?
NO! Not to exploit Jason so I look like a hero! Which I'm not!
DRY
I just don't know how...
Oh, Veronica, of course!
Gee! A two dollar tip on a one hundred dollar bill! Aren't you generous!
You're lucky to get that!
You were texting throughout our entire order!
And we had a hair in our pie!
Sorry! But do you want this beautiful hair imprisoned in a hairnet?
VERONICA!!
VERMONT
Kevin! What brings you here?
I can't believe you leaked that whole story!

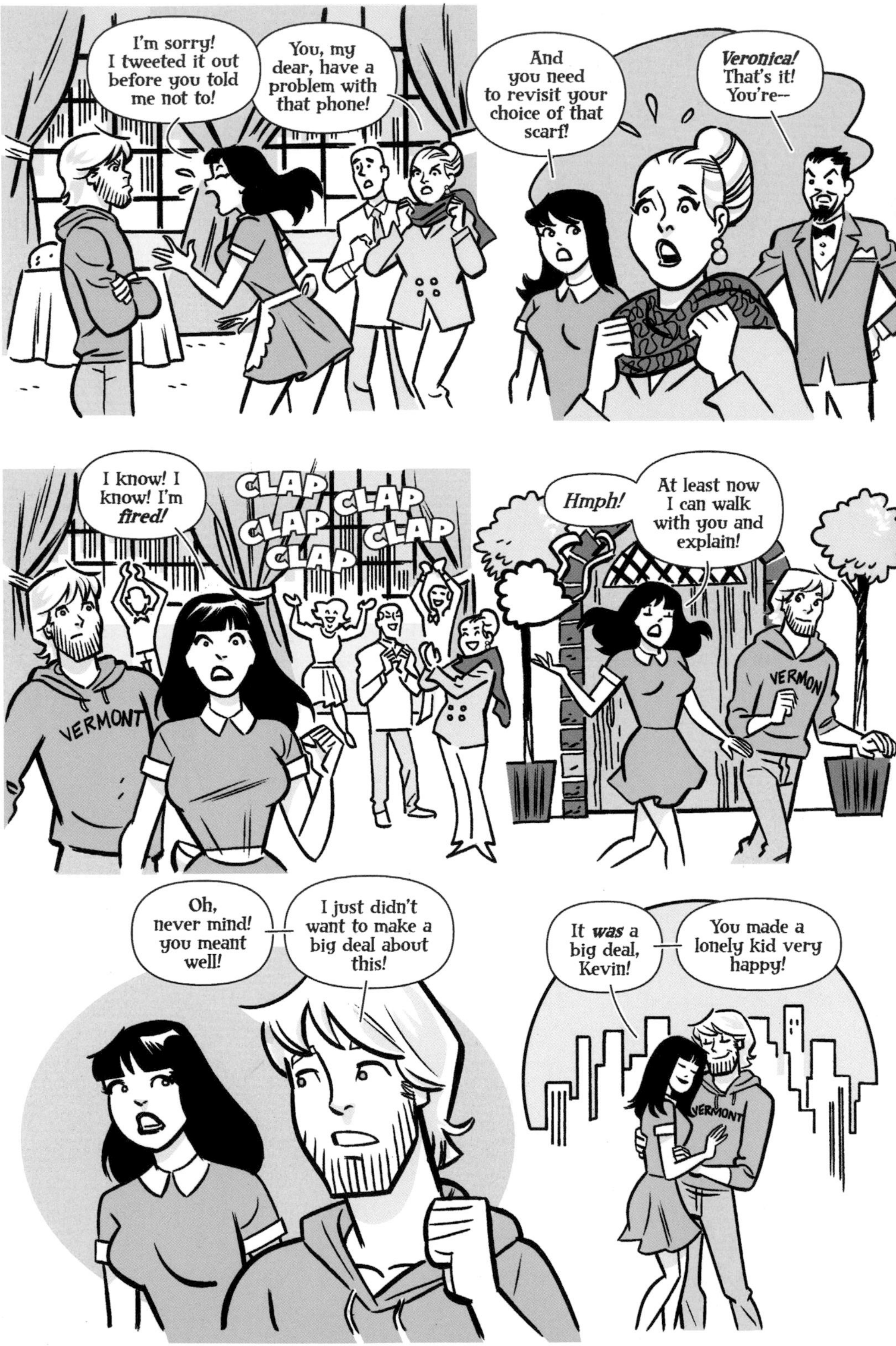
I'm sorry! I tweeted it out before you told me not to!
You, my dear, have a problem with that phone!
And you need to revisit your choice of that scarf!
Veronica! That's it! You're--
I know! I know! I'm *fired!*
CLAP CLAP CLAP CLAP CLAP
Hmph!
At least now I can walk with you and explain!
Oh, never mind! you meant well!
I just didn't want to make a big deal about this!
It *was* a big deal, Kevin!
You made a lonely kid very happy!
VERMONT

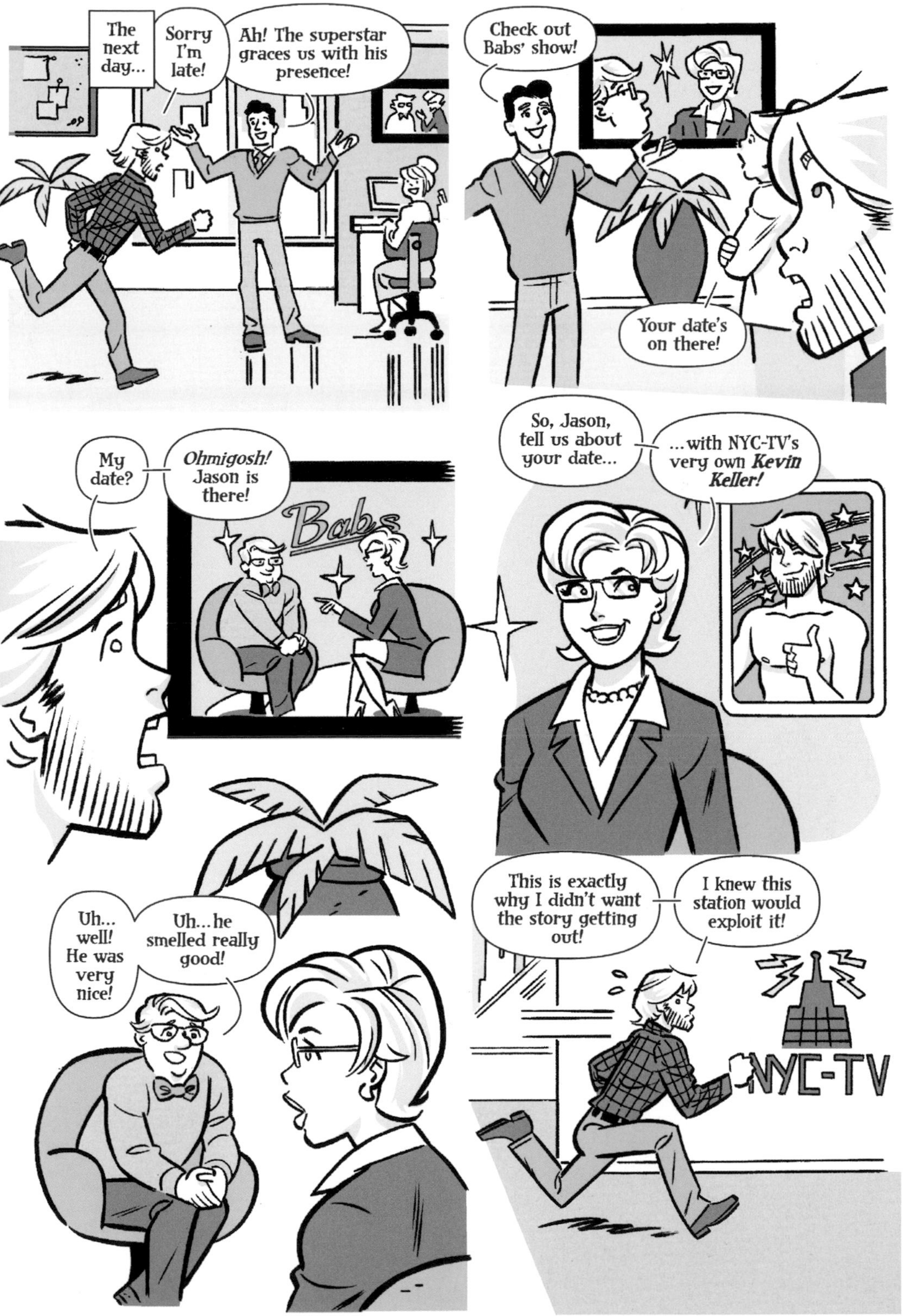

The next day...
Sorry I'm late!
Ah! The superstar graces us with his presence!
Check out Babs' show!
Your date's on there!
My date?
Ohmigosh! Jason is there!
Babs
So, Jason, tell us about your date...
...with NYC-TV's very own Kevin Keller!
Uh... well! He was very nice!
Uh... he smelled really good!
This is exactly why I didn't want the story getting out!
I knew this station would exploit it!
NYC-TV

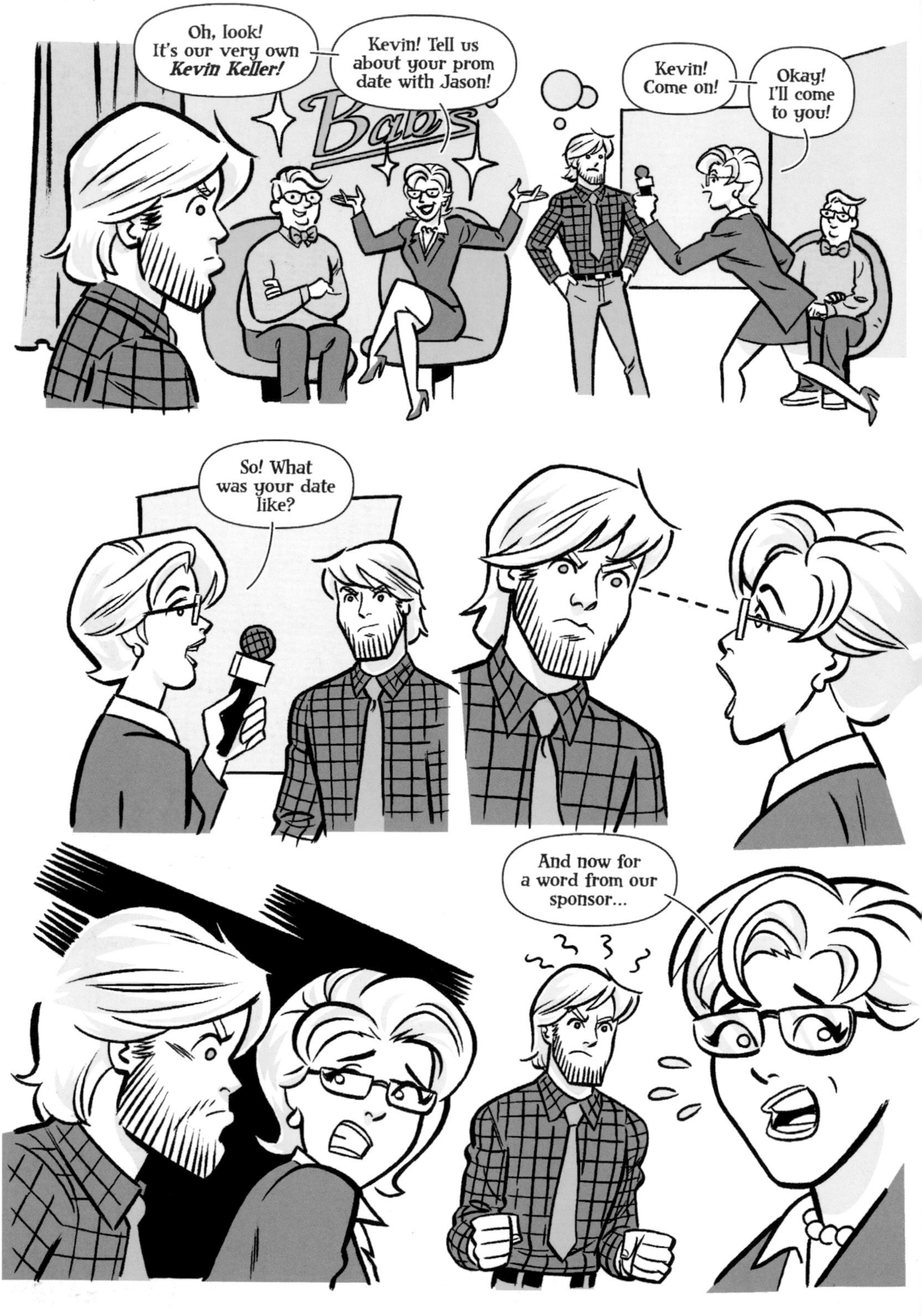
Oh, look! It's our very own *Kevin Keller!*
Kevin! Tell us about your prom date with Jason!
Kevin! Come on!
Okay! I'll come to you!
So! What was your date like?
And now for a word from our sponsor...

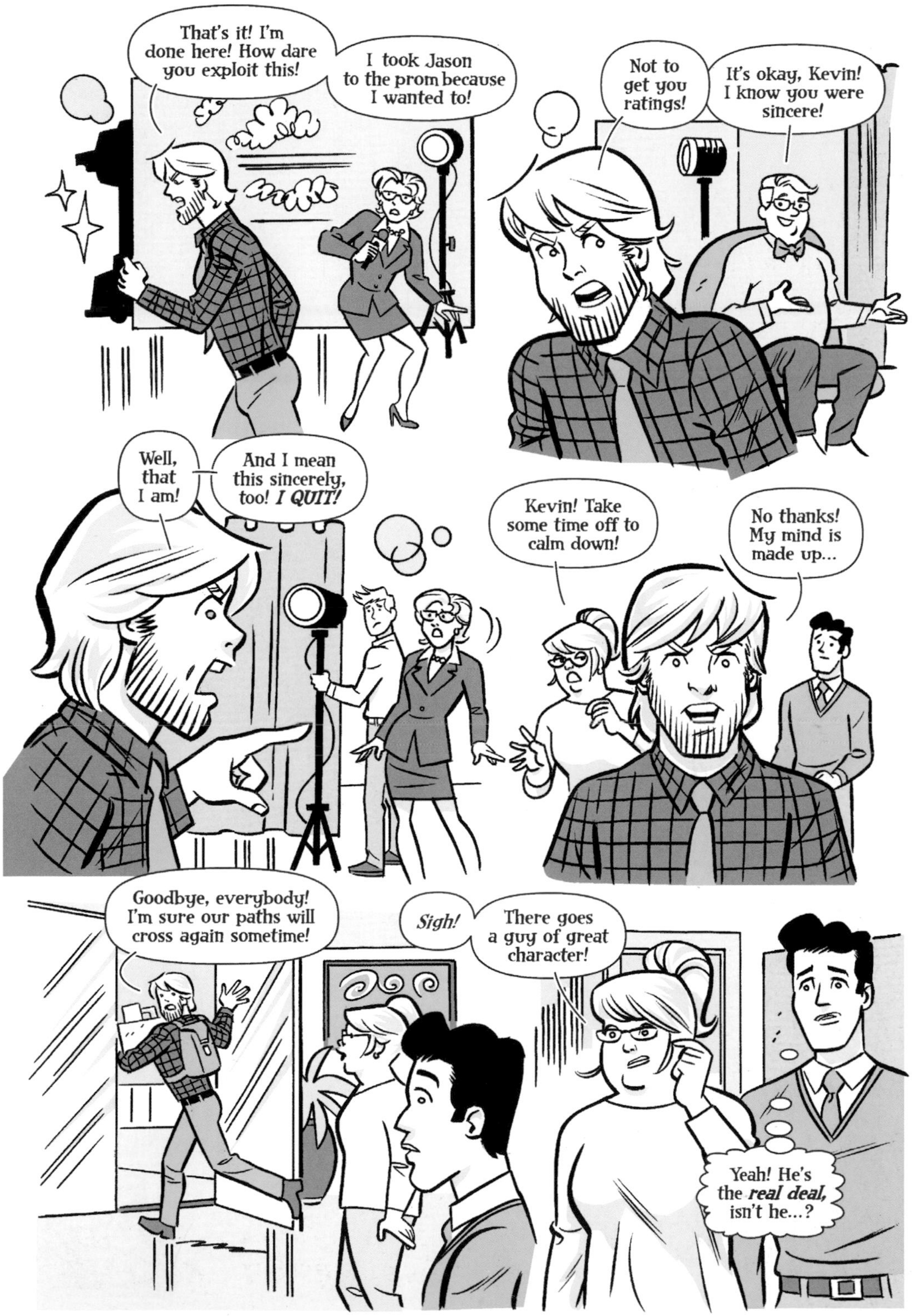
That's it! I'm done here! How dare you exploit this!
I took Jason to the prom because I wanted to!
Not to get you ratings!
It's okay, Kevin! I know you were sincere!
Well, that I am!
And I mean this sincerely, too! *I QUIT!*
Kevin! Take some time off to calm down!
No thanks! My mind is made up...
Goodbye, everybody! I'm sure our paths will cross again sometime!
Sigh!
There goes a guy of great character!
Yeah! He's the *real deal,* isn't he...?

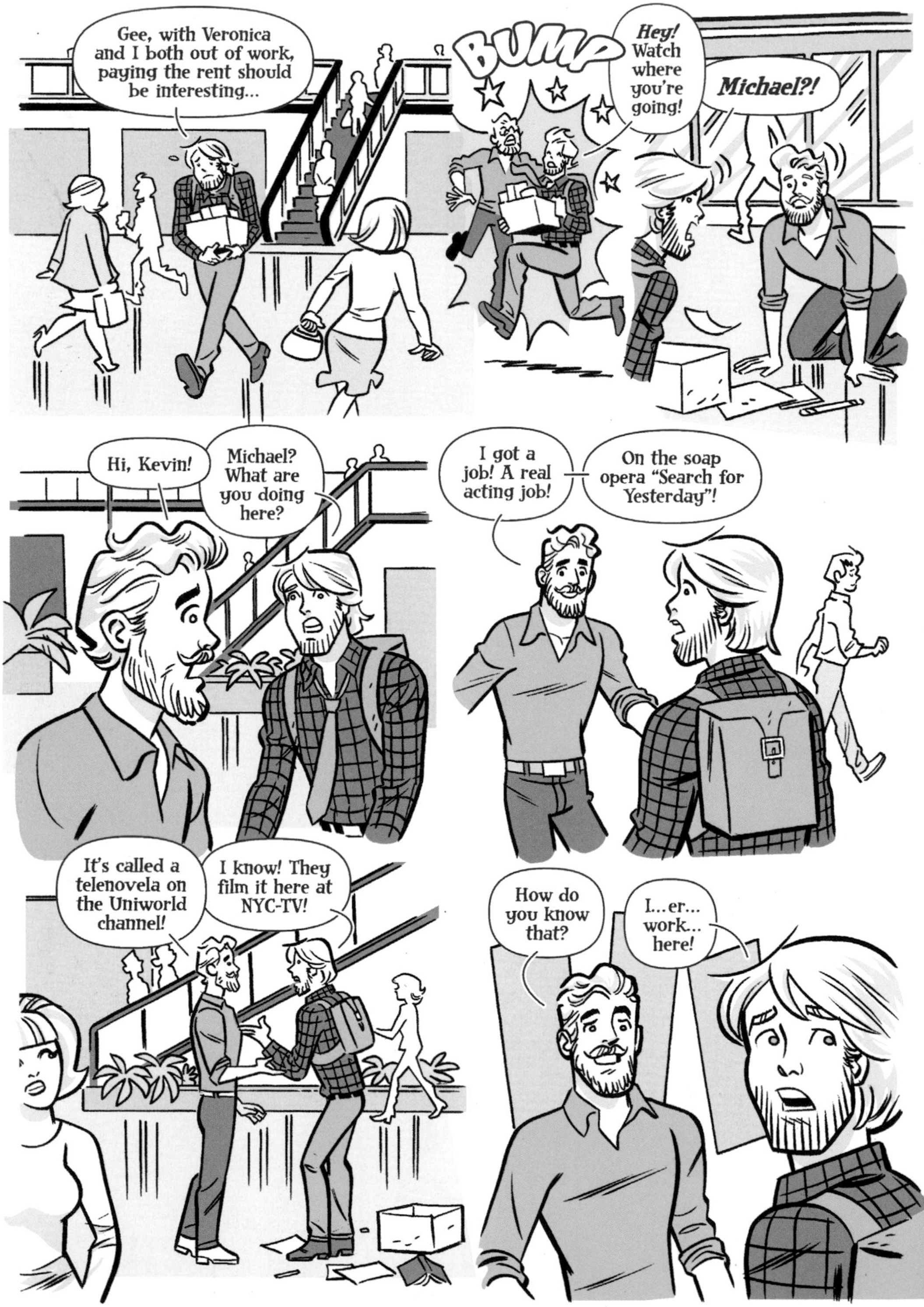
Gee, with Veronica and I both out of work, paying the rent should be interesting...
BUMP
Hey! Watch where you're going!
Michael?!
Hi, Kevin!
Michael? What are you doing here?
I got a job! A real acting job!
On the soap opera "Search for Yesterday"!
It's called a telenovela on the Uniworld channel!
I know! They film it here at NYC-TV!
How do you know that?
I...er... work... here!

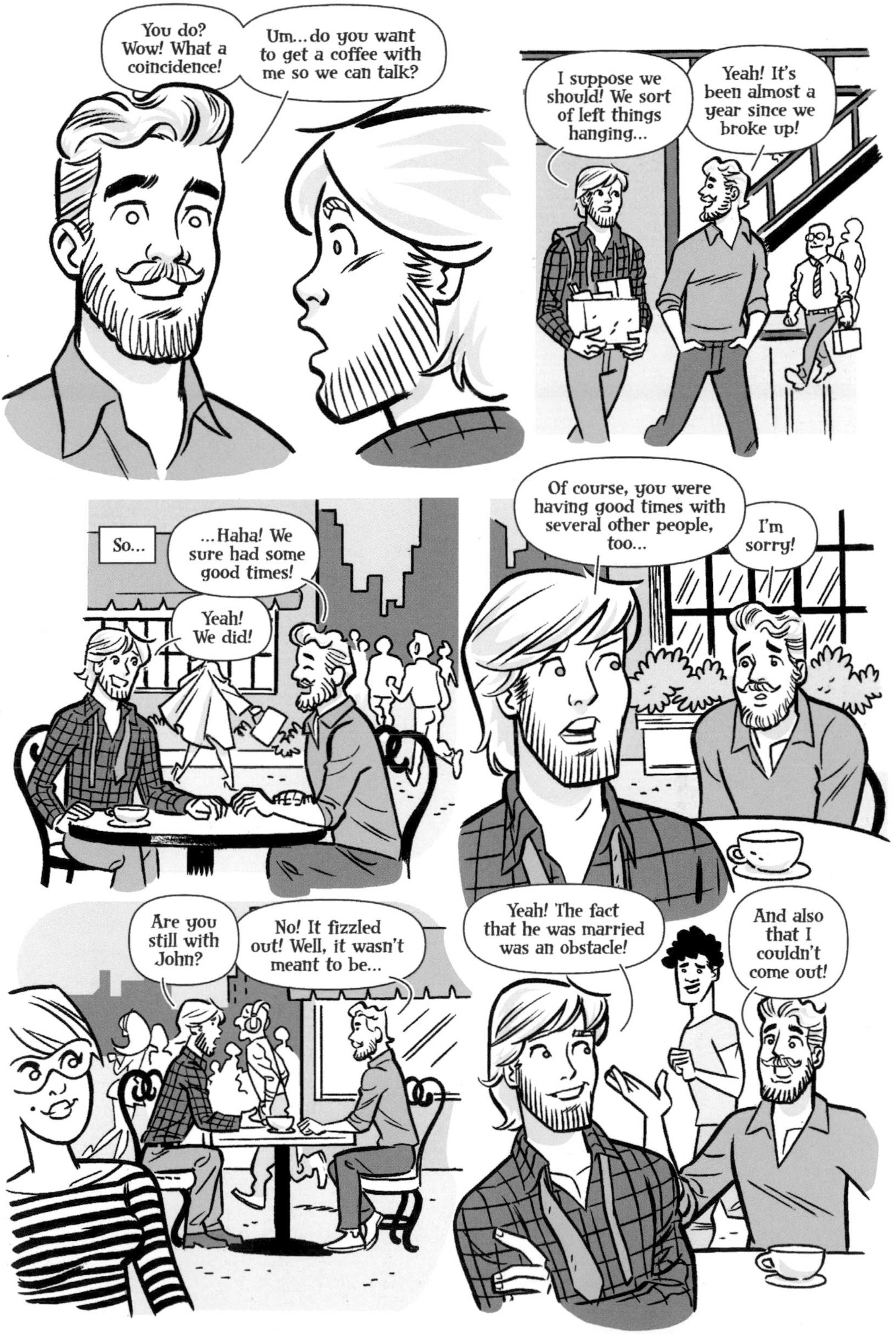
You do? Wow! What a coincidence!
Um...do you want to get a coffee with me so we can talk?
I suppose we should! We sort of left things hanging...
Yeah! It's been almost a year since we broke up!
So...
...Haha! We sure had some good times!
Yeah! We did!
Of course, you were having good times with several other people, too...
I'm sorry!
Are you still with John?
No! It fizzled out! Well, it wasn't meant to be...
Yeah! The fact that he was married was an obstacle!
And also that I couldn't come out!

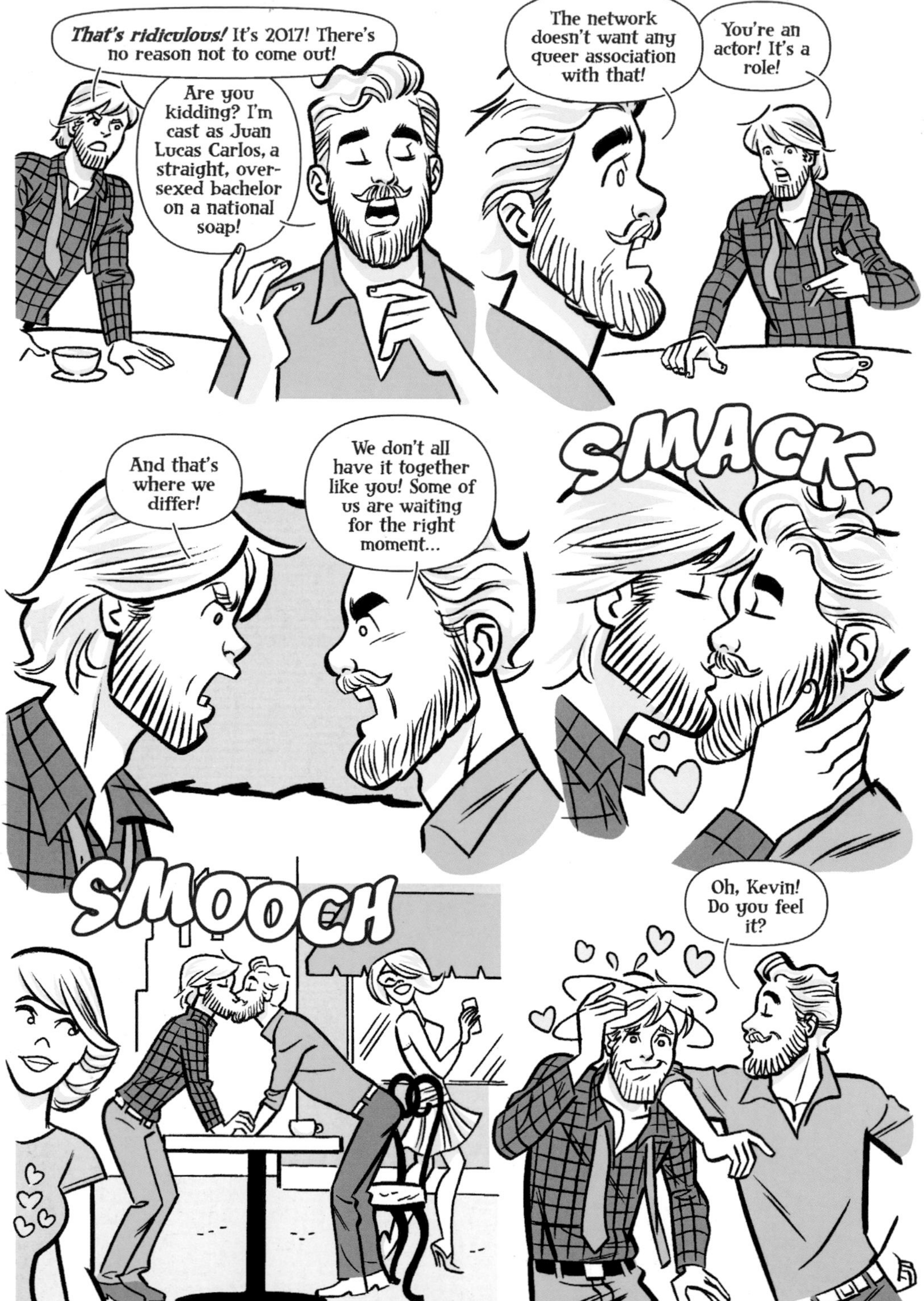
That's ridiculous! It's 2017! There's no reason not to come out!
Are you kidding? I'm cast as Juan Lucas Carlos, a straight, over-sexed bachelor on a national soap!
The network doesn't want any queer association with that!
You're an actor! It's a role!
And that's where we differ!
We don't all have it together like you! Some of us are waiting for the right moment...
SMACK
SMOOCH
Oh, Kevin! Do you feel it?

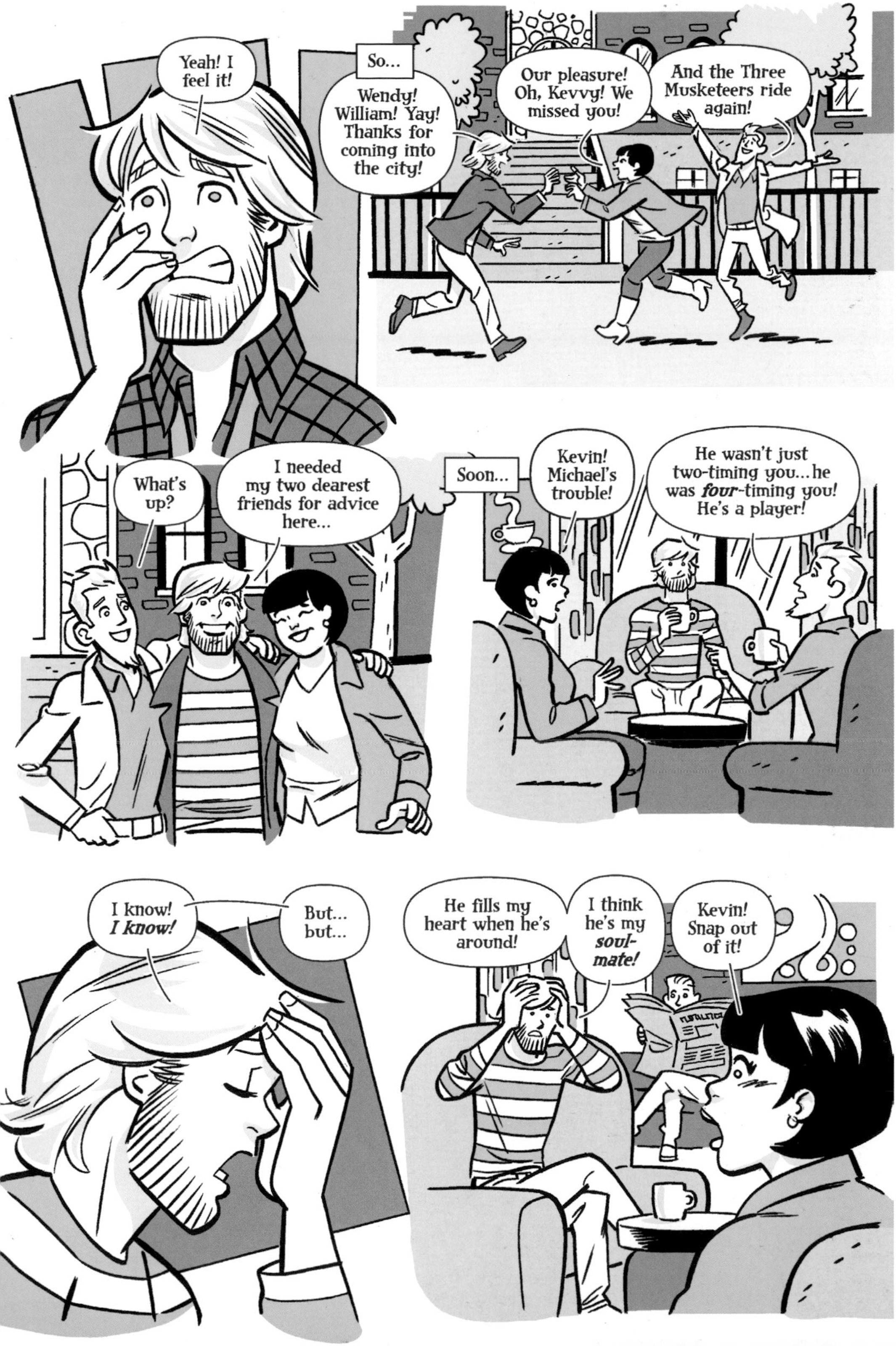

Yeah! I feel it!
So...
Wendy! William! Yay! Thanks for coming into the city!
Our pleasure! Oh, Kevvy! We missed you!
And the Three Musketeers ride again!
What's up?
I needed my two dearest friends for advice here...
Soon...
Kevin! Michael's trouble!
He wasn't just two-timing you...he was *four*-timing you! He's a player!
I know! *I know!*
But... but...
He fills my heart when he's around!
I think he's my *soul-mate!*
Kevin! Snap out of it!

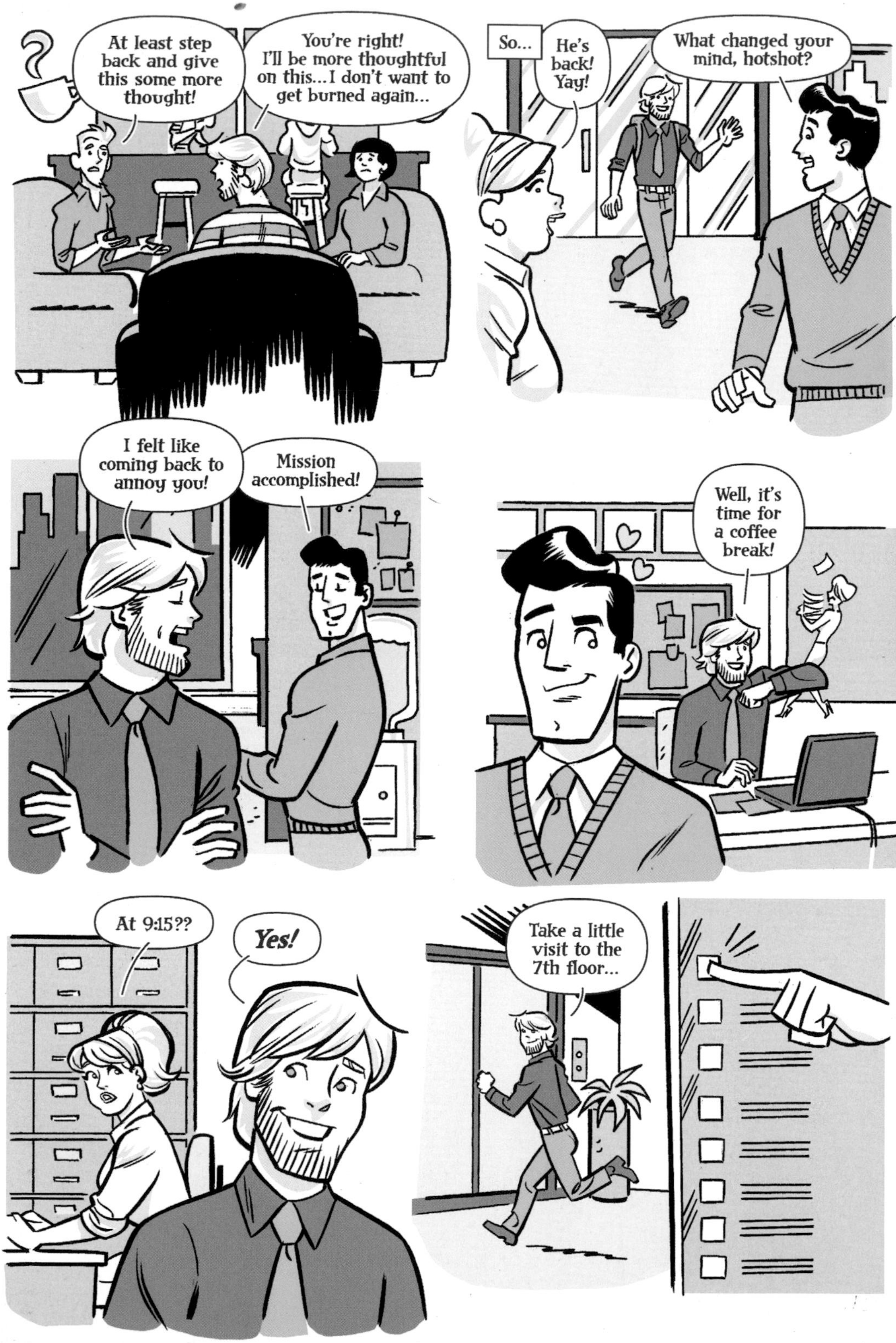
At least step back and give this some more thought!
You're right! I'll be more thoughtful on this...I don't want to get burned again...
So...
He's back! Yay!
What changed your mind, hotshot?
I felt like coming back to annoy you!
Mission accomplished!
Well, it's time for a coffee break!
At 9:15??
Yes!
Take a little visit to the 7th floor...

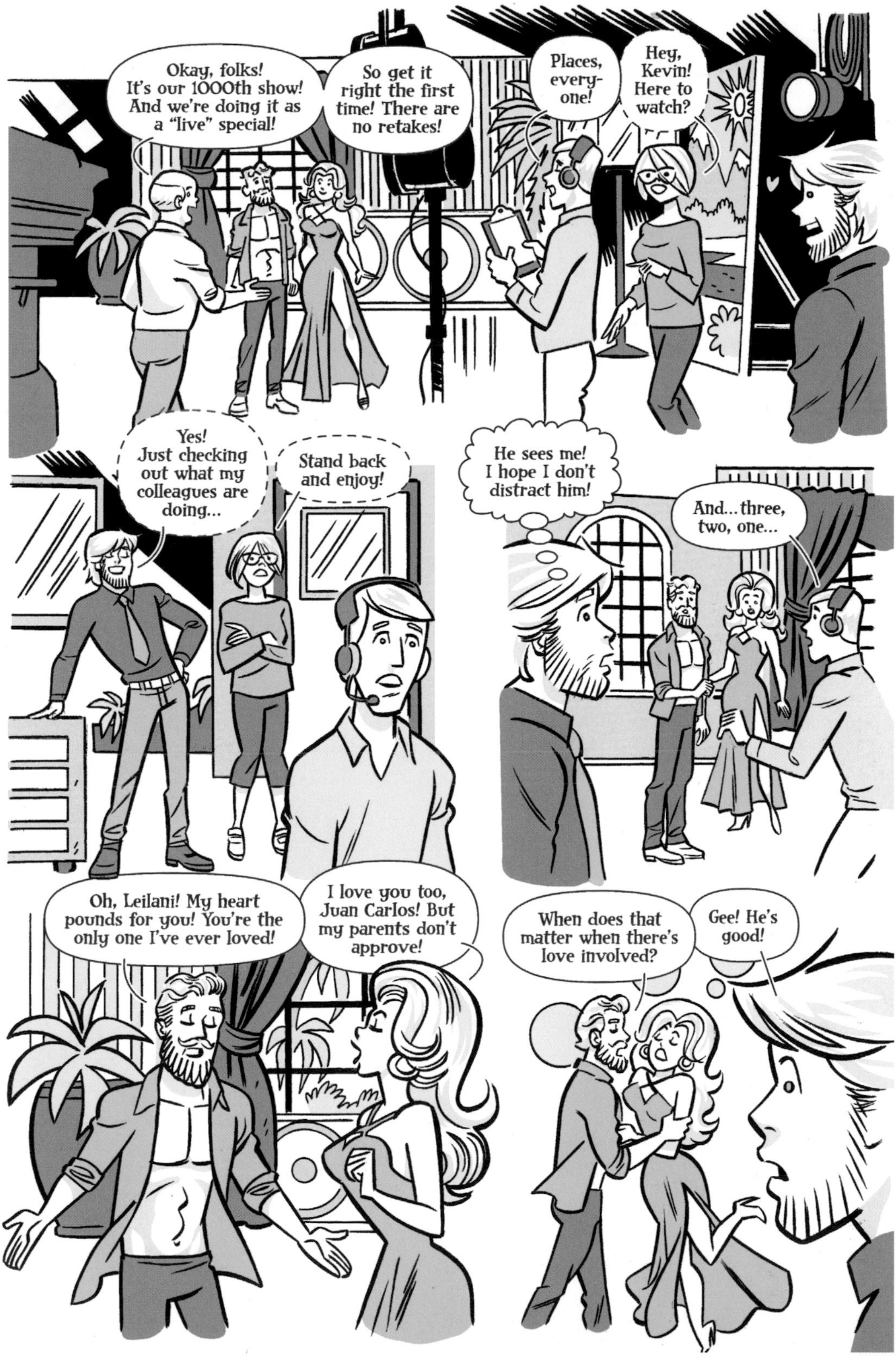
Okay, folks! It's our 1000th show! And we're doing it as a "live" special!
So get it right the first time! There are no retakes!
Places, every-one!
Hey, Kevin! Here to watch?
Yes! Just checking out what my colleagues are doing...
Stand back and enjoy!
He sees me! I hope I don't distract him!
And...three, two, one...
Oh, Leilani! My heart pounds for you! You're the only one I've ever loved!
I love you too, Juan Carlos! But my parents don't approve!
When does that matter when there's love involved?
Gee! He's good!

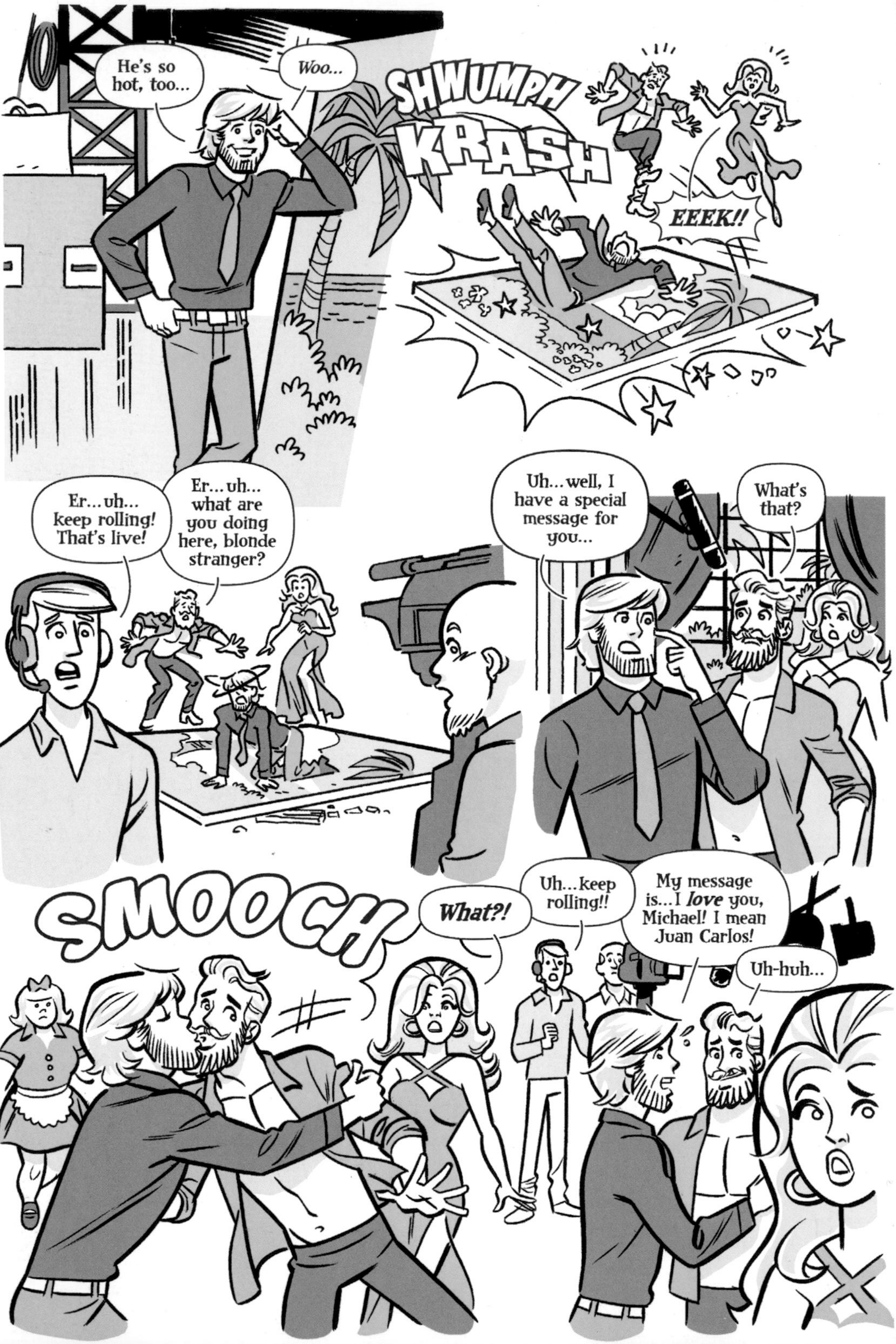
He's so hot, too...
Woo...
SHWUMPH
KRASH
EEEK!!
Er...uh... keep rolling! That's live!
Er...uh... what are you doing here, blonde stranger?
Uh...well, I have a special message for you...
What's that?
SMOOCH
What?!
Uh...keep rolling!!
My message is...I *love* you, Michael! I mean Juan Carlos!
Uh-huh...

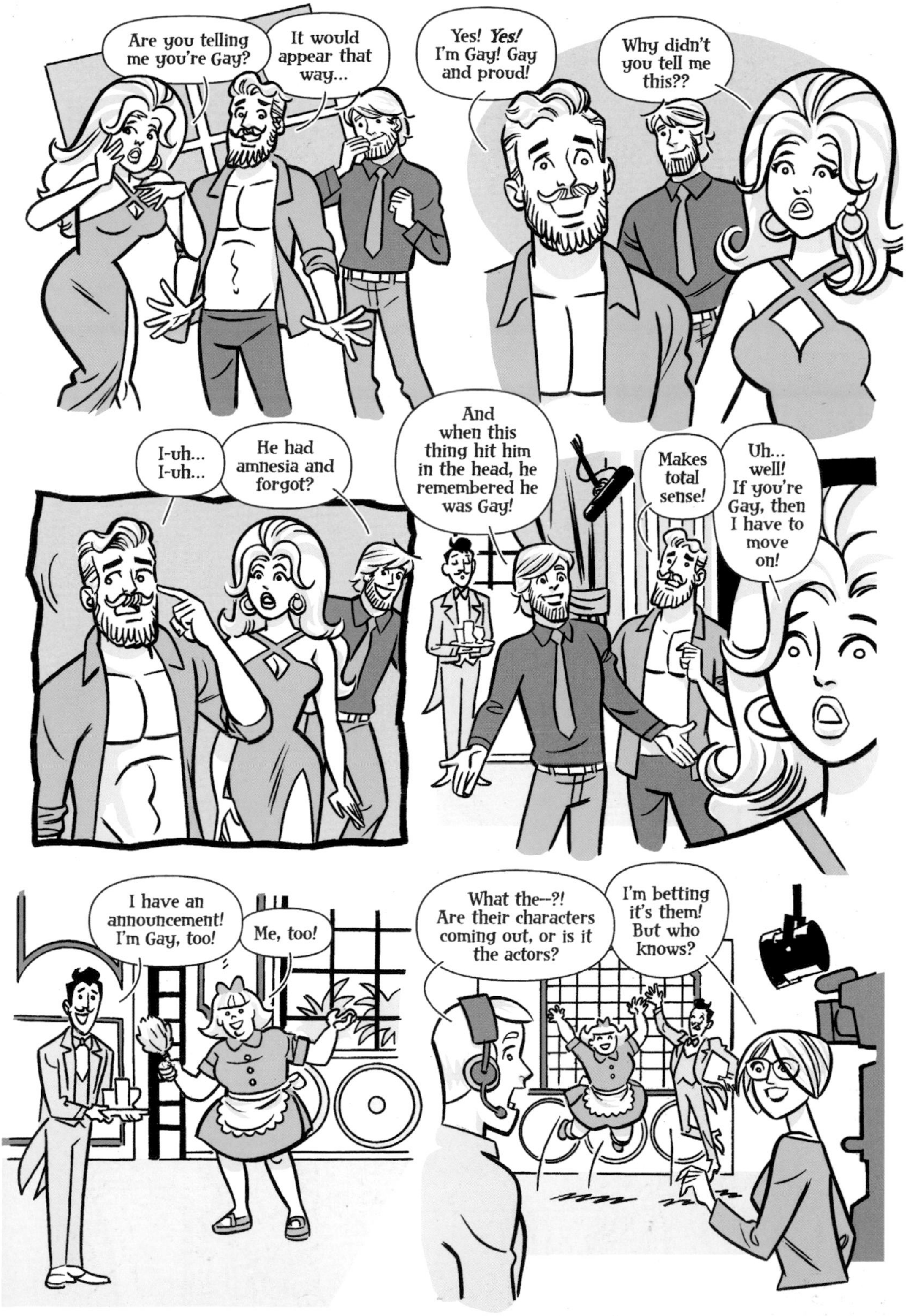

Are you telling me you're Gay?
It would appear that way...
Yes! *Yes!* I'm Gay! Gay and proud!
Why didn't you tell me this??
I-uh... I-uh...
He had amnesia and forgot?
And when this thing hit him in the head, he remembered he was Gay!
Makes total sense!
Uh... well! If you're Gay, then I have to move on!
I have an announcement! I'm Gay, too!
Me, too!
What the--?! Are their characters coming out, or is it the actors?
I'm betting it's them! But who knows?

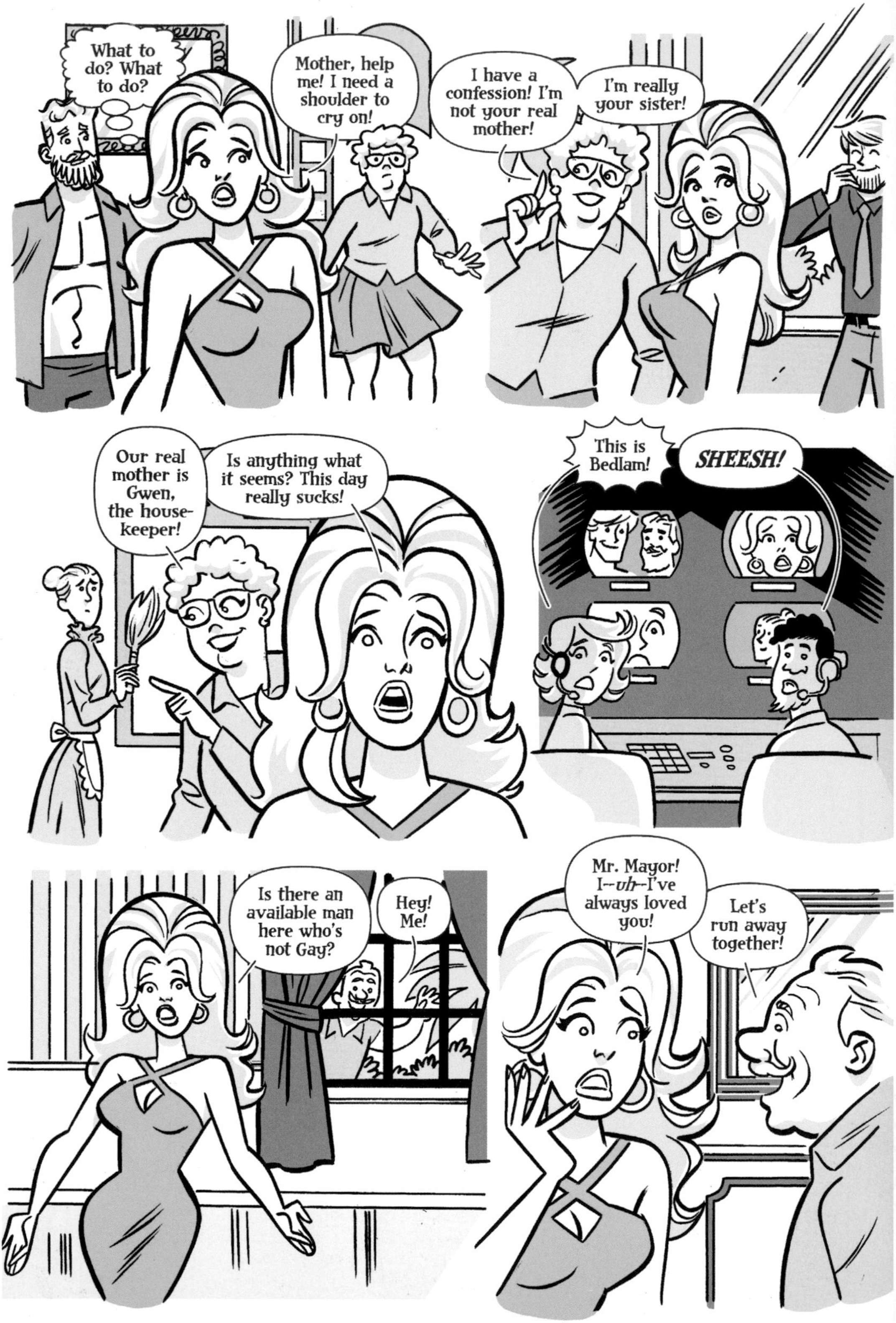
What to do? What to do?
Mother, help me! I need a shoulder to cry on!
I have a confession! I'm not your real mother!
I'm really your sister!
Our real mother is Gwen, the house-keeper!
Is anything what it seems? This day really sucks!
This is Bedlam!
SHEESH!
Is there an available man here who's not Gay?
Hey! Me!
Mr. Mayor! I--*uh*--I've always loved you!
Let's run away together!

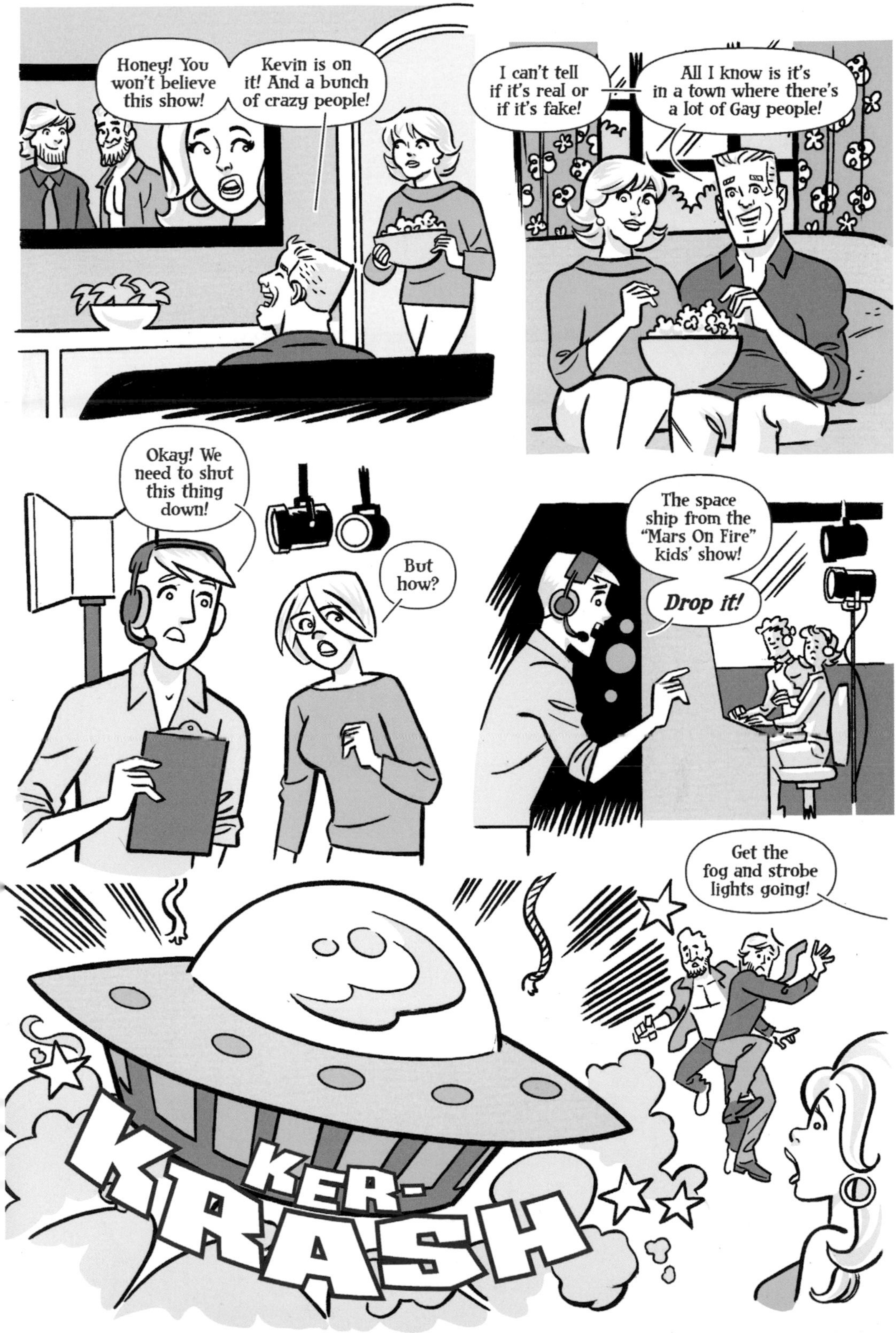
Honey! You won't believe this show!
Kevin is on it! And a bunch of crazy people!
I can't tell if it's real or if it's fake!
All I know is it's in a town where there's a lot of Gay people!
Okay! We need to shut this thing down!
But how?
The space ship from the "Mars On Fire" kids' show!
Drop it!
Get the fog and strobe lights going!
KER-KRASH

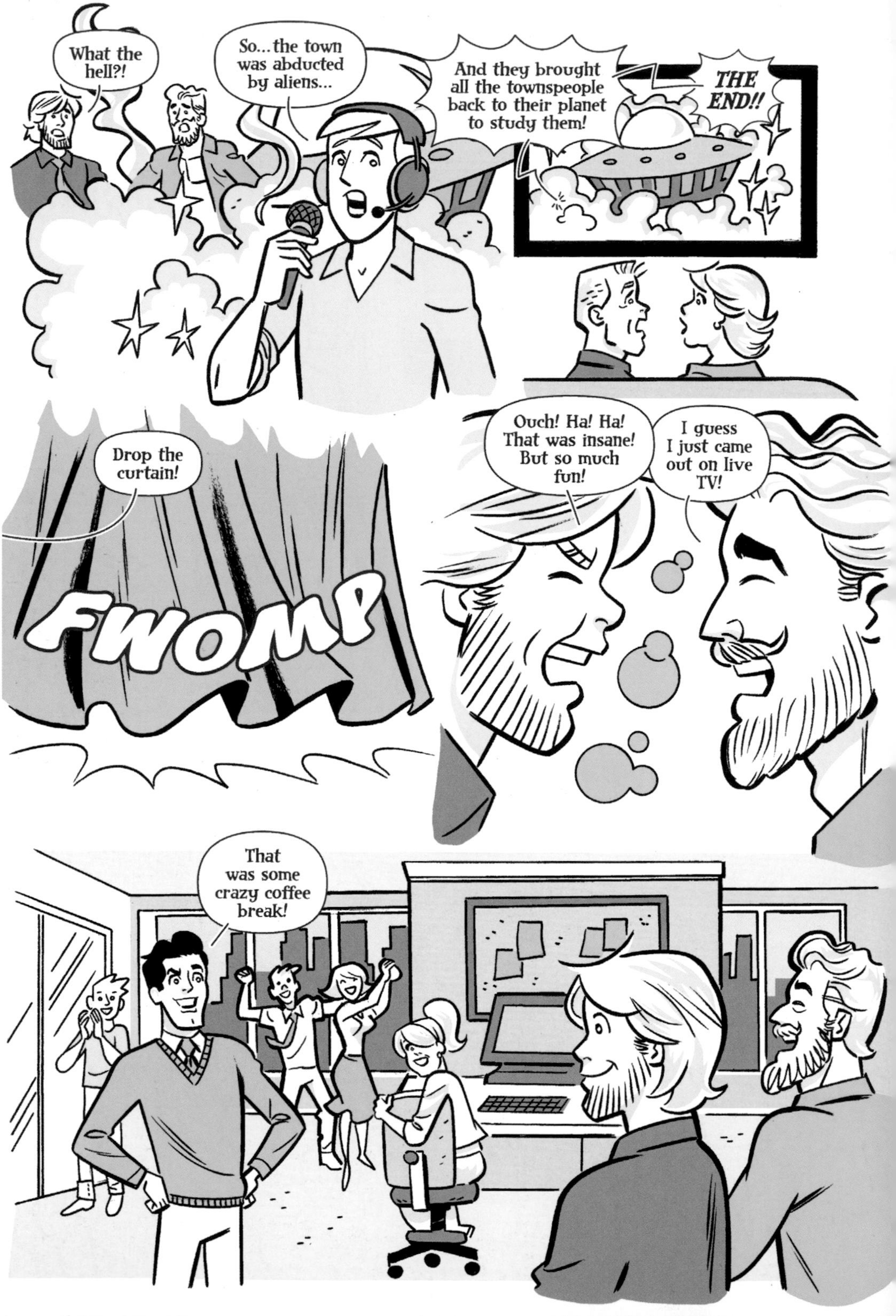
What the hell?!
So...the town was abducted by aliens...
And they brought all the townspeople back to their planet to study them!
THE END!!
Drop the curtain!
FWOMP
Ouch! Ha! Ha! That was insane! But so much fun!
I guess I just came out on live TV!
That was some crazy coffee break!

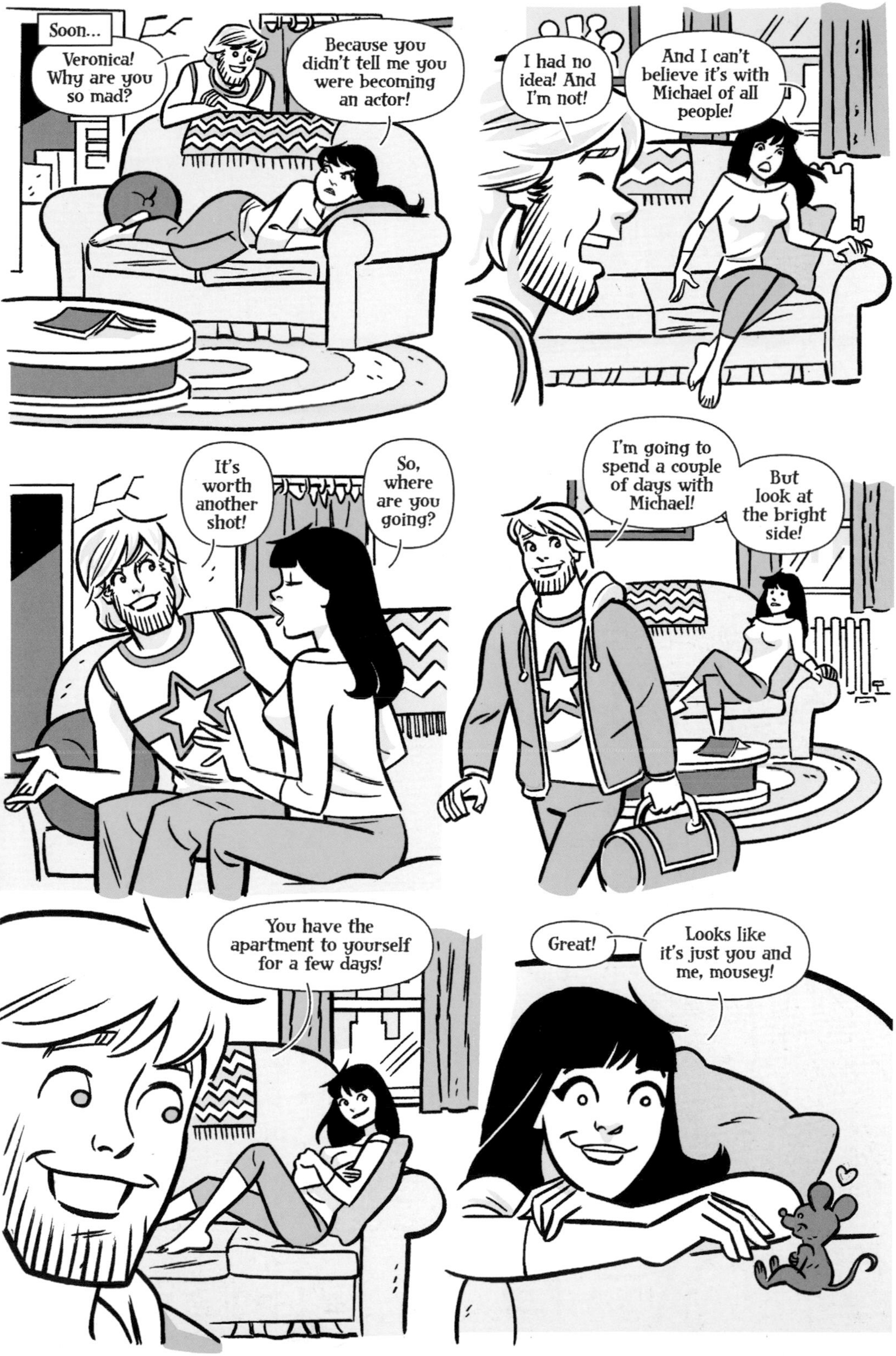
Soon...
Veronica! Why are you so mad?
Because you didn't tell me you were becoming an actor!
I had no idea! And I'm not!
And I can't believe it's with Michael of all people!
It's worth another shot!
So, where are you going?
I'm going to spend a couple of days with Michael!
But look at the bright side!
You have the apartment to yourself for a few days!
Great!
Looks like it's just you and me, mousey!

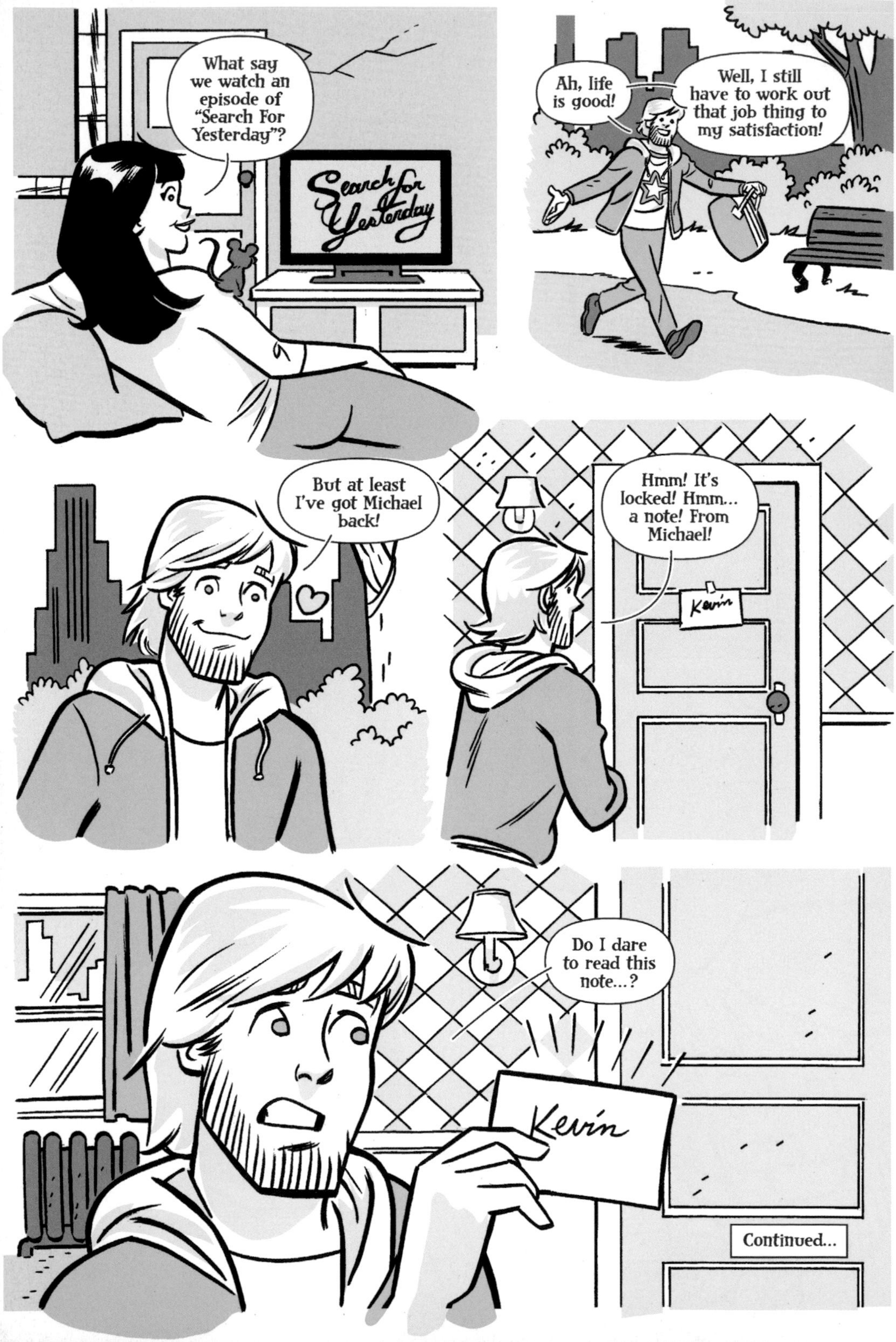
What say we watch an episode of "Search For Yesterday"?
Search for Yesterday
Ah, life is good!
Well, I still have to work out that job thing to my satisfaction!
But at least I've got Michael back!
Hmm! It's locked! Hmm... a note! From Michael!
Kevin
Do I dare to read this note...?
Kevin
Continued...

CHAPTER 5

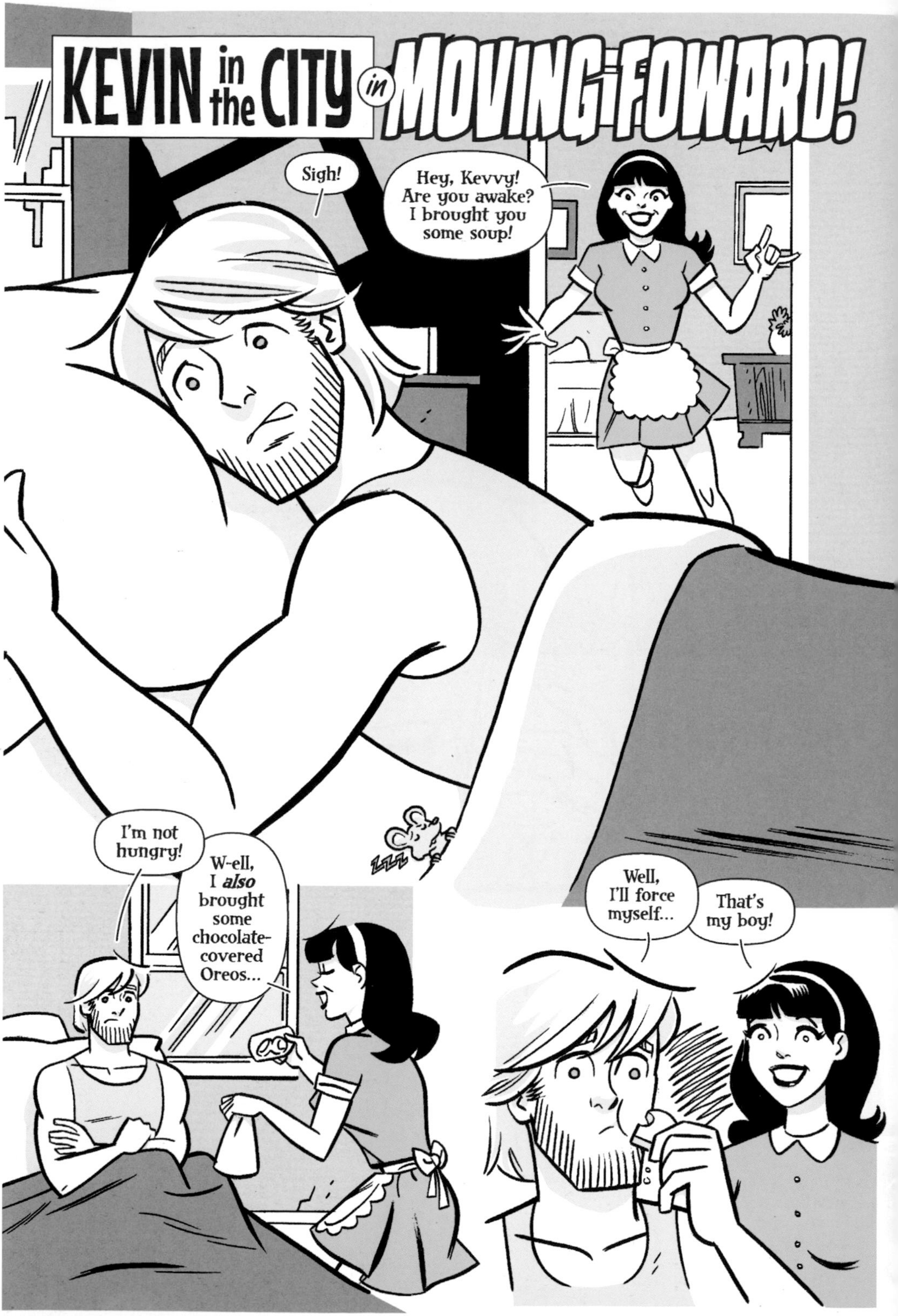
KEVIN in the CITY in MOVING FOWARD!
Sigh!
Hey, Kevvy! Are you awake? I brought you some soup!
I'm not hungry!
W-ell, I *also* brought some chocolate-covered Oreos...
Well, I'll force myself...
That's my boy!

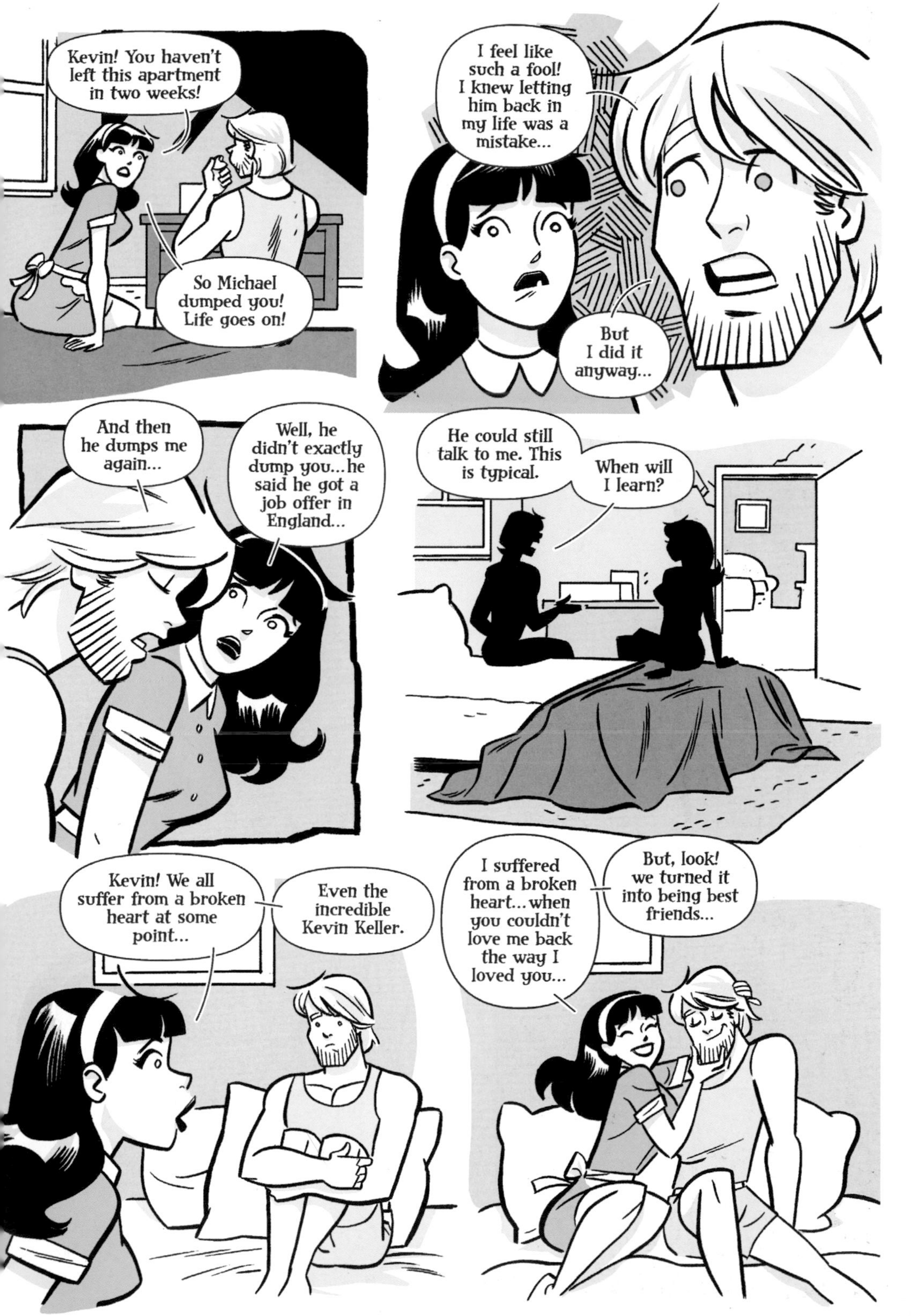
Kevin! You haven't left this apartment in two weeks!
So Michael dumped you! Life goes on!
I feel like such a fool! I knew letting him back in my life was a mistake...
But I did it anyway...
And then he dumps me again...
Well, he didn't exactly dump you...he said he got a job offer in England...
He could still talk to me. This is typical.
When will I learn?
Kevin! We all suffer from a broken heart at some point...
Even the incredible Kevin Keller.
I suffered from a broken heart...when you couldn't love me back the way I loved you...
But, look! we turned it into being best friends...

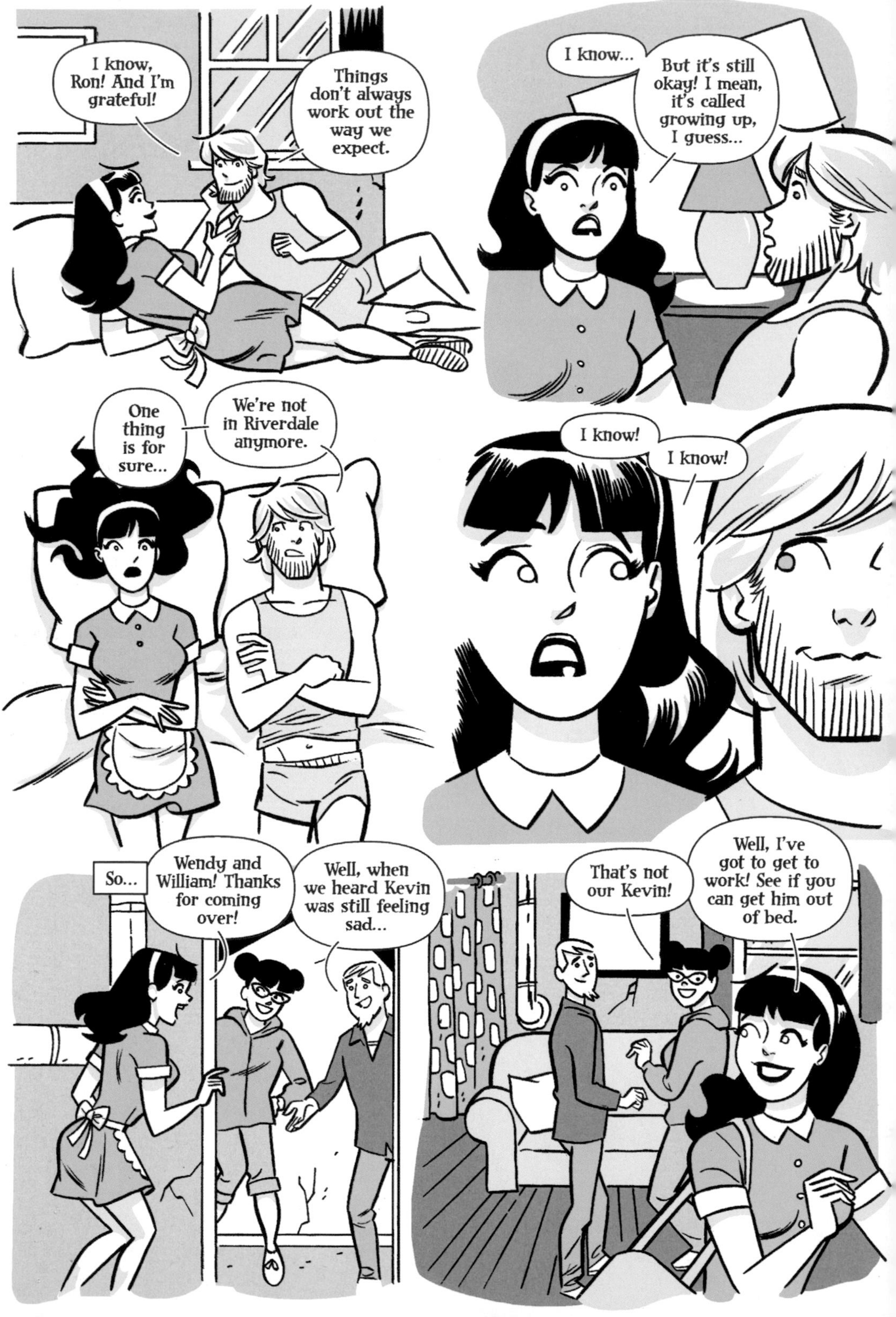
I know, Ron! And I'm grateful!
Things don't always work out the way we expect.
I know...
But it's still okay! I mean, it's called growing up, I guess...
One thing is for sure...
We're not in Riverdale anymore.
I know!
I know!
So...
Wendy and William! Thanks for coming over!
Well, when we heard Kevin was still feeling sad...
That's not our Kevin!
Well, I've got to get to work! See if you can get him out of bed.

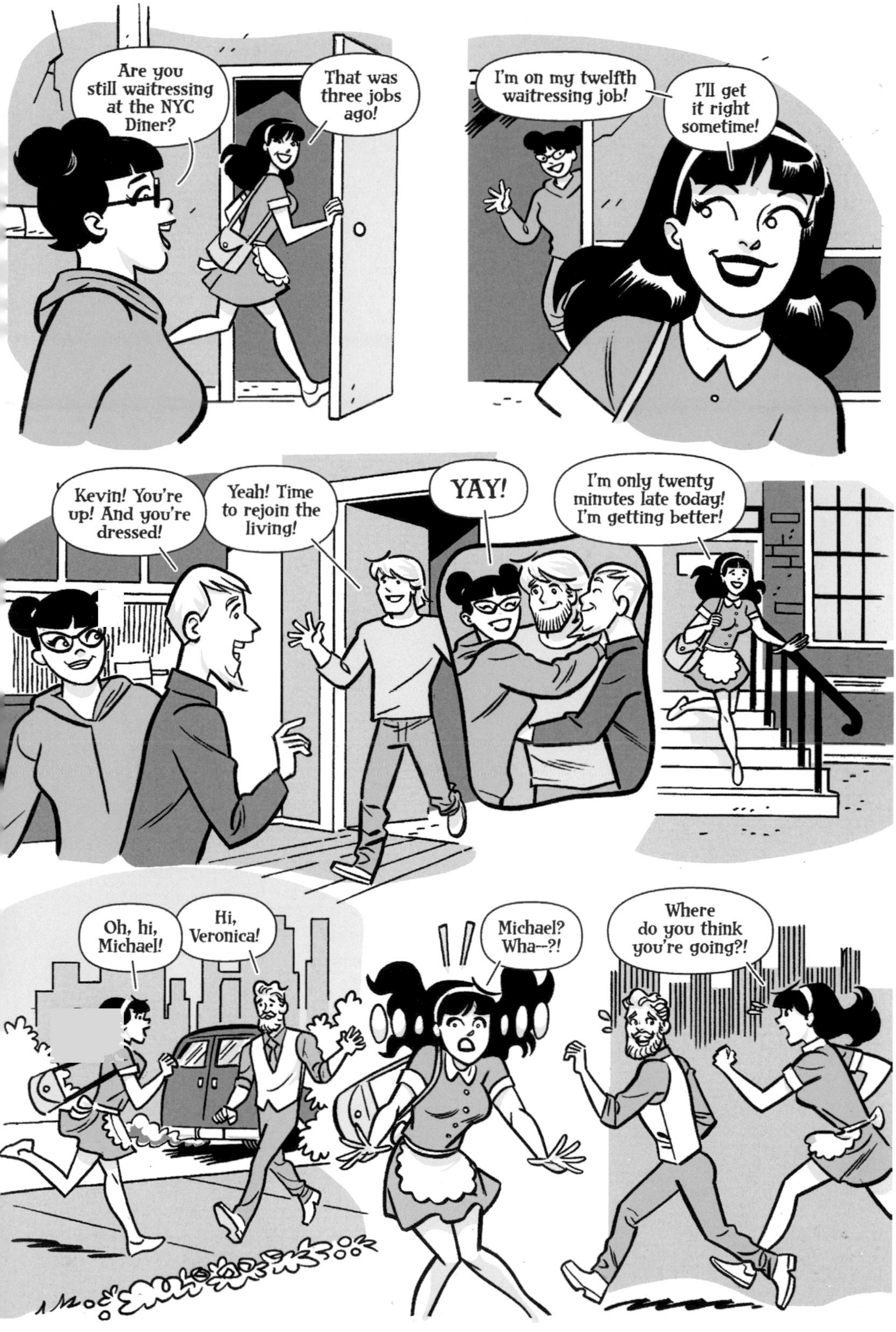
Are you still waitressing at the NYC Diner?
That was three jobs ago!
I'm on my twelfth waitressing job!
I'll get it right sometime!
Kevin! You're up! And you're dressed!
Yeah! Time to rejoin the living!
YAY!
I'm only twenty minutes late today! I'm getting better!
Oh, hi, Michael!
Hi, Veronica!
Michael? Wha--?!
Where do you think you're going?!

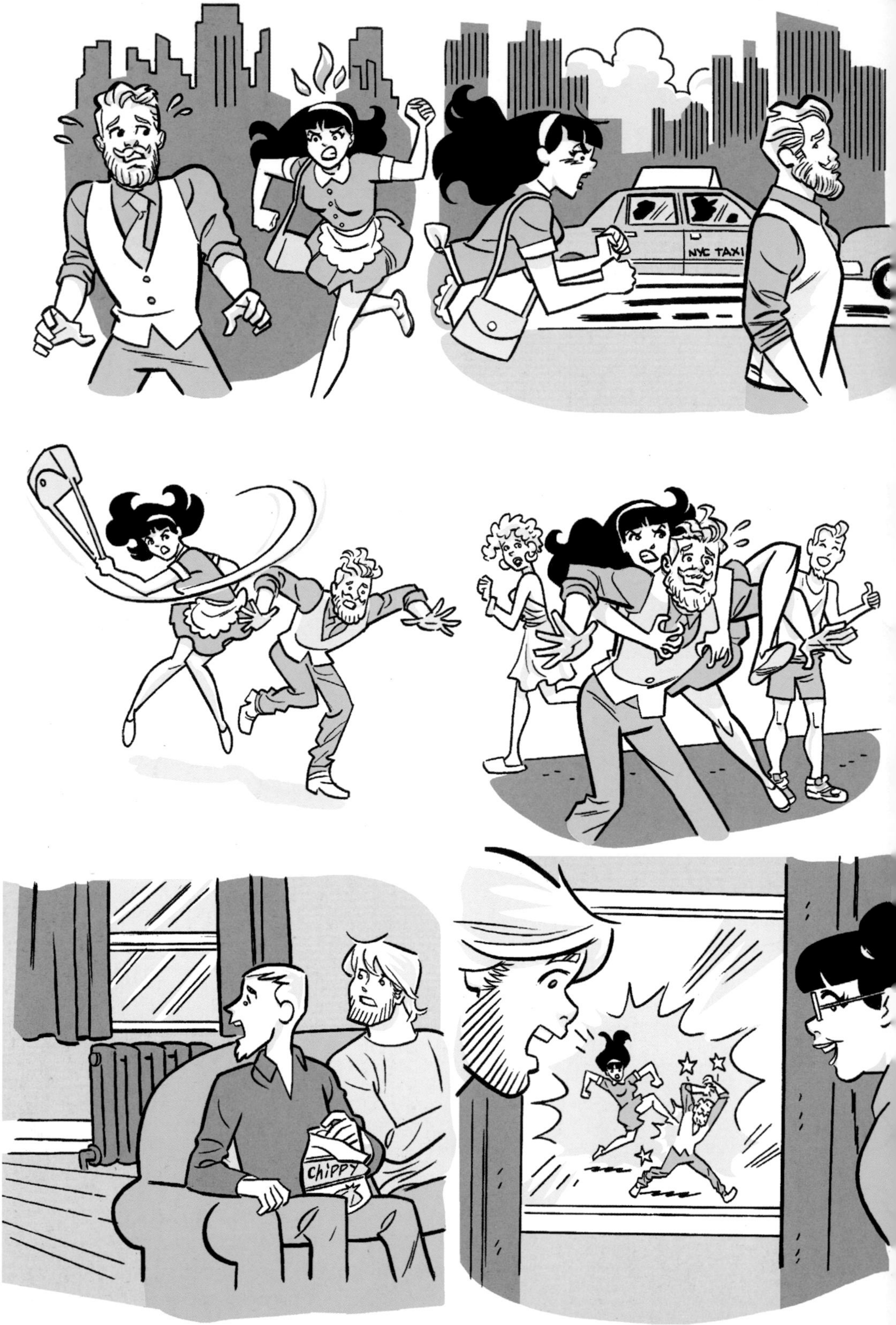
NYC TAXI
CHIPPY

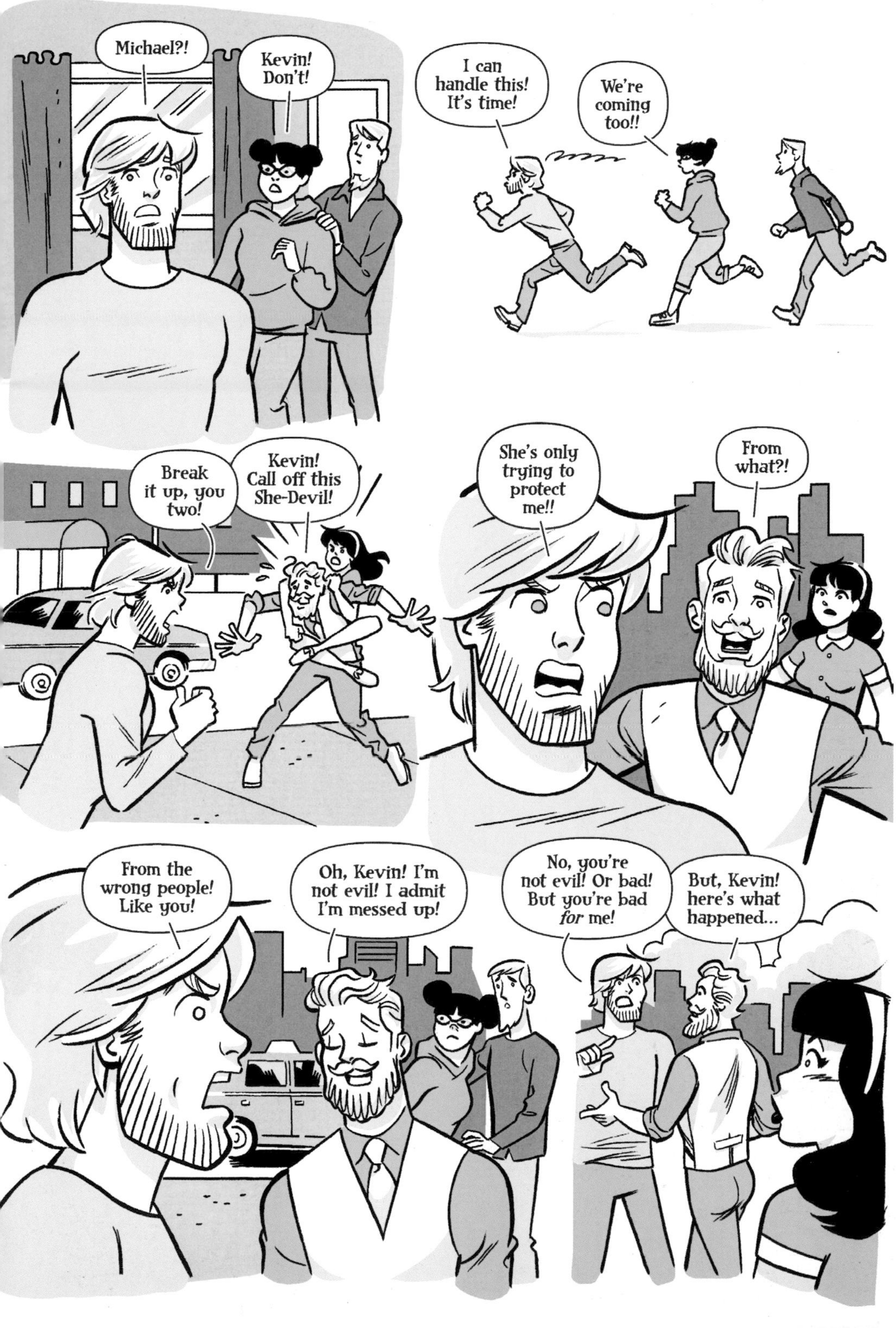
Michael?!
Kevin! Don't!
I can handle this! It's time!
We're coming too!!
Break it up, you two!
Kevin! Call off this She-Devil!
She's only trying to protect me!!
From what?!
From the wrong people! Like you!
Oh, Kevin! I'm not evil! I admit I'm messed up!
No, you're not evil! Or bad! But you're bad *for* me!
But, Kevin! here's what happened...

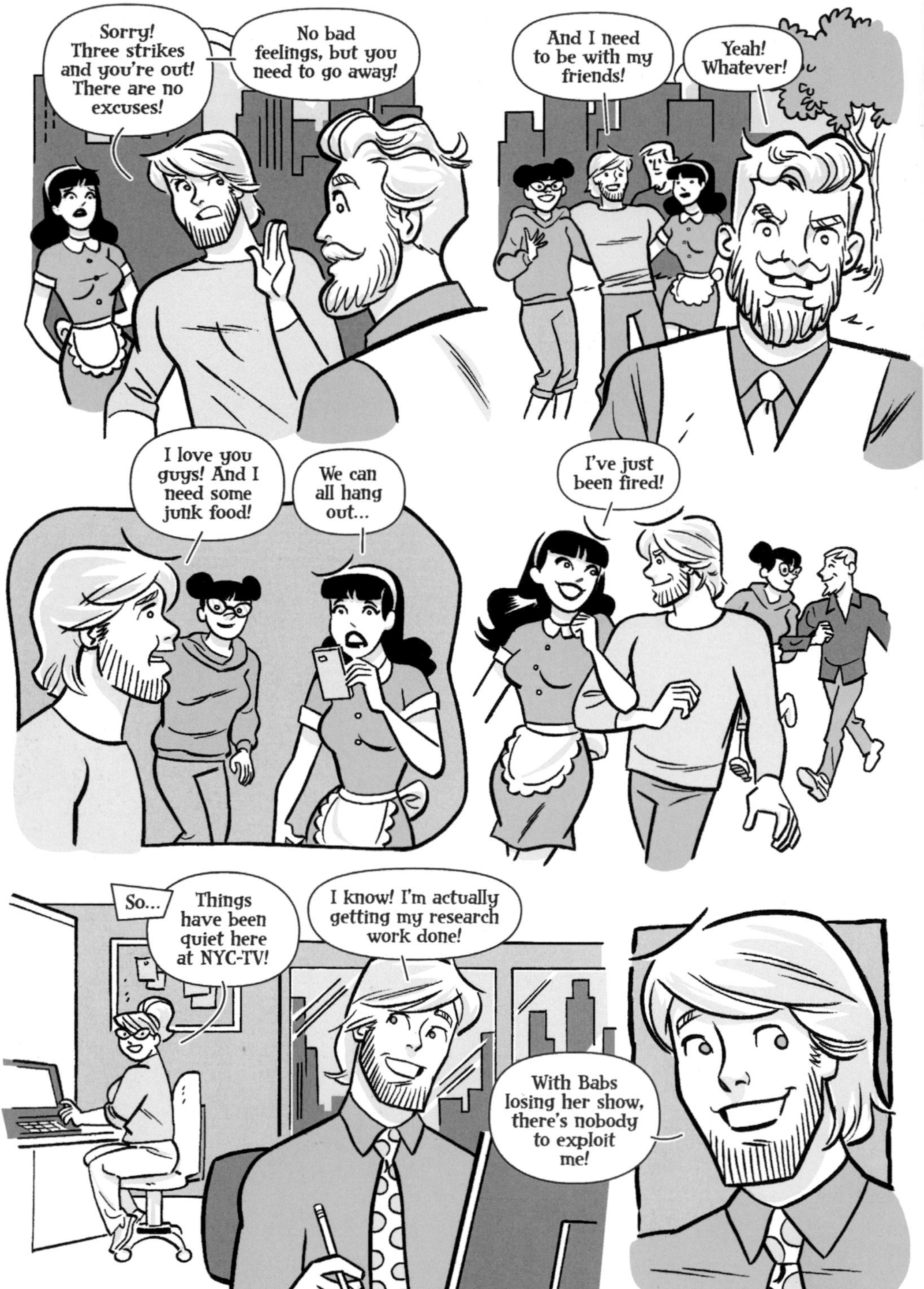
Sorry! Three strikes and you're out! There are no excuses!
No bad feelings, but you need to go away!
And I need to be with my friends!
Yeah! Whatever!
I love you guys! And I need some junk food!
We can all hang out...
I've just been fired!
So...
Things have been quiet here at NYC-TV!
I know! I'm actually getting my research work done!
With Babs losing her show, there's nobody to exploit me!

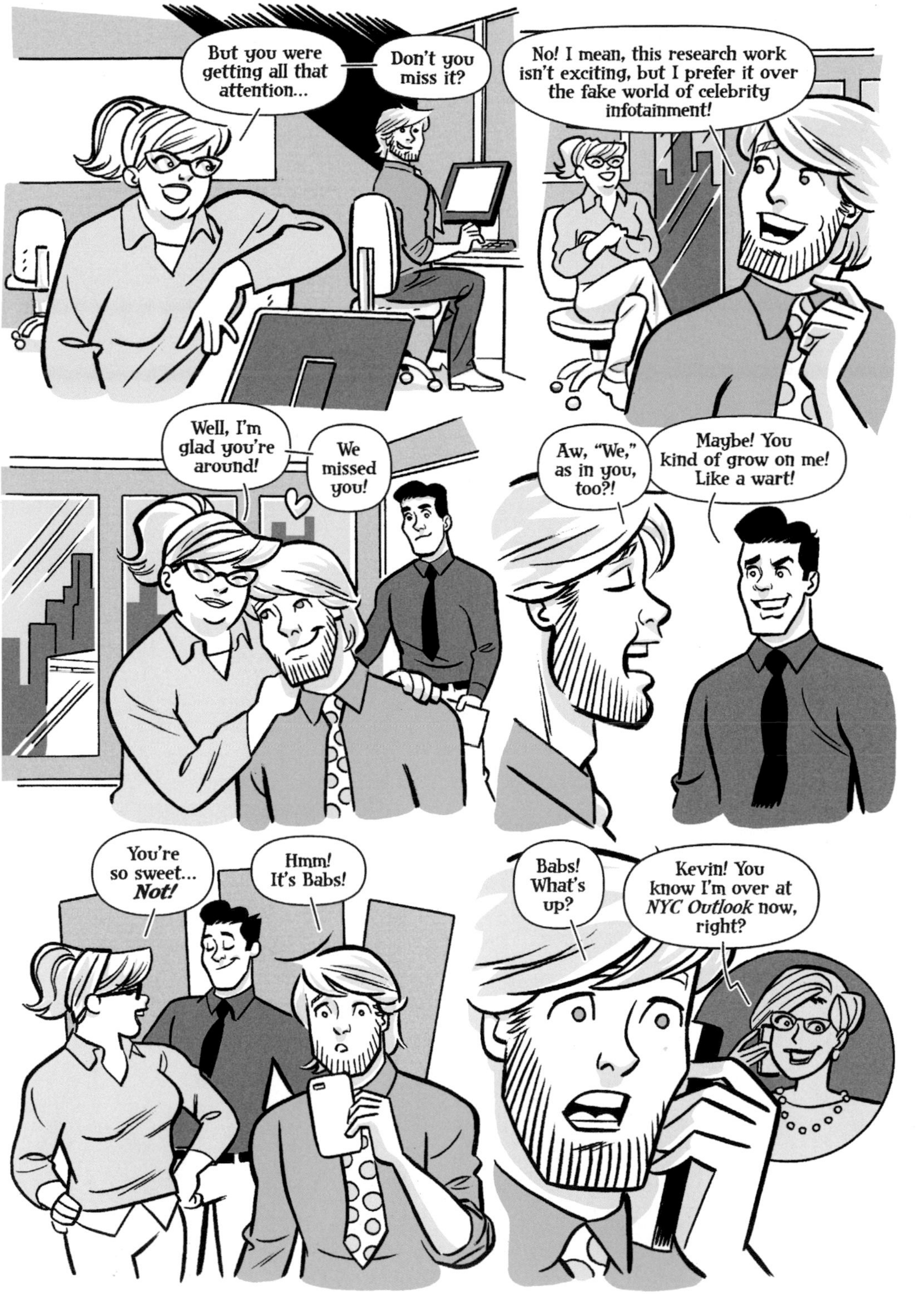
But you were getting all that attention...
Don't you miss it?
No! I mean, this research work isn't exciting, but I prefer it over the fake world of celebrity infotainment!
Well, I'm glad you're around!
We missed you!
Aw, "We," as in you, too?!
Maybe! You kind of grow on me! Like a wart!
You're so sweet... ***Not!***
Hmm! It's Babs!
Babs! What's up?
Kevin! You know I'm over at *NYC Outlook* now, right?

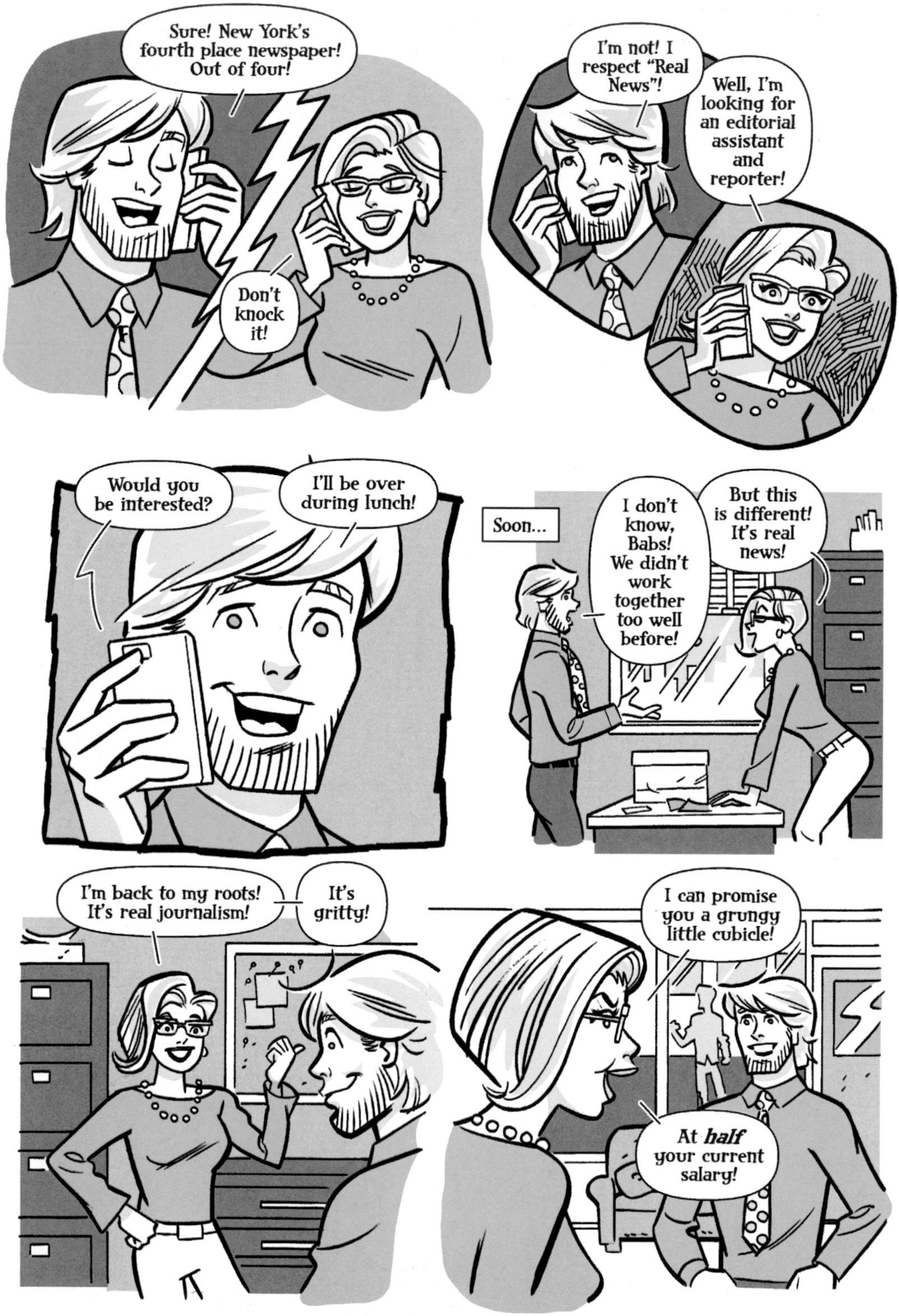

Sure! New York's fourth place newspaper! Out of four!
Don't knock it!
I'm not! I respect "Real News"!
Well, I'm looking for an editorial assistant and reporter!
Would you be interested?
I'll be over during lunch!
Soon...
I don't know, Babs! We didn't work together too well before!
But this is different! It's real news!
I'm back to my roots! It's real journalism!
It's gritty!
I can promise you a grungy little cubicle!
At *half* your current salary!

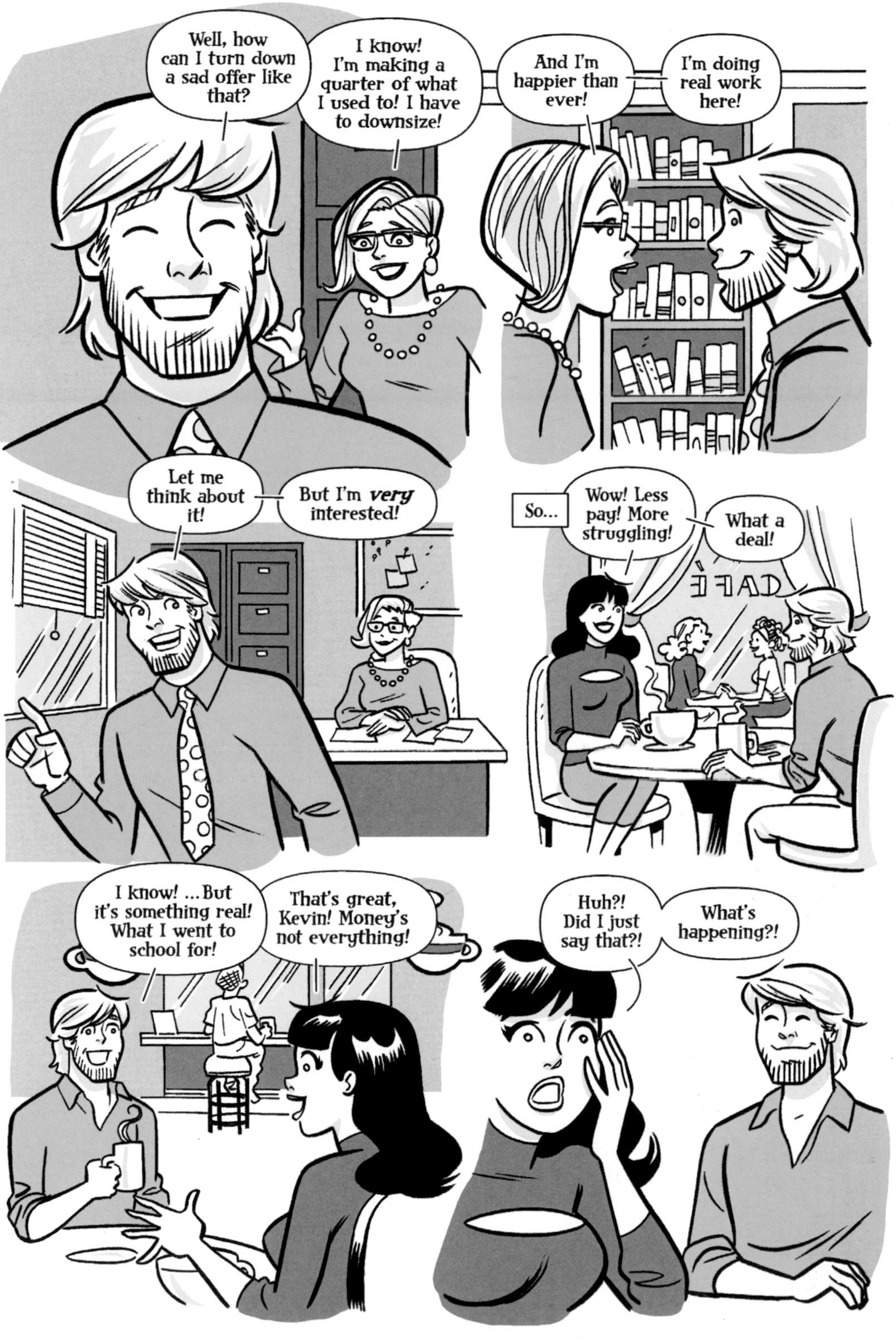
Well, how can I turn down a sad offer like that?
I know! I'm making a quarter of what I used to! I have to downsize!
And I'm happier than ever!
I'm doing real work here!
Let me think about it!
But I'm *very* interested!
So...
Wow! Less pay! More struggling!
What a deal!
I know! ...But it's something real! What I went to school for!
That's great, Kevin! Money's not everything!
Huh?! Did I just say that?!
What's happening?!

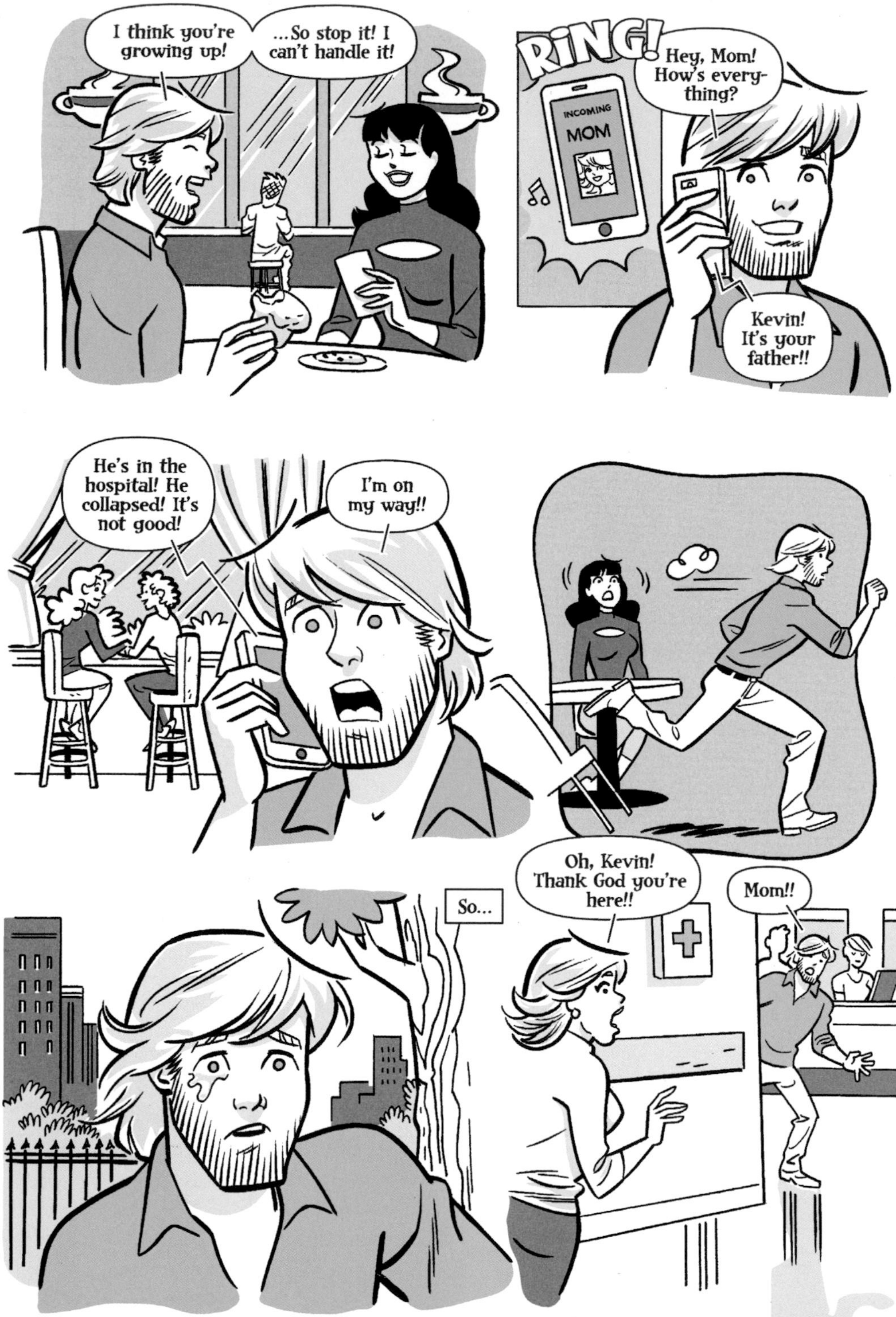
I think you're growing up!
...So stop it! I can't handle it!
RING!
INCOMING
MOM
Hey, Mom! How's every-thing?
Kevin! It's your father!!
He's in the hospital! He collapsed! It's not good!
I'm on my way!!
So...
Oh, Kevin! Thank God you're here!!
Mom!!

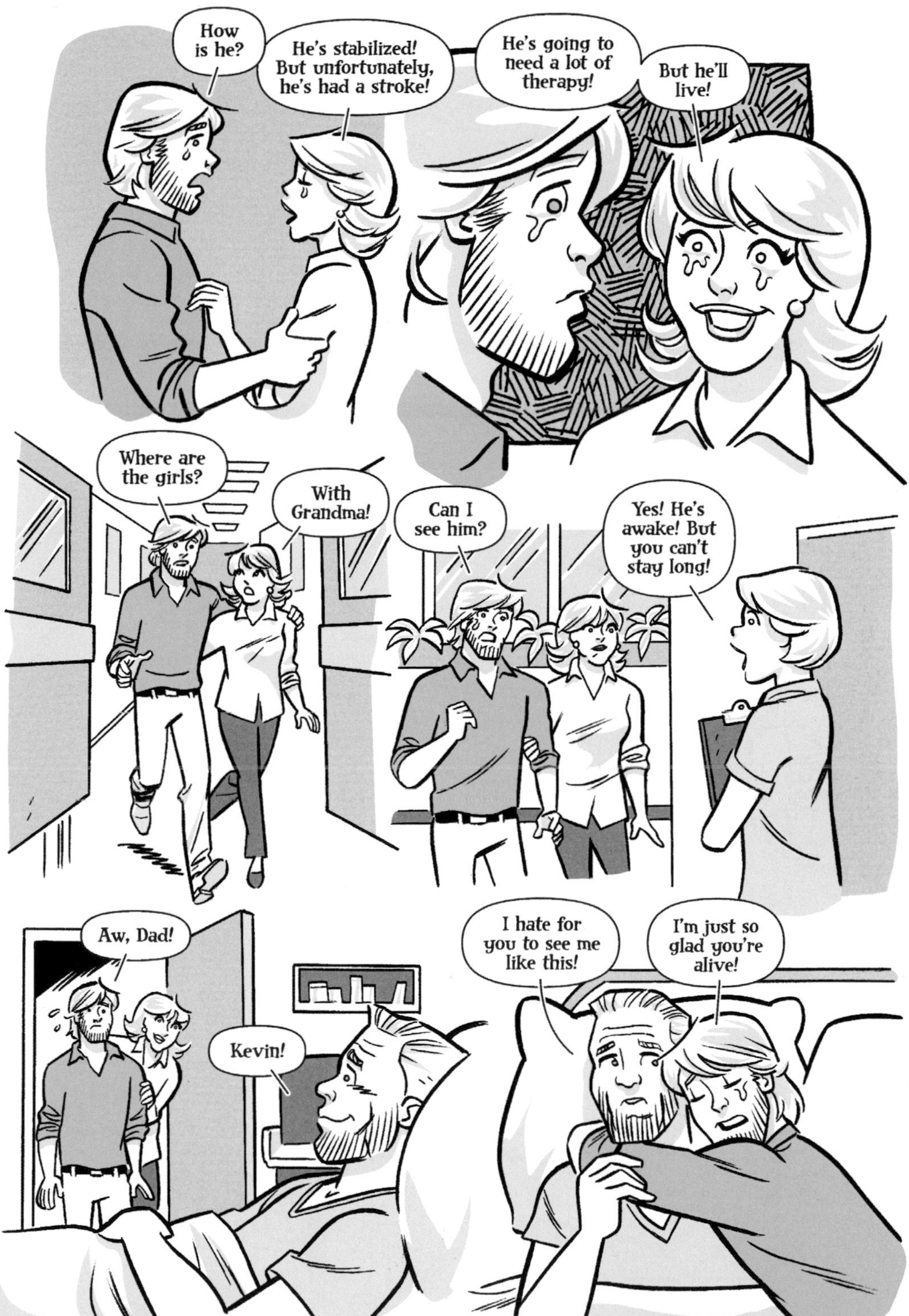
How is he?
He's stabilized! But unfortunately, he's had a stroke!
He's going to need a lot of therapy!
But he'll live!
Where are the girls?
With Grandma!
Can I see him?
Yes! He's awake! But you can't stay long!
Aw, Dad!
Kevin!
I hate for you to see me like this!
I'm just so glad you're alive!

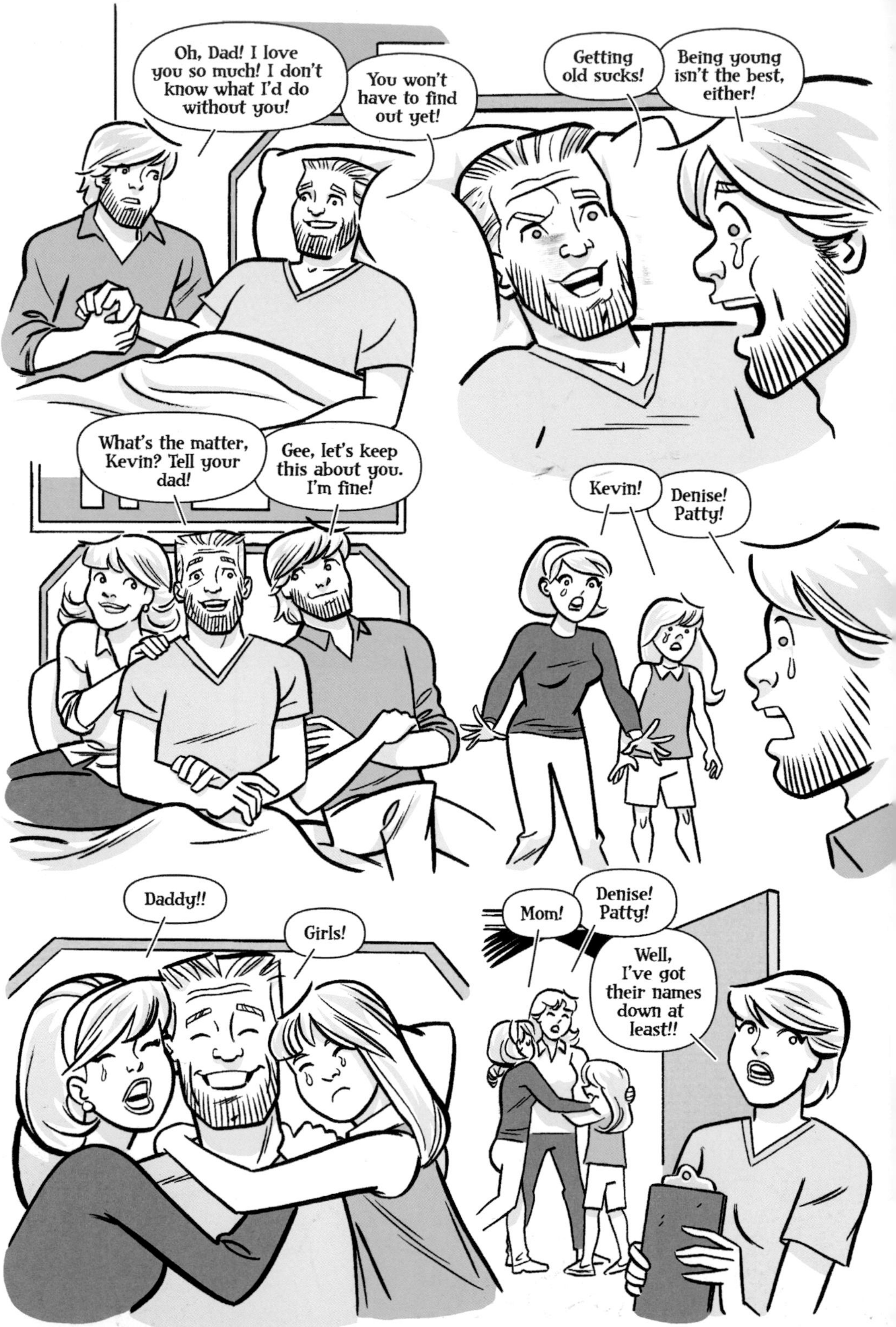
Oh, Dad! I love you so much! I don't know what I'd do without you!
You won't have to find out yet!
Getting old sucks!
Being young isn't the best, either!
What's the matter, Kevin? Tell your dad!
Gee, let's keep this about you. I'm fine!
Kevin!
Denise! Patty!
Daddy!!
Girls!
Mom!
Denise! Patty!
Well, I've got their names down at least!!

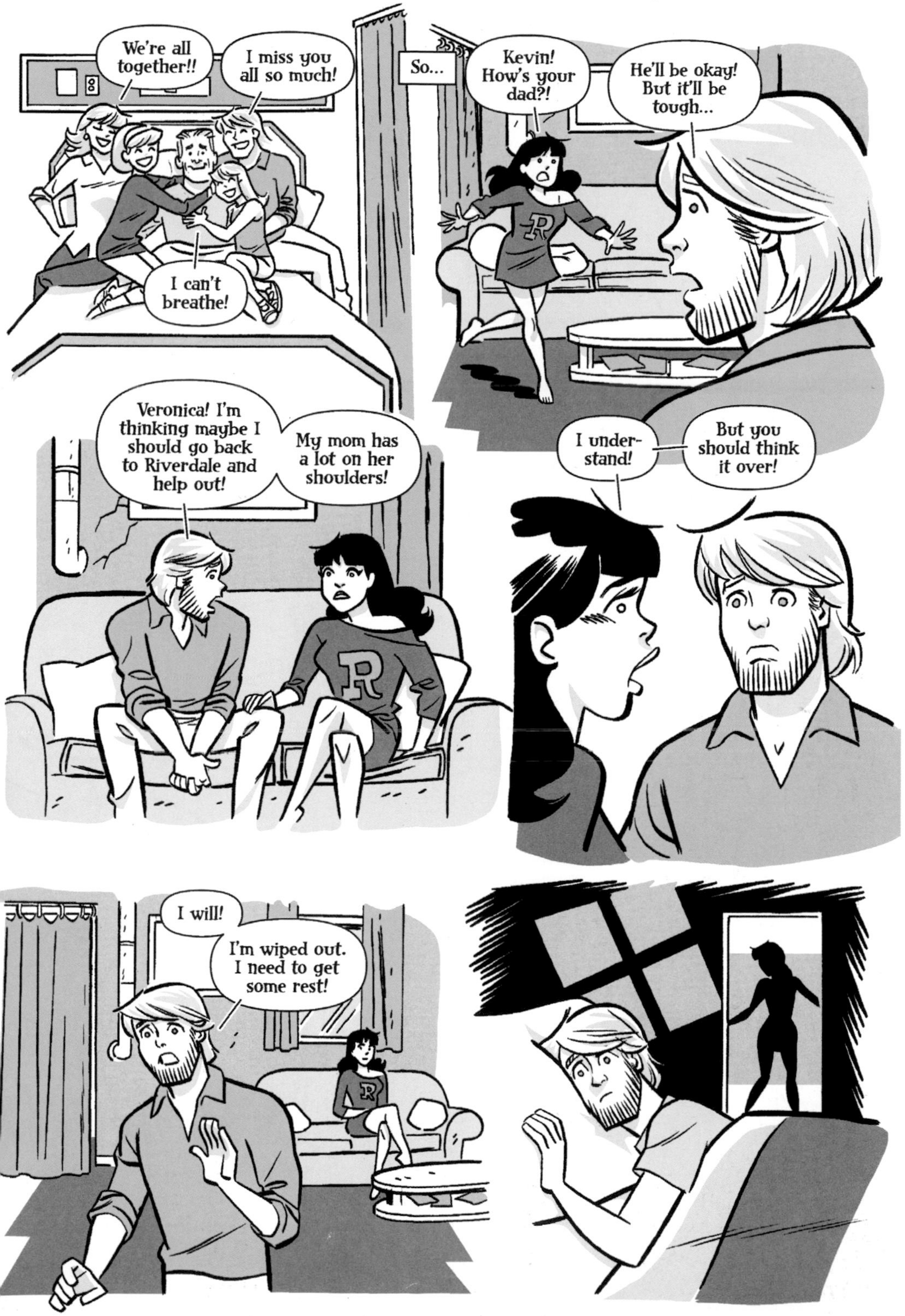
We're all together!!
I miss you all so much!
I can't breathe!
So...
Kevin! How's your dad?!
He'll be okay! But it'll be tough...
Veronica! I'm thinking maybe I should go back to Riverdale and help out!
My mom has a lot on her shoulders!
I under-stand!
But you should think it over!
I will!
I'm wiped out. I need to get some rest!

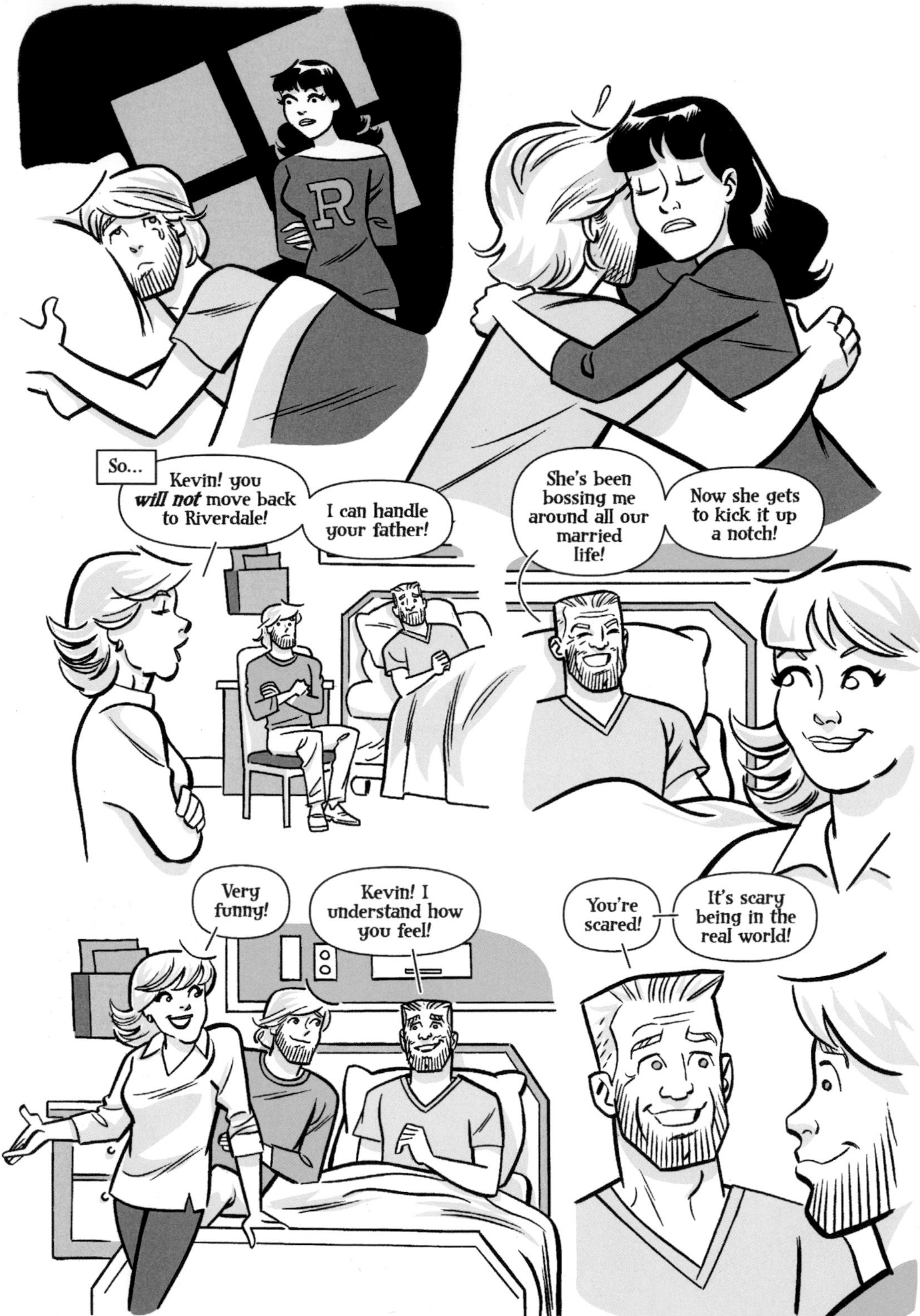
So...
Kevin! you *will not* move back to Riverdale!
I can handle your father!
She's been bossing me around all our married life!
Now she gets to kick it up a notch!
Very funny!
Kevin! I understand how you feel!
You're scared!
It's scary being in the real world!

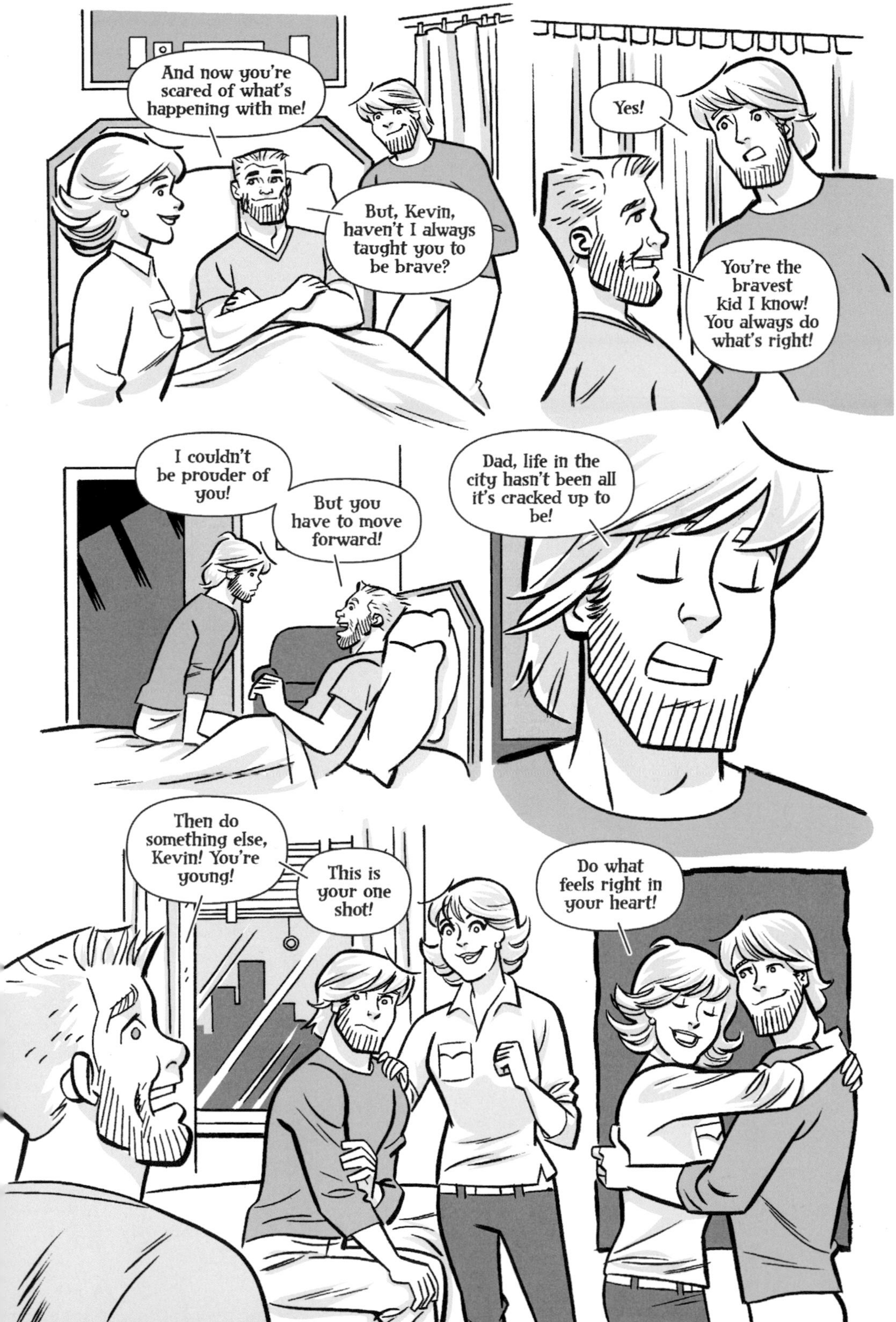
And now you're scared of what's happening with me!
But, Kevin, haven't I always taught you to be brave?
Yes!
You're the bravest kid I know! You always do what's right!
I couldn't be prouder of you!
But you have to move forward!
Dad, life in the city hasn't been all it's cracked up to be!
Then do something else, Kevin! You're young!
This is your one shot!
Do what feels right in your heart!

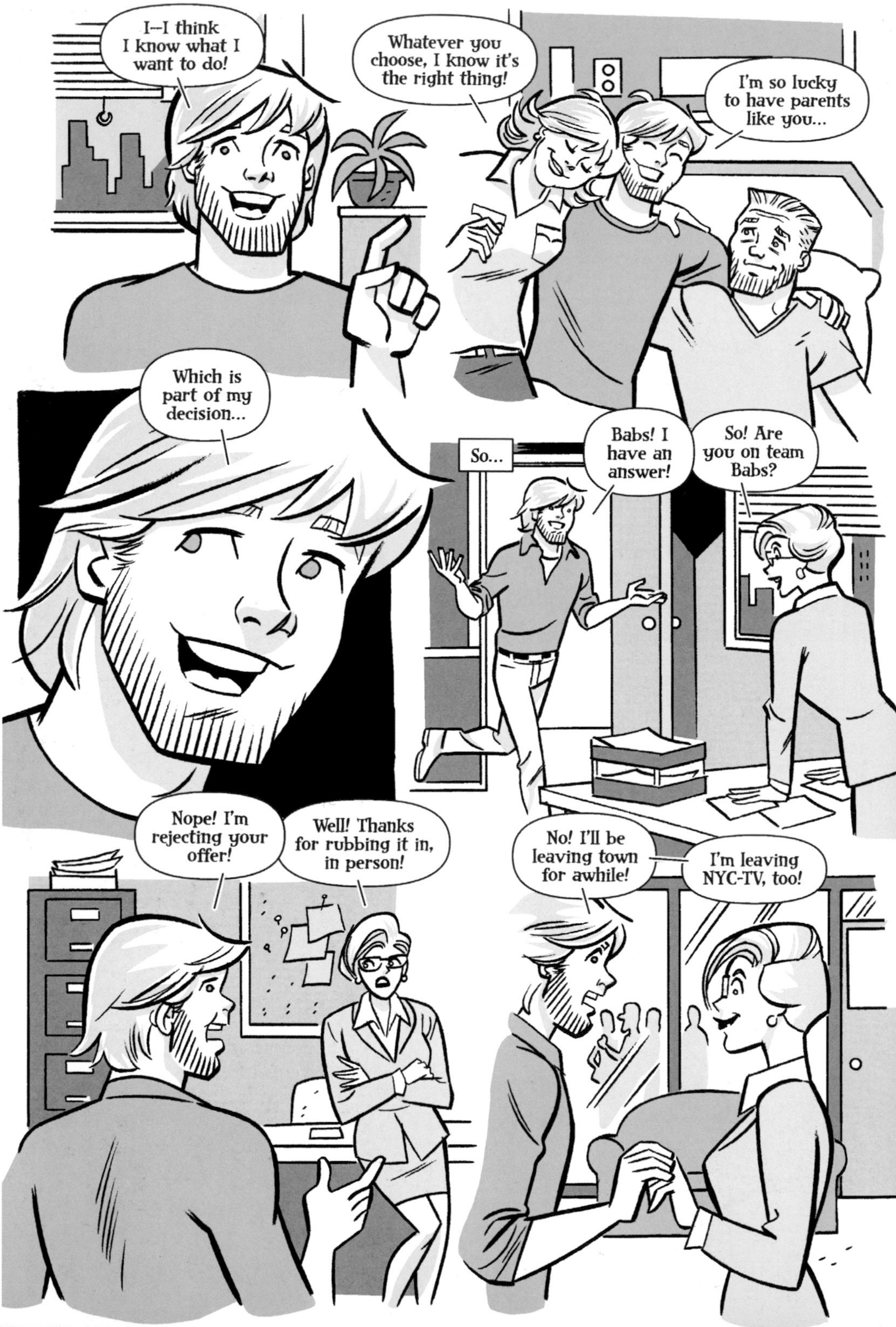
I--I think I know what I want to do!
Whatever you choose, I know it's the right thing!
I'm so lucky to have parents like you...
Which is part of my decision...
So...
Babs! I have an answer!
So! Are you on team Babs?
Nope! I'm rejecting your offer!
Well! Thanks for rubbing it in, in person!
No! I'll be leaving town for awhile!
I'm leaving NYC-TV, too!

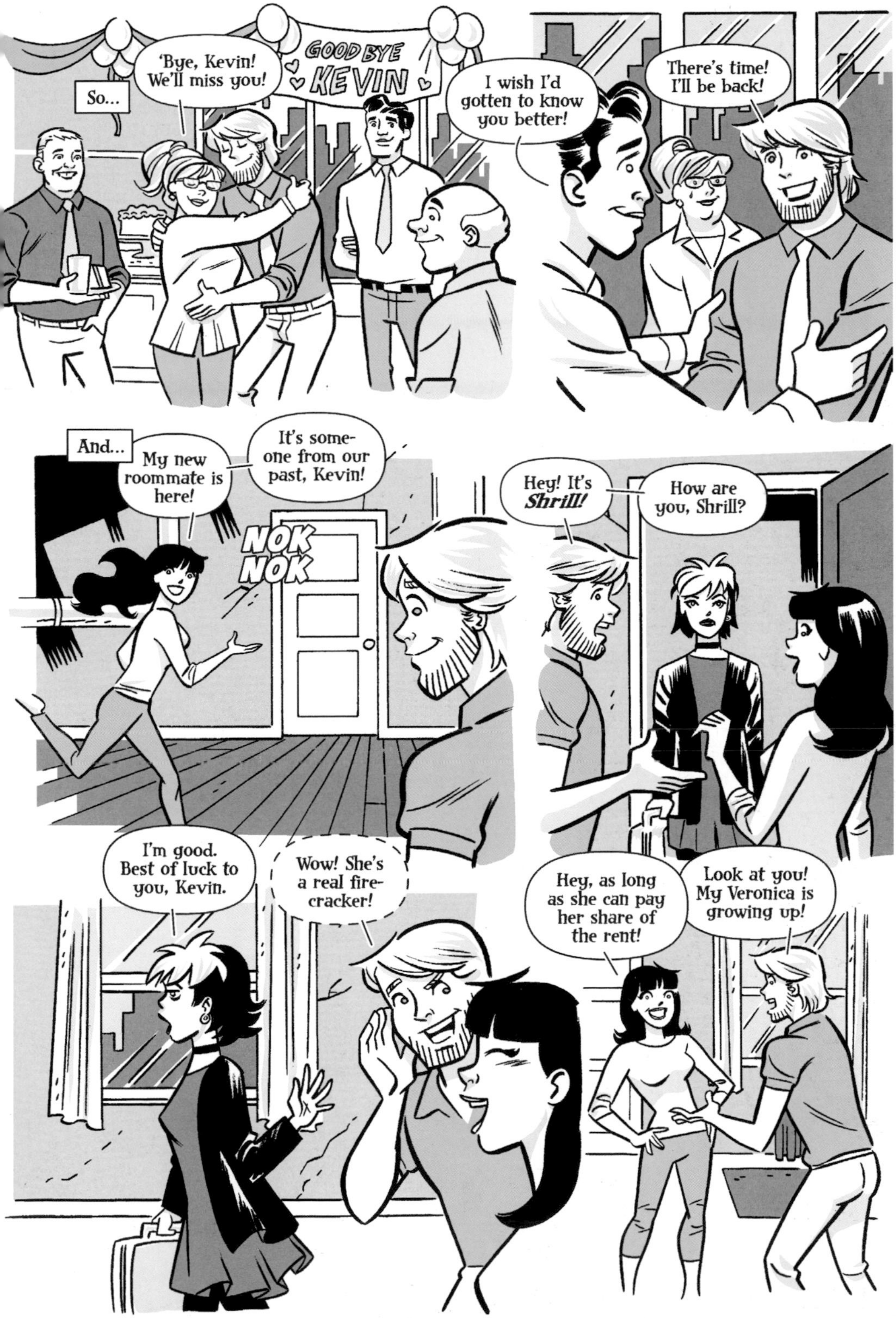

So...
GOOD BYE KEVIN
'Bye, Kevin! We'll miss you!
I wish I'd gotten to know you better!
There's time! I'll be back!
And...
My new roommate is here!
It's someone from our past, Kevin!
NOK NOK
Hey! It's Shrill!
How are you, Shrill?
I'm good. Best of luck to you, Kevin.
Wow! She's a real firecracker!
Hey, as long as she can pay her share of the rent!
Look at you! My Veronica is growing up!

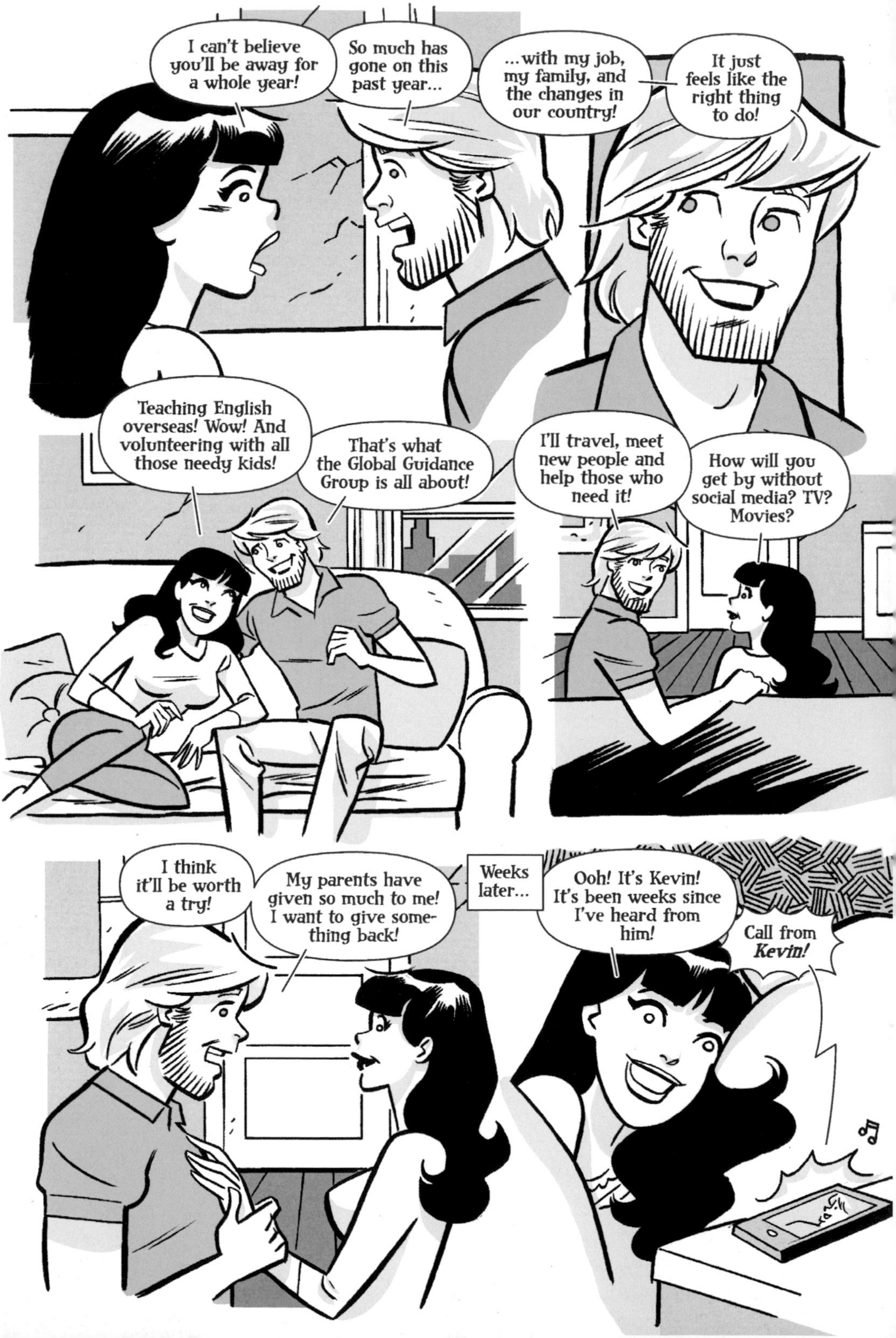
I can't believe you'll be away for a whole year!
So much has gone on this past year...
...with my job, my family, and the changes in our country!
It just feels like the right thing to do!
Teaching English overseas! Wow! And volunteering with all those needy kids!
That's what the Global Guidance Group is all about!
I'll travel, meet new people and help those who need it!
How will you get by without social media? TV? Movies?
I think it'll be worth a try!
My parents have given so much to me! I want to give something back!
Weeks later...
Ooh! It's Kevin! It's been weeks since I've heard from him!
Call from *Kevin!*

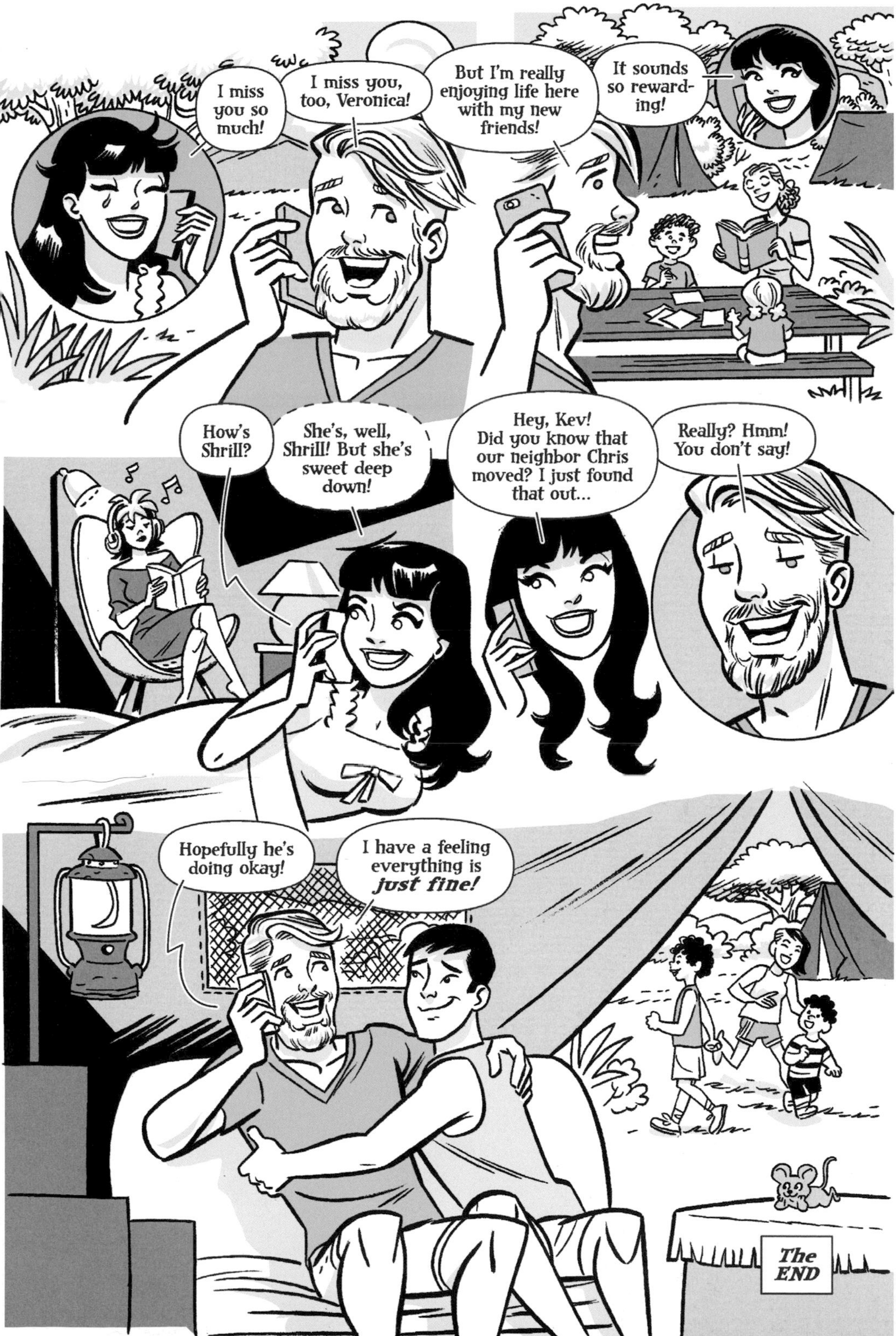
I miss you so much!
I miss you, too, Veronica!
But I'm really enjoying life here with my new friends!
It sounds so reward-ing!
How's Shrill?
She's, well, Shrill! But she's sweet deep down!
Hey, Kev! Did you know that our neighbor Chris moved? I just found that out...
Really? Hmm! You don't say!
Hopefully he's doing okay!
I have a feeling everything is *just fine!*
The END

Life with Kevin

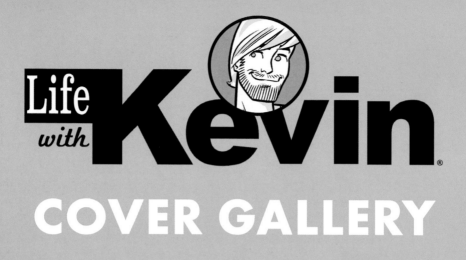

COVER GALLERY

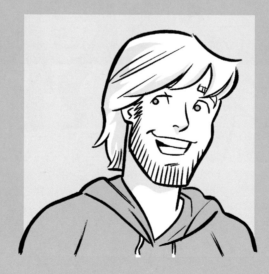

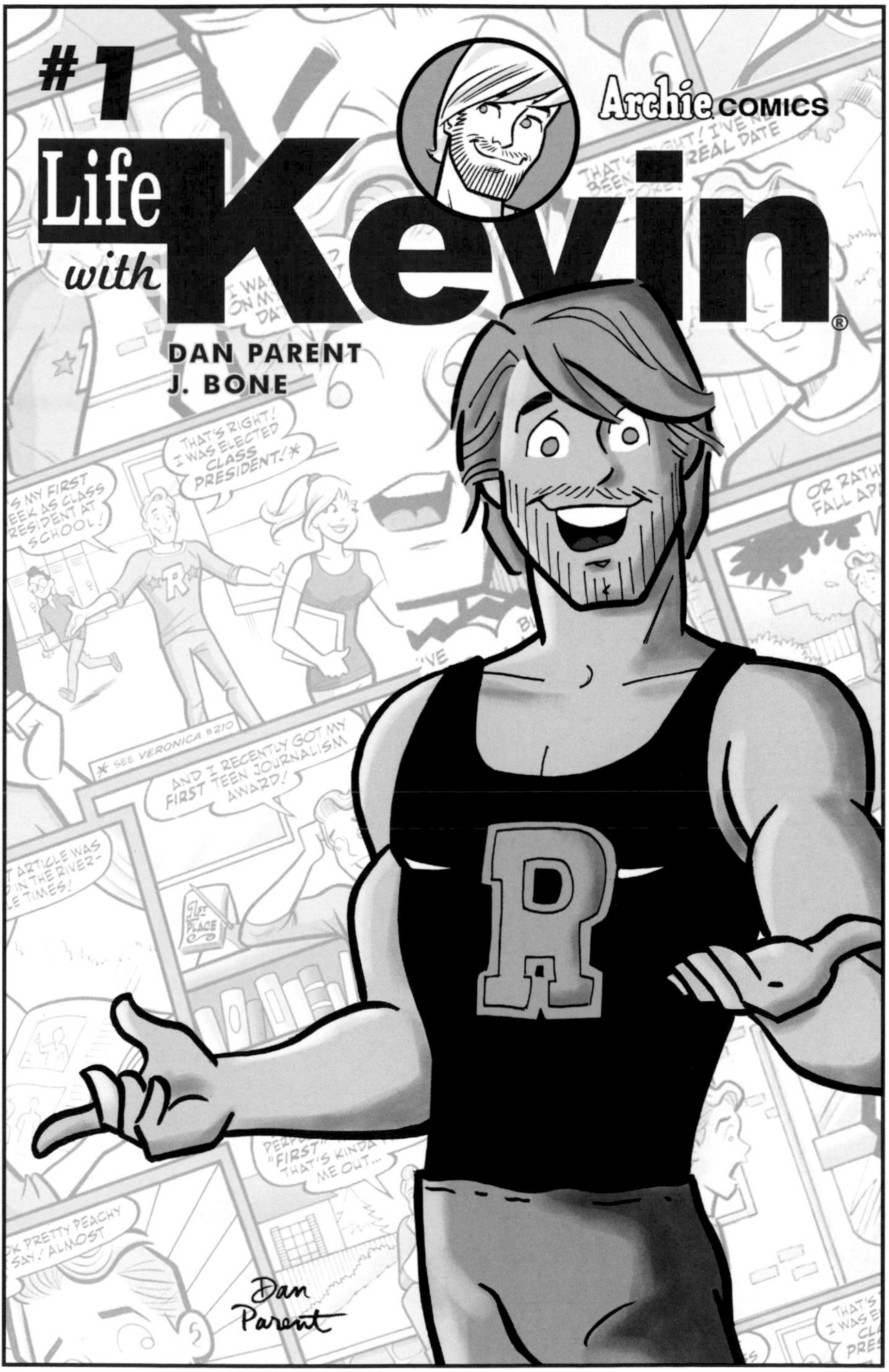
#1
Archie COMICS
Life with Kevin
DAN PARENT
J. BONE
THAT'S RIGHT! I WAS ELECTED CLASS PRESIDENT!*
* SEE VERONICA #210
AND I RECENTLY GOT MY FIRST TEEN JOURNALISM AWARD!
Dan Parent

LIFE WITH KEVIN #1 DAN PARENT

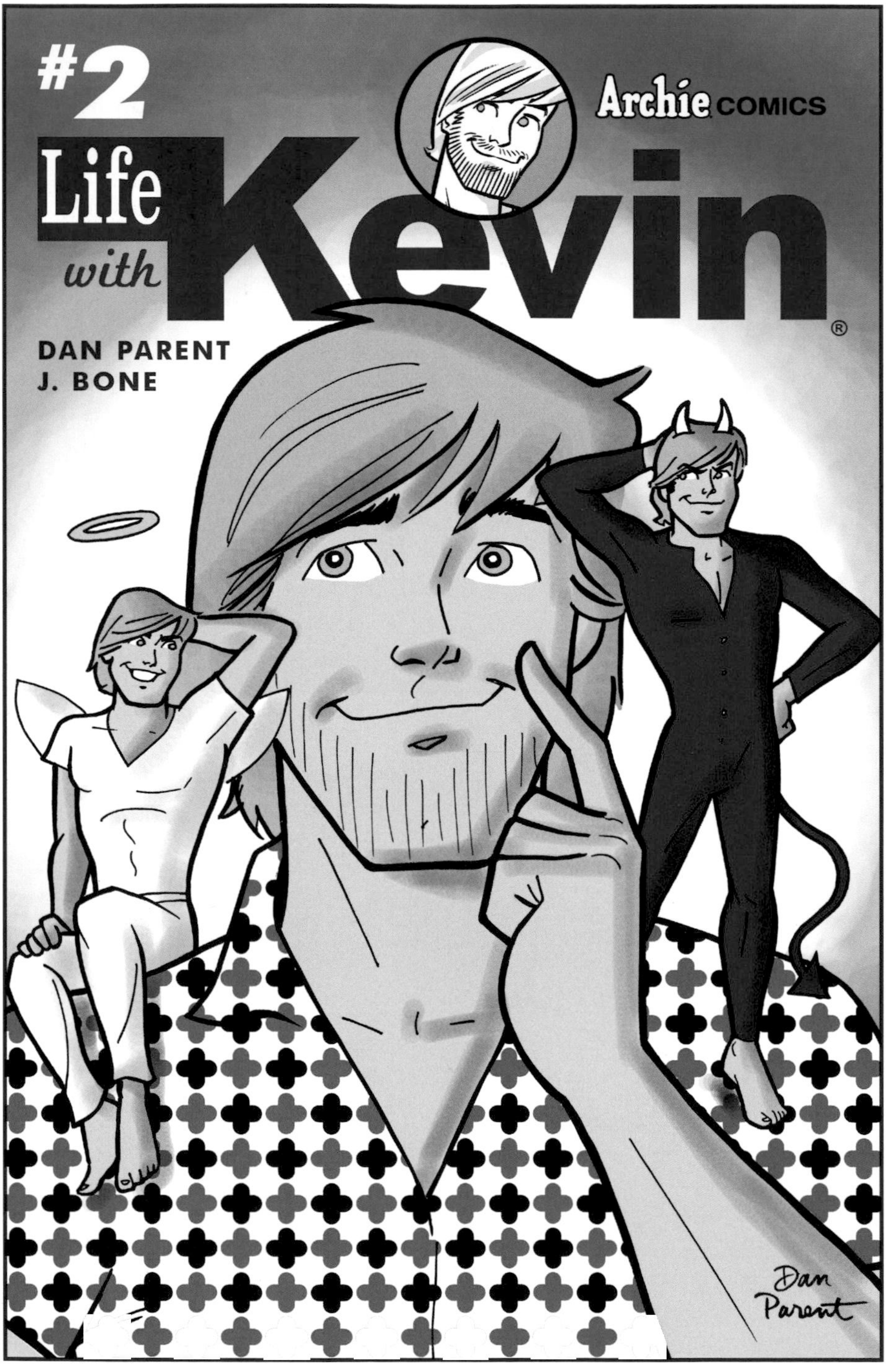
#2
Archie COMICS
Life with Kevin®
DAN PARENT
J. BONE
Dan Parent

LIFE WITH KEVIN #2 DAN PARENT

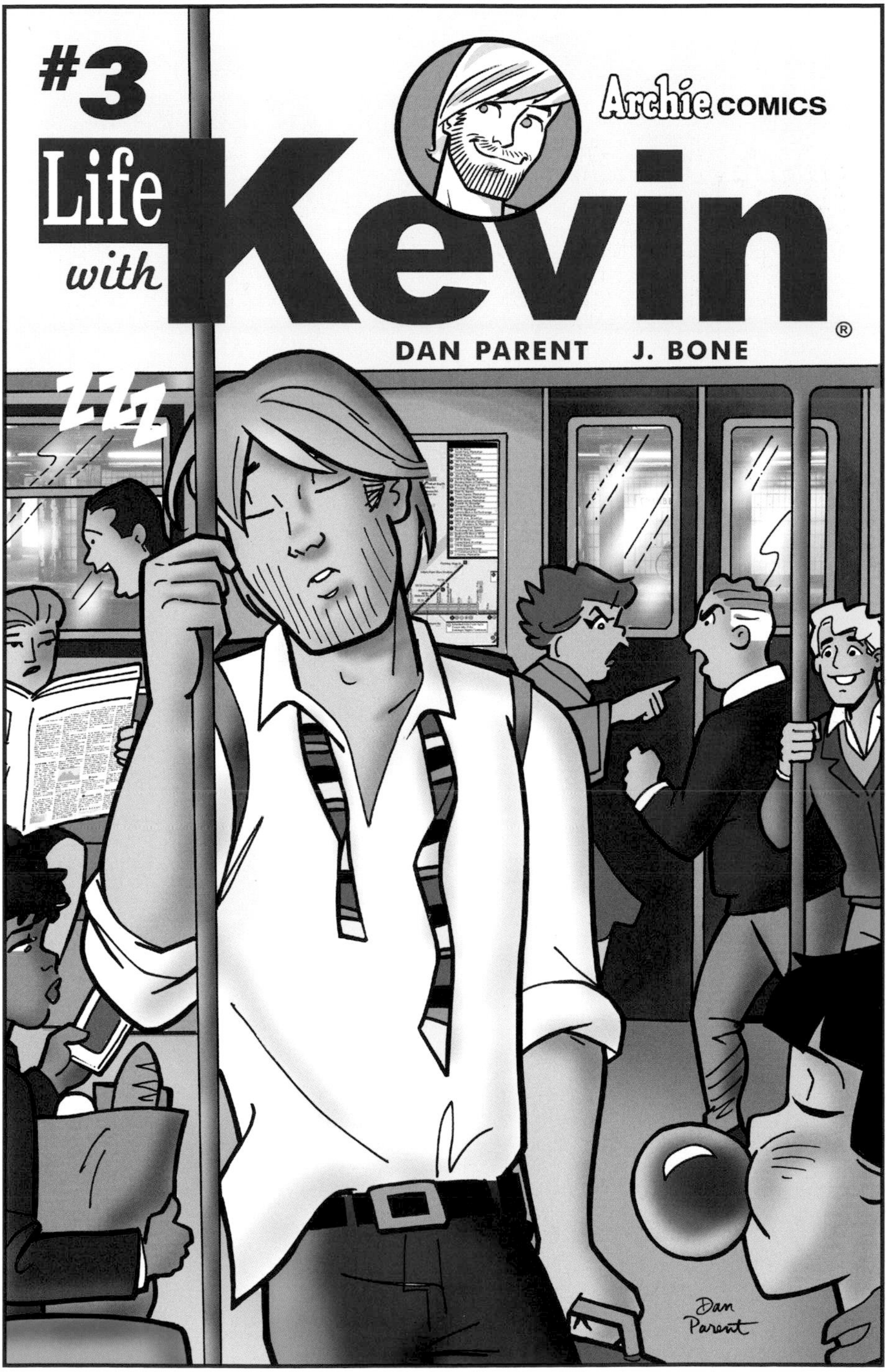
#3
Archie COMICS
Life with Kevin
DAN PARENT J. BONE
ZZZ
Dan Parent

LIFE WITH KEVIN #3 DAN PARENT

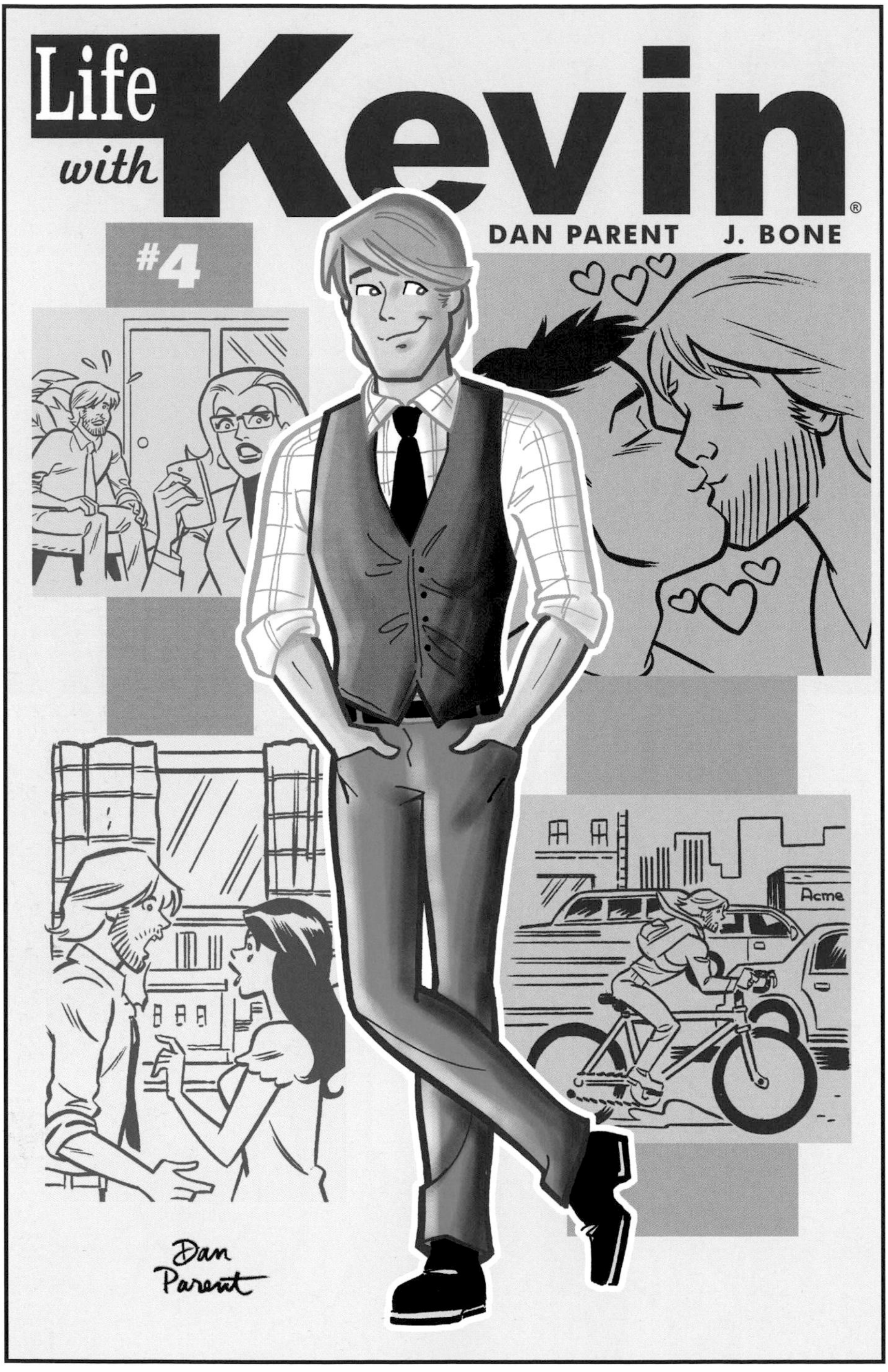
Life with Kevin®
DAN PARENT J. BONE
#4
Acme
Dan Parent

LIFE WITH KEVIN #4 DAN PARENT

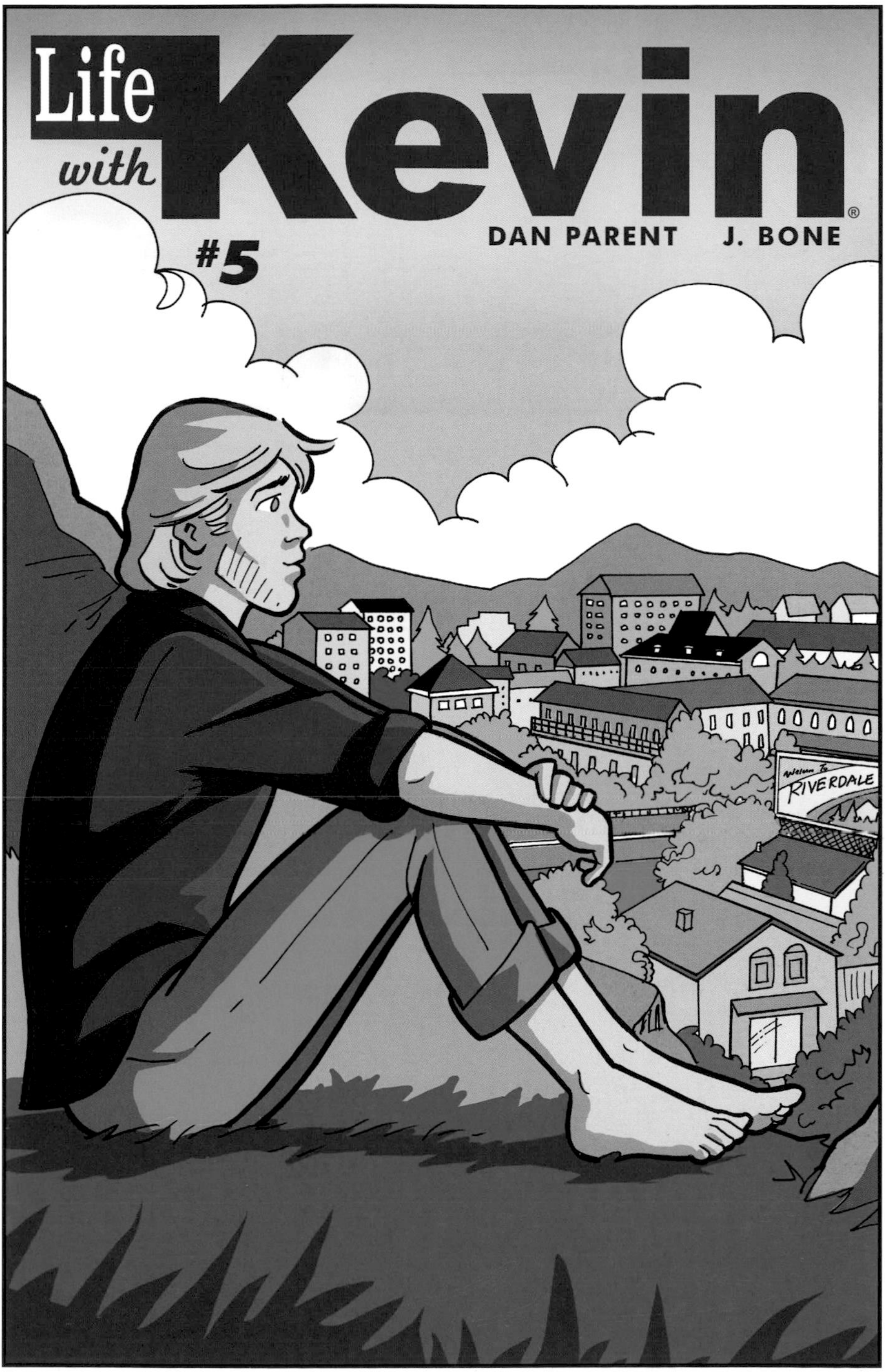
Life with Kevin
#5
DAN PARENT J. BONE
RIVERDALE

LIFE WITH KEVIN #5 DAN PARENT

Your Pal Archie

Classic-style Archie makes his return in this ALL-NEW, ALL-AGES comic featuring two stories from Eisner Award-winning writer **TY TEMPLETON** (Batman and Robin Adventures) and fan-favorite Archie Comics artist **DAN PARENT** (Life with Kevin)!

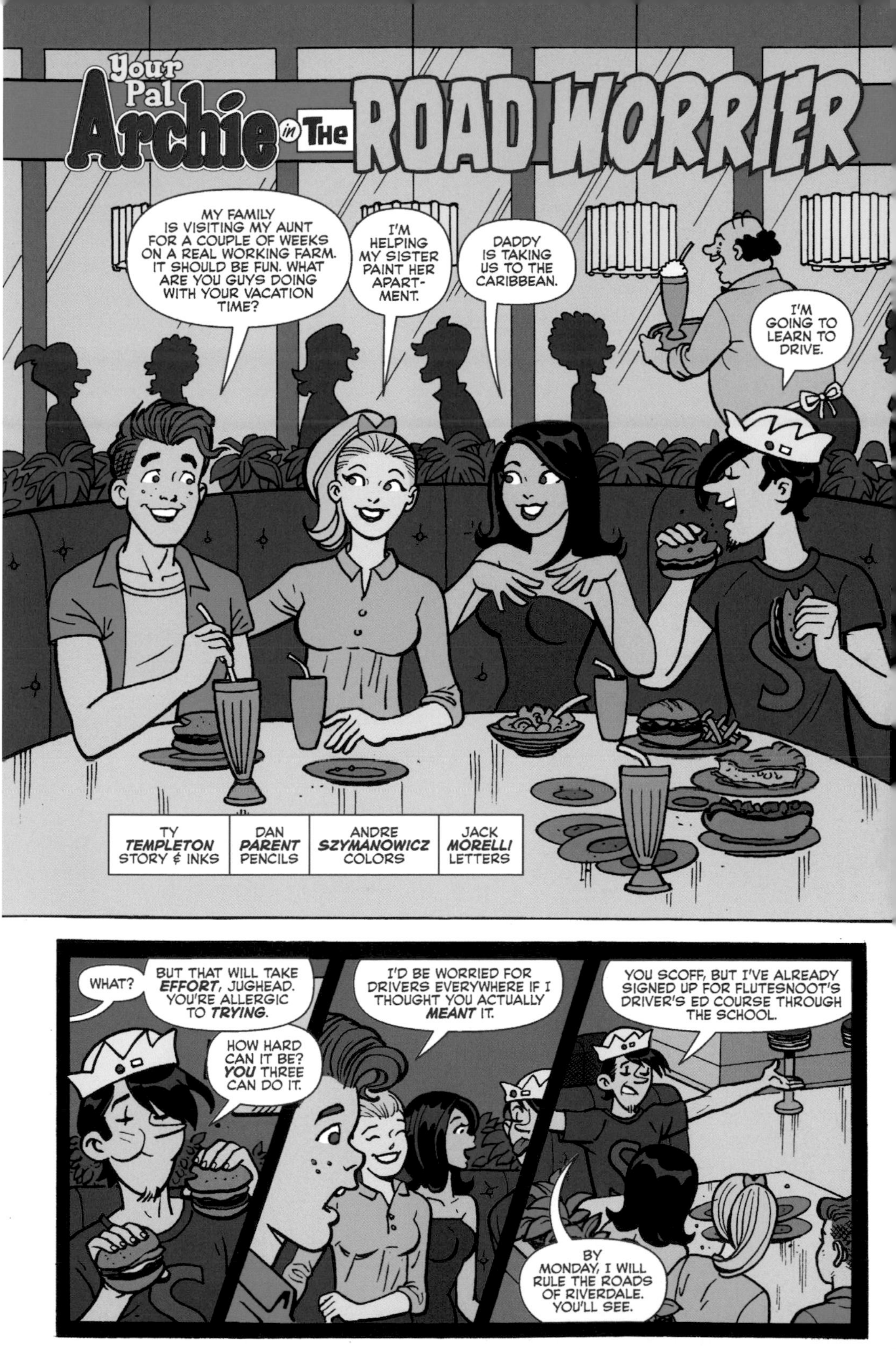
Your Pal Archie in THE ROAD WORRIER
MY FAMILY IS VISITING MY AUNT FOR A COUPLE OF WEEKS ON A REAL WORKING FARM. IT SHOULD BE FUN. WHAT ARE YOU GUYS DOING WITH YOUR VACATION TIME?
I'M HELPING MY SISTER PAINT HER APART- MENT.
DADDY IS TAKING US TO THE CARIBBEAN.
I'M GOING TO LEARN TO DRIVE.
TY TEMPLETON STORY & INKS
DAN PARENT PENCILS
ANDRE SZYMANOWICZ COLORS
JACK MORELLI LETTERS
WHAT?
BUT THAT WILL TAKE EFFORT, JUGHEAD. YOU'RE ALLERGIC TO TRYING.
HOW HARD CAN IT BE? YOU THREE CAN DO IT.
I'D BE WORRIED FOR DRIVERS EVERYWHERE IF I THOUGHT YOU ACTUALLY MEANT IT.
YOU SCOFF, BUT I'VE ALREADY SIGNED UP FOR FLUTESNOOT'S DRIVER'S ED COURSE THROUGH THE SCHOOL.
BY MONDAY, I WILL RULE THE ROADS OF RIVERDALE. YOU'LL SEE.

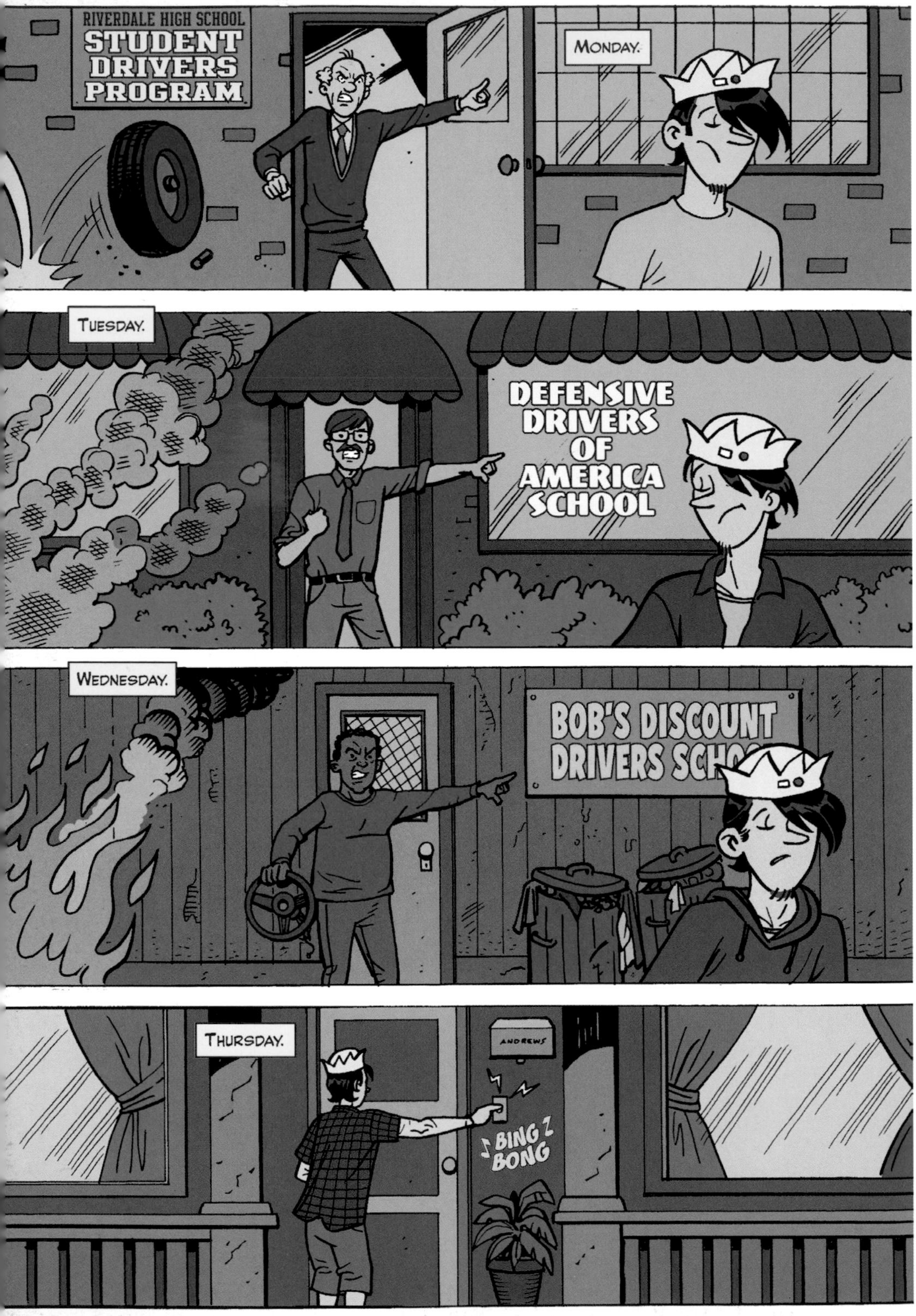
RIVERDALE HIGH SCHOOL
STUDENT DRIVERS PROGRAM
MONDAY.
TUESDAY.
DEFENSIVE DRIVERS OF AMERICA SCHOOL
WEDNESDAY.
BOB'S DISCOUNT DRIVERS SCHO
THURSDAY.
ANDREWS
BING BONG

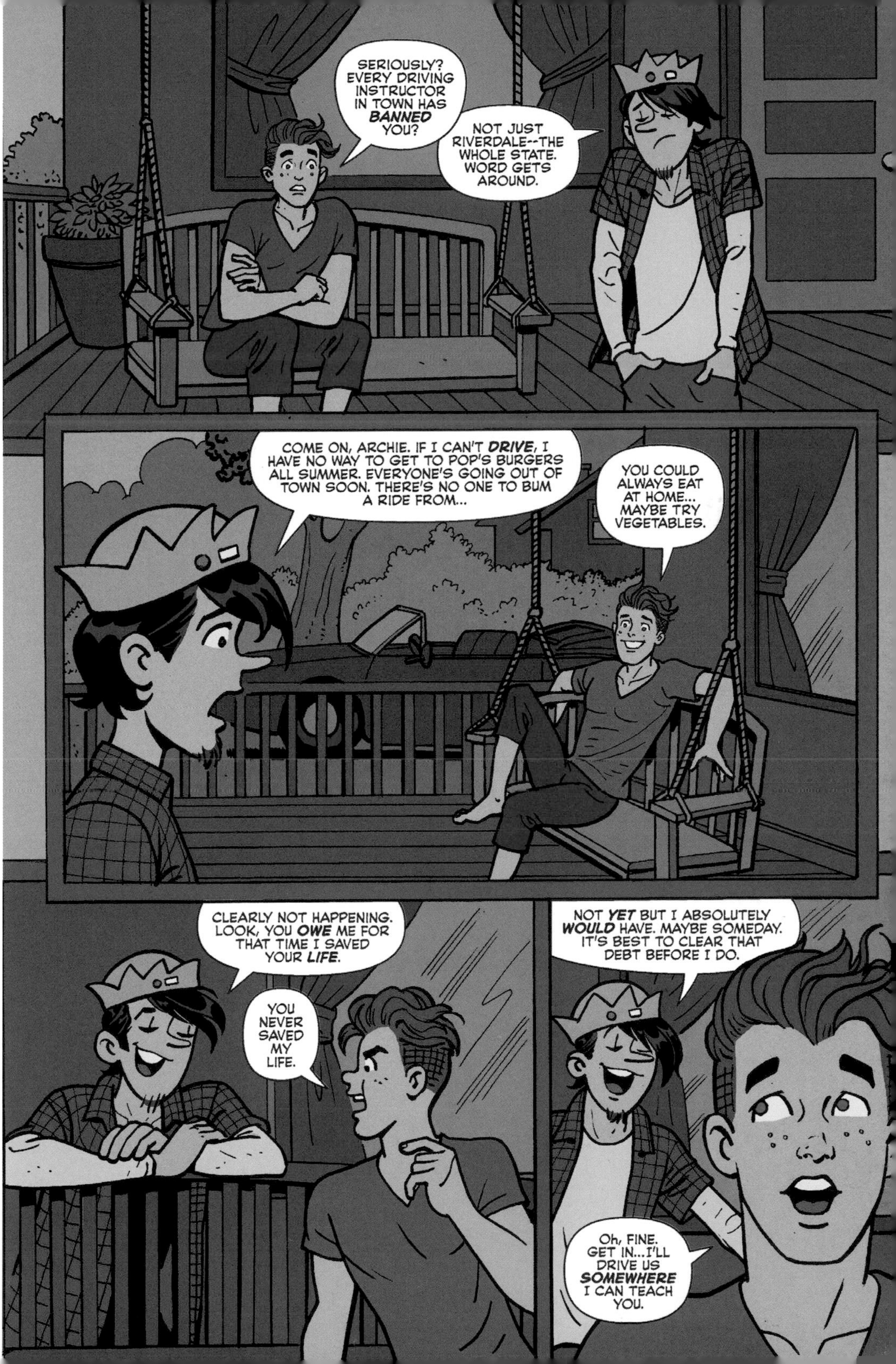
SERIOUSLY? EVERY DRIVING INSTRUCTOR IN TOWN HAS BANNED YOU?
NOT JUST RIVERDALE--THE WHOLE STATE. WORD GETS AROUND.
COME ON, ARCHIE. IF I CAN'T DRIVE, I HAVE NO WAY TO GET TO POP'S BURGERS ALL SUMMER. EVERYONE'S GOING OUT OF TOWN SOON. THERE'S NO ONE TO BUM A RIDE FROM...
YOU COULD ALWAYS EAT AT HOME... MAYBE TRY VEGETABLES.
CLEARLY NOT HAPPENING. LOOK, YOU OWE ME FOR THAT TIME I SAVED YOUR LIFE.
YOU NEVER SAVED MY LIFE.
NOT YET BUT I ABSOLUTELY WOULD HAVE. MAYBE SOMEDAY. IT'S BEST TO CLEAR THAT DEBT BEFORE I DO.
Oh, FINE. GET IN...I'LL DRIVE US SOMEWHERE I CAN TEACH YOU.

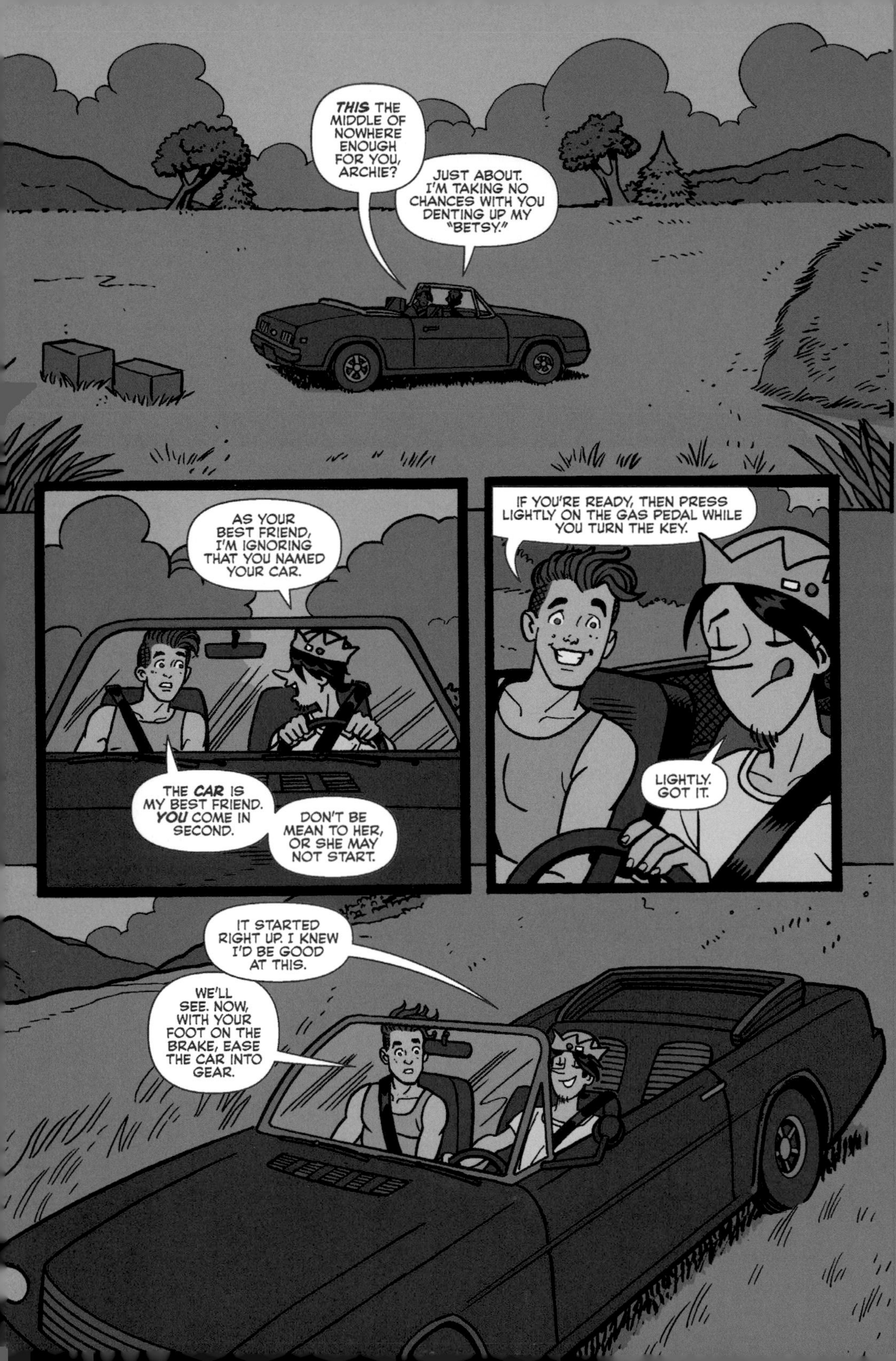
THIS THE MIDDLE OF NOWHERE ENOUGH FOR YOU, ARCHIE?
JUST ABOUT. I'M TAKING NO CHANCES WITH YOU DENTING UP MY "BETSY."
AS YOUR BEST FRIEND, I'M IGNORING THAT YOU NAMED YOUR CAR.
THE CAR IS MY BEST FRIEND. YOU COME IN SECOND.
DON'T BE MEAN TO HER, OR SHE MAY NOT START.
IF YOU'RE READY, THEN PRESS LIGHTLY ON THE GAS PEDAL WHILE YOU TURN THE KEY.
LIGHTLY. GOT IT.
IT STARTED RIGHT UP. I KNEW I'D BE GOOD AT THIS.
WE'LL SEE. NOW, WITH YOUR FOOT ON THE BRAKE, EASE THE CAR INTO GEAR.

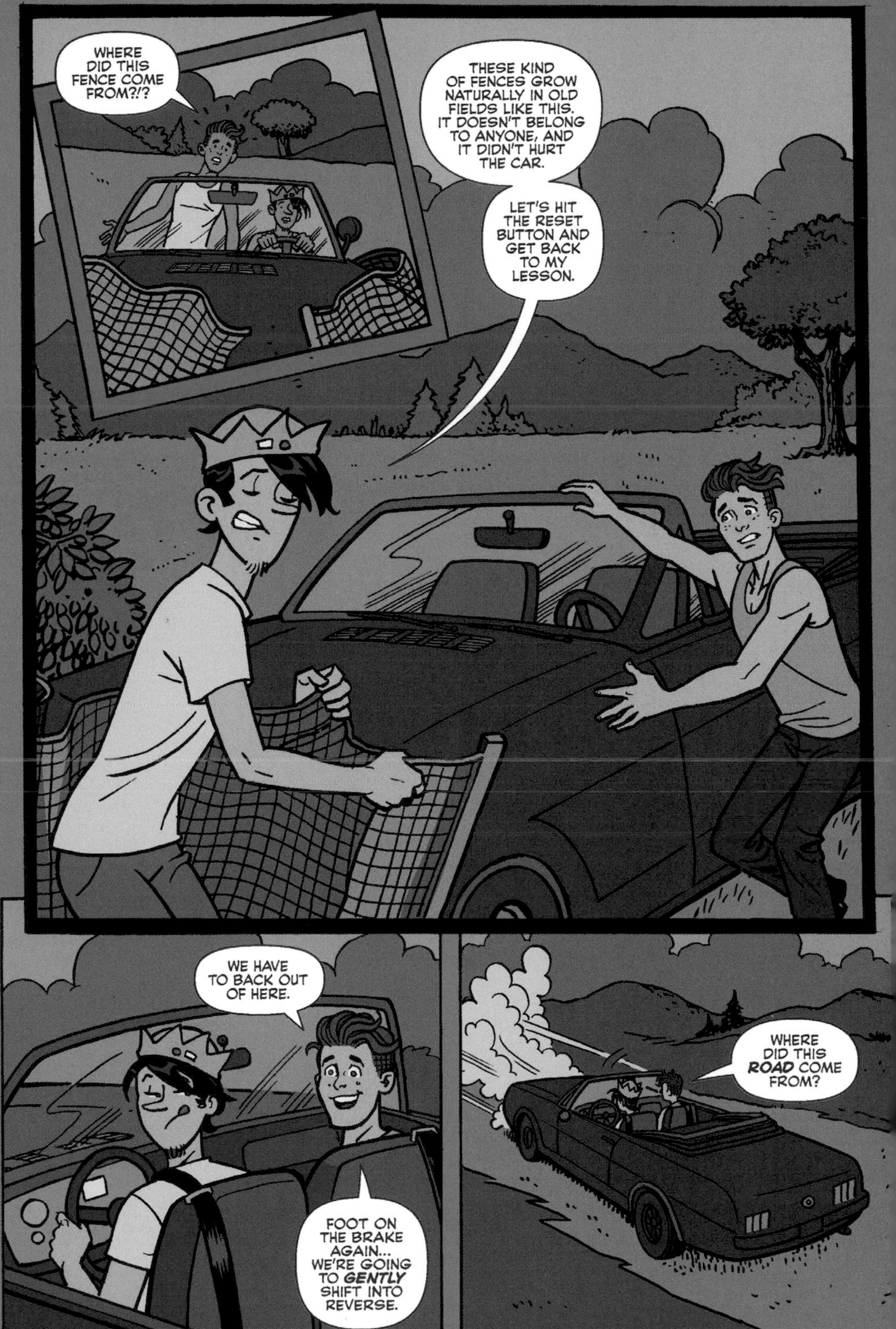
WHERE DID THIS FENCE COME FROM?!?
THESE KIND OF FENCES GROW NATURALLY IN OLD FIELDS LIKE THIS. IT DOESN'T BELONG TO ANYONE, AND IT DIDN'T HURT THE CAR.
LET'S HIT THE RESET BUTTON AND GET BACK TO MY LESSON.
WE HAVE TO BACK OUT OF HERE.
FOOT ON THE BRAKE AGAIN... WE'RE GOING TO *GENTLY* SHIFT INTO REVERSE.
WHERE DID THIS *ROAD* COME FROM?

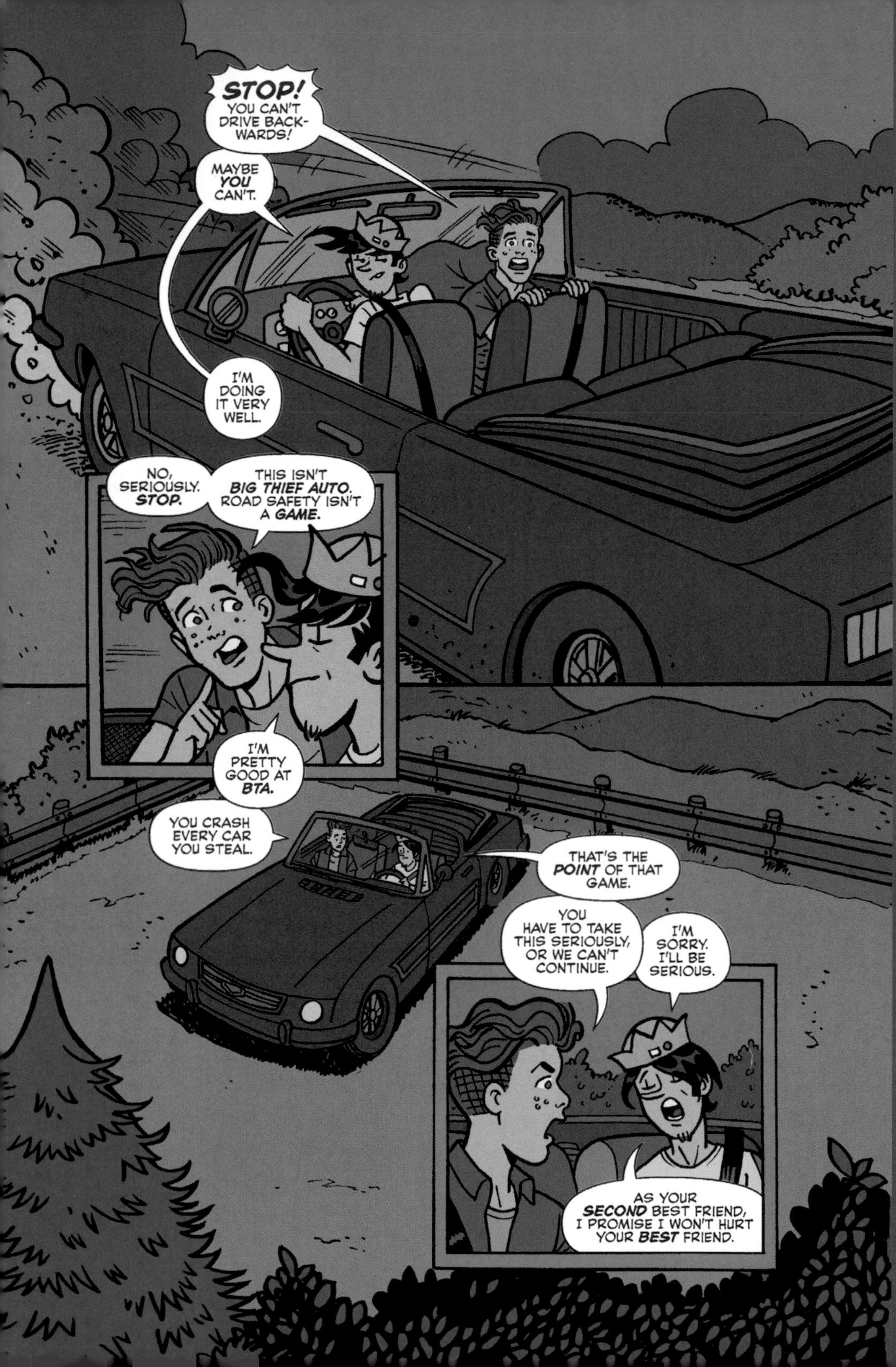
STOP! YOU CAN'T DRIVE BACK-WARDS!
MAYBE YOU CAN'T.
I'M DOING IT VERY WELL.
NO, SERIOUSLY. STOP.
THIS ISN'T BIG THIEF AUTO. ROAD SAFETY ISN'T A GAME.
I'M PRETTY GOOD AT BTA.
YOU CRASH EVERY CAR YOU STEAL.
THAT'S THE POINT OF THAT GAME.
YOU HAVE TO TAKE THIS SERIOUSLY, OR WE CAN'T CONTINUE.
I'M SORRY. I'LL BE SERIOUS.
AS YOUR SECOND BEST FRIEND, I PROMISE I WON'T HURT YOUR BEST FRIEND.

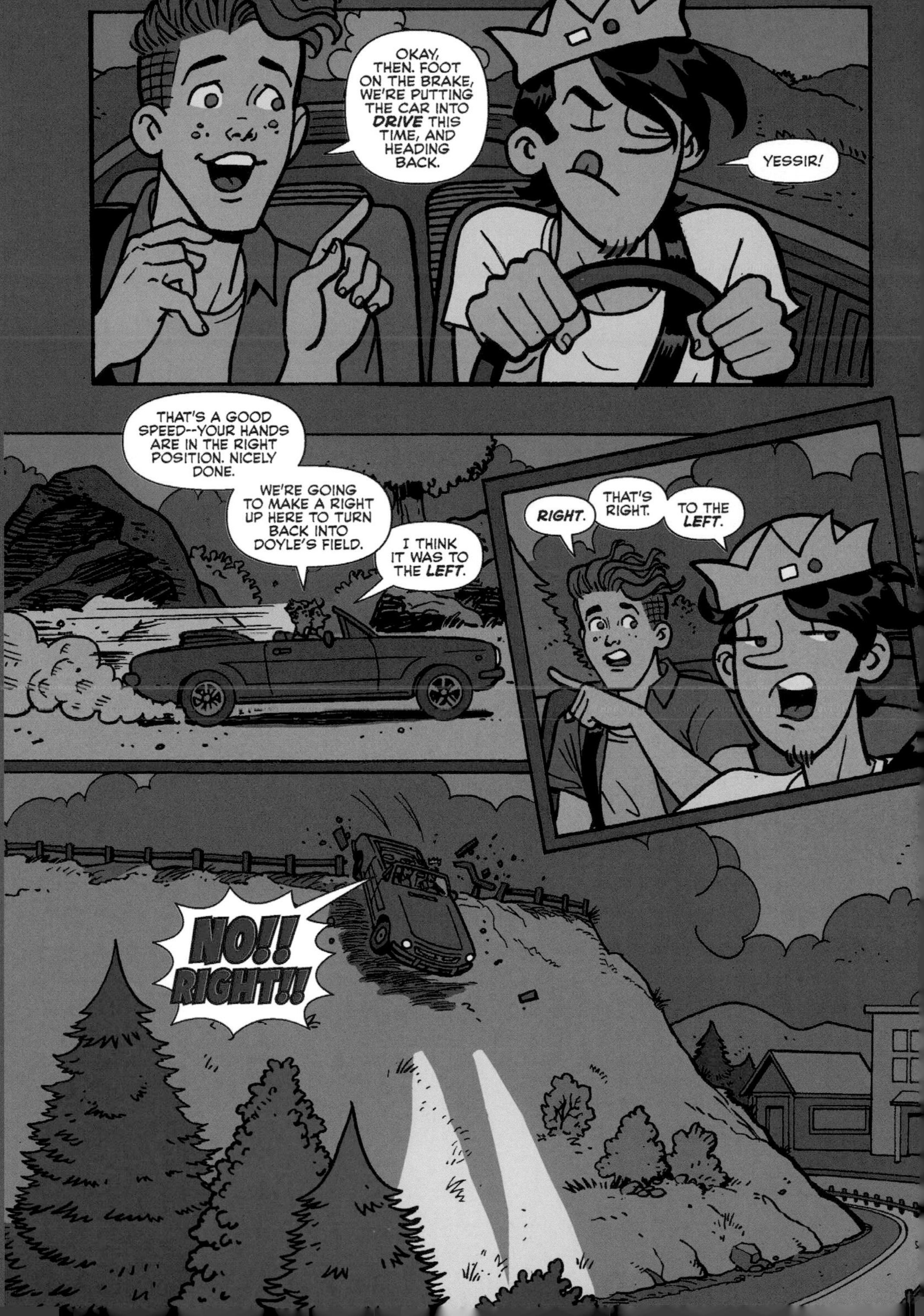
OKAY, THEN. FOOT ON THE BRAKE, WE'RE PUTTING THE CAR INTO *DRIVE* THIS TIME, AND HEADING BACK.
YESSIR!
THAT'S A GOOD SPEED--YOUR HANDS ARE IN THE RIGHT POSITION. NICELY DONE.
WE'RE GOING TO MAKE A RIGHT UP HERE TO TURN BACK INTO DOYLE'S FIELD.
I THINK IT WAS TO THE *LEFT*.
RIGHT.
THAT'S RIGHT.
TO THE *LEFT*.
NO!! RIGHT!!

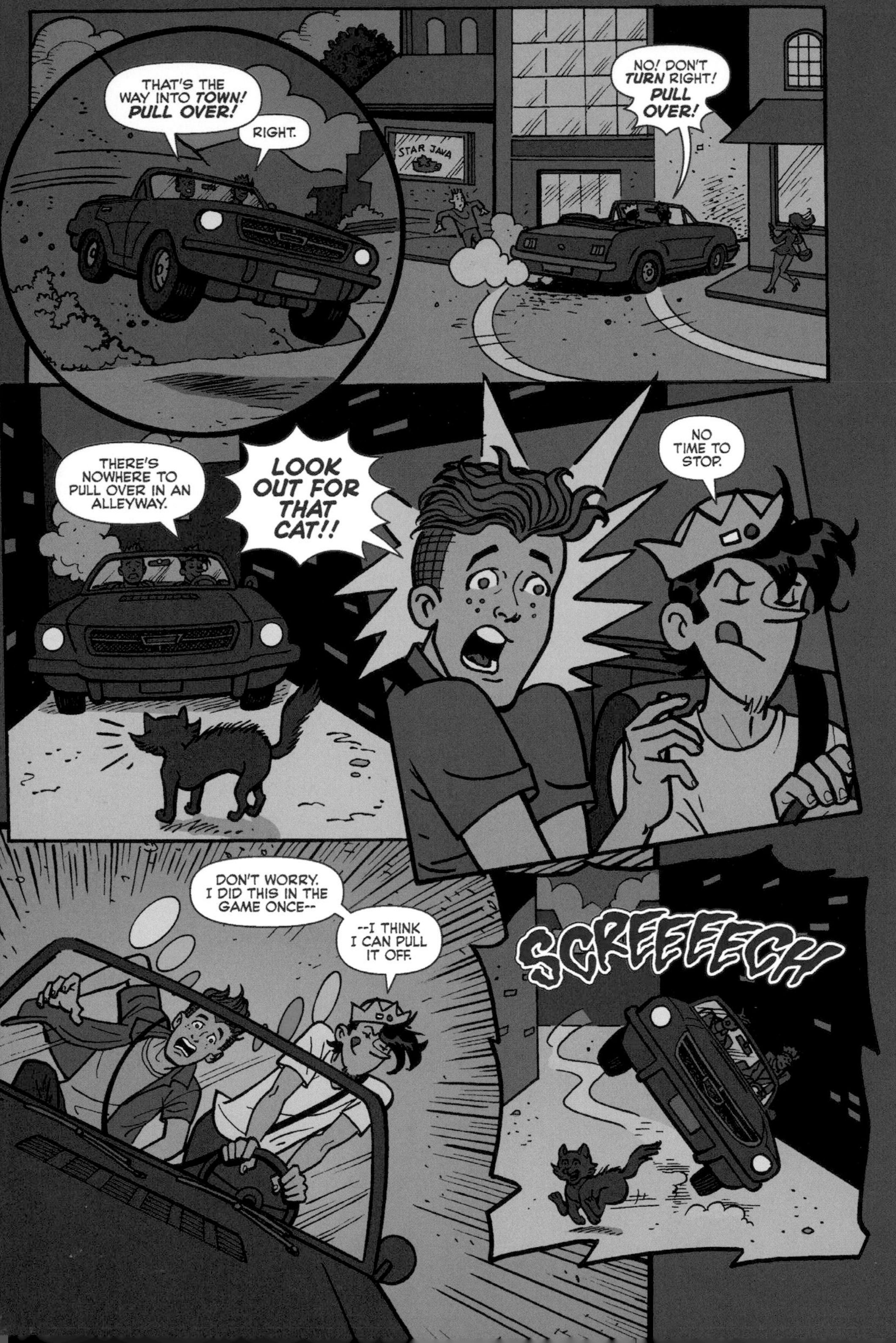
THAT'S THE WAY INTO TOWN! PULL OVER!
RIGHT.
STAR JAVA
NO! DON'T TURN RIGHT! PULL OVER!
THERE'S NOWHERE TO PULL OVER IN AN ALLEYWAY.
LOOK OUT FOR THAT CAT!!
NO TIME TO STOP.
DON'T WORRY. I DID THIS IN THE GAME ONCE--
--I THINK I CAN PULL IT OFF.
SCREEEECH

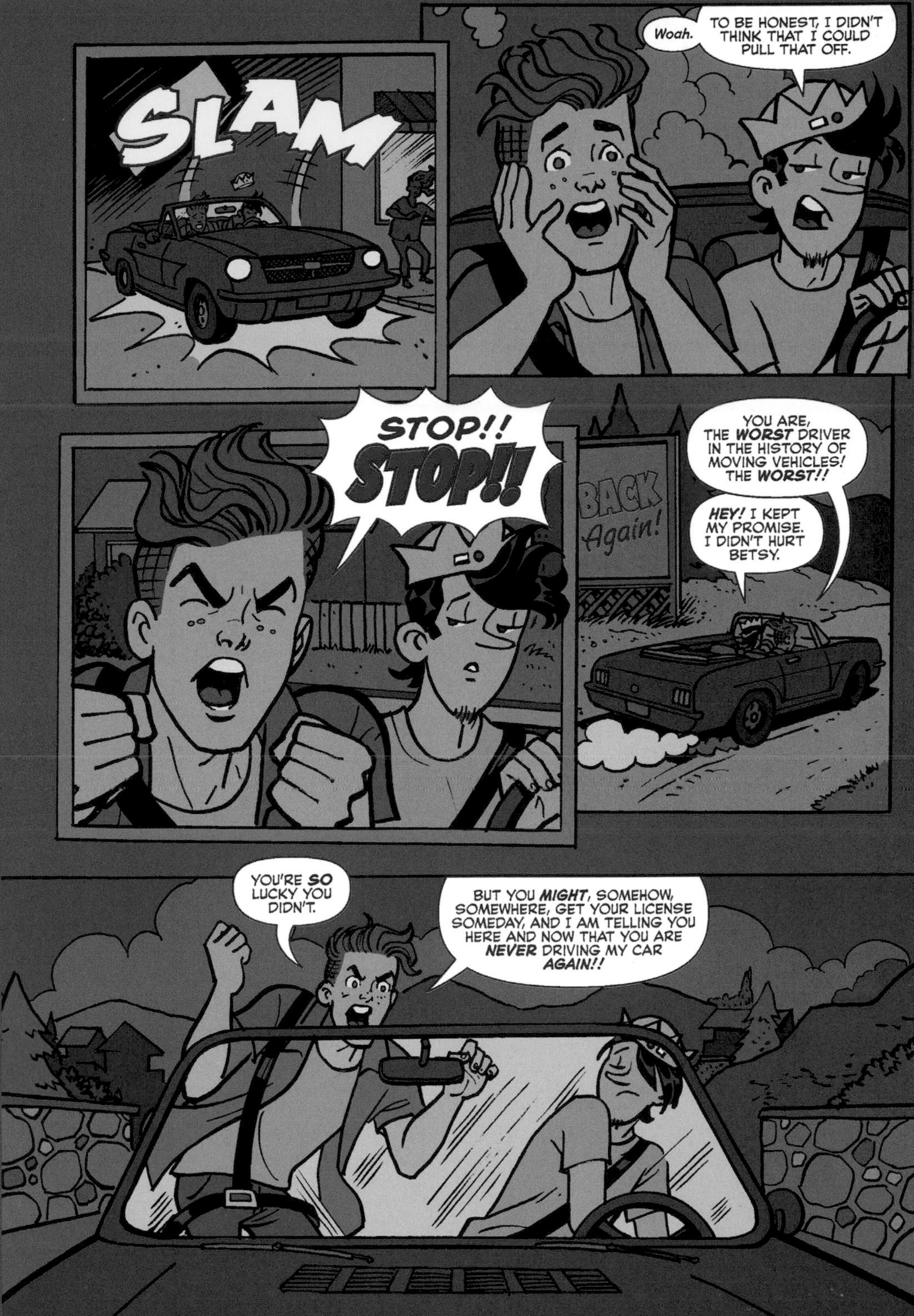
SLAM
Woah.
TO BE HONEST, I DIDN'T THINK THAT I COULD PULL THAT OFF.
STOP!! STOP!!
BACK Again!
YOU ARE, THE WORST DRIVER IN THE HISTORY OF MOVING VEHICLES! THE WORST!!
HEY! I KEPT MY PROMISE. I DIDN'T HURT BETSY.
YOU'RE SO LUCKY YOU DIDN'T.
BUT YOU MIGHT, SOMEHOW, SOMEWHERE, GET YOUR LICENSE SOMEDAY, AND I AM TELLING YOU HERE AND NOW THAT YOU ARE NEVER DRIVING MY CAR AGAIN!!

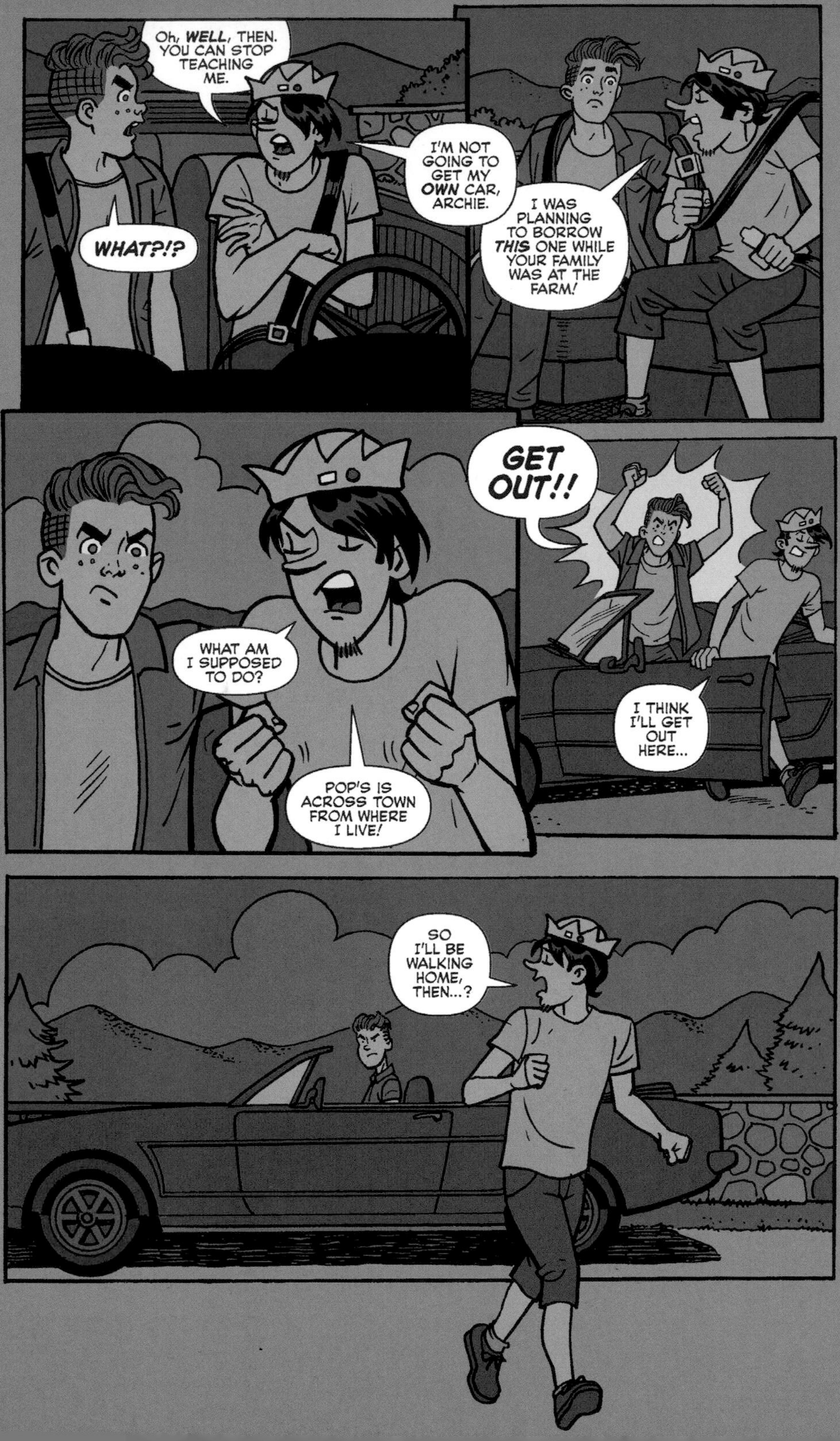
Oh, WELL, THEN. YOU CAN STOP TEACHING ME.
WHAT?!?
I'M NOT GOING TO GET MY OWN CAR, ARCHIE.
I WAS PLANNING TO BORROW THIS ONE WHILE YOUR FAMILY WAS AT THE FARM!
WHAT AM I SUPPOSED TO DO?
POP'S IS ACROSS TOWN FROM WHERE I LIVE!
GET OUT!!
I THINK I'LL GET OUT HERE...
SO I'LL BE WALKING HOME, THEN...?

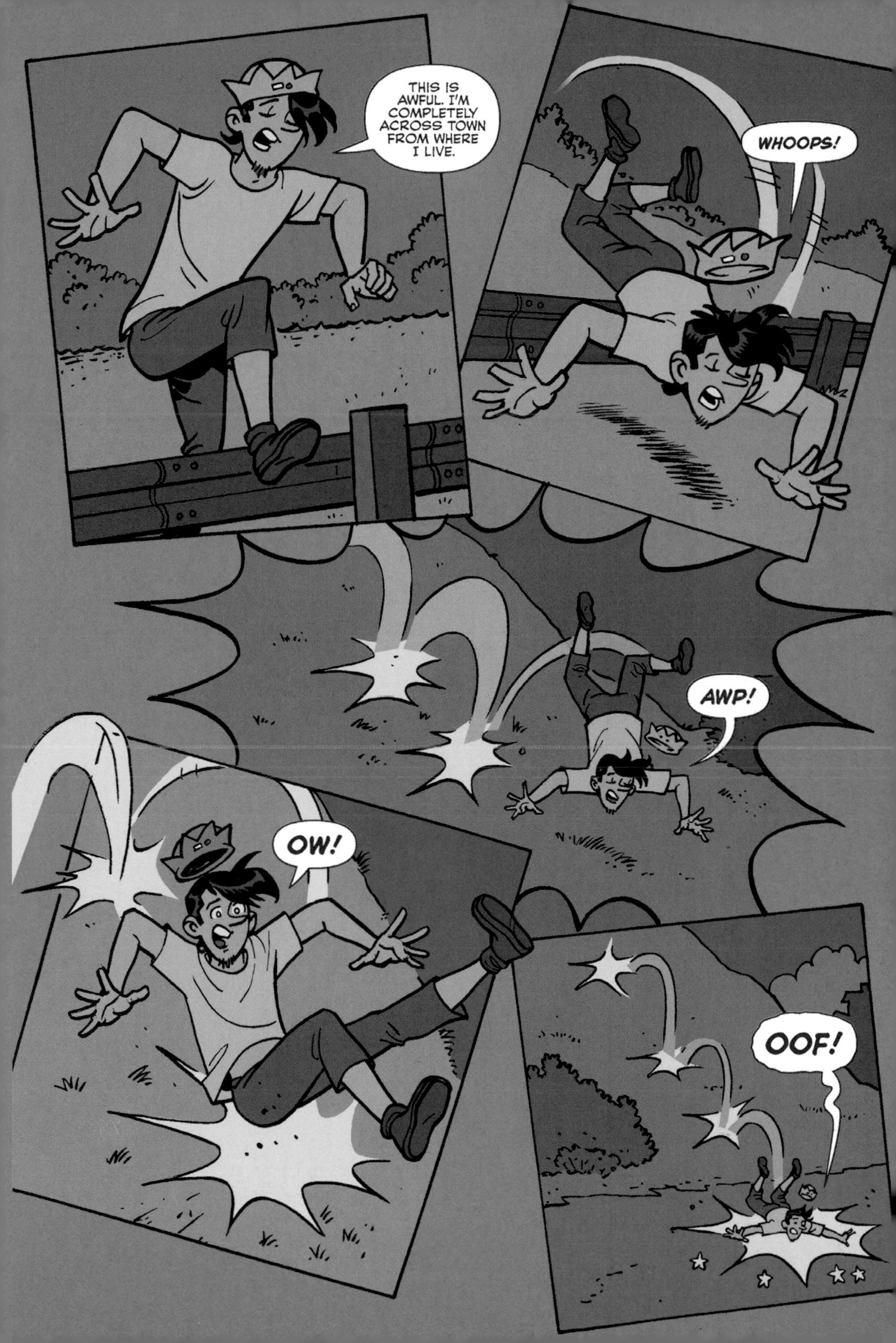
THIS IS AWFUL. I'M COMPLETELY ACROSS TOWN FROM WHERE I LIVE.
WHOOPS!
AWP!
OW!
OOF!

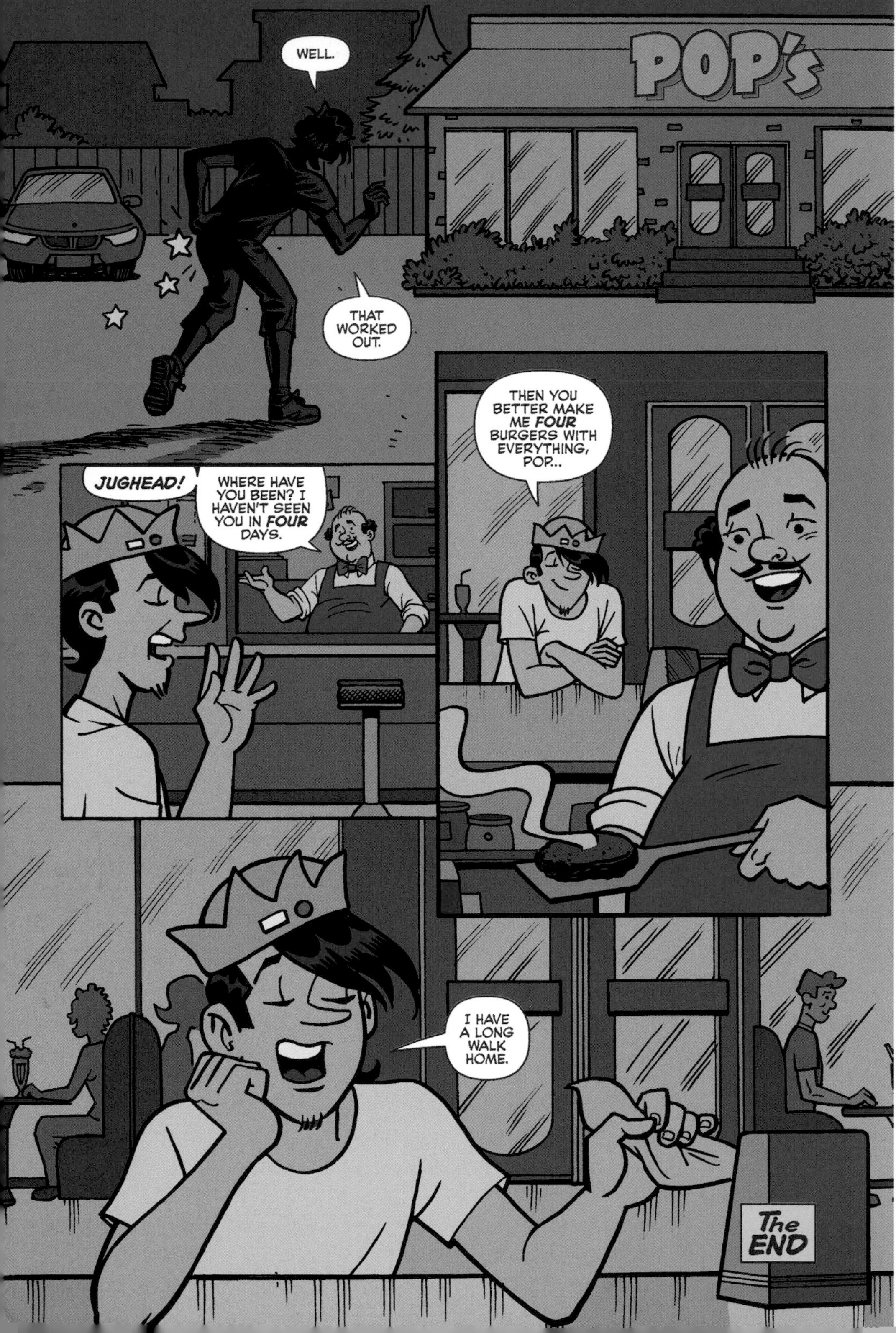
POP's
WELL.
THAT WORKED OUT.
JUGHEAD!
WHERE HAVE YOU BEEN? I HAVEN'T SEEN YOU IN FOUR DAYS.
THEN YOU BETTER MAKE ME FOUR BURGERS WITH EVERYTHING, POP...
I HAVE A LONG WALK HOME.
The END

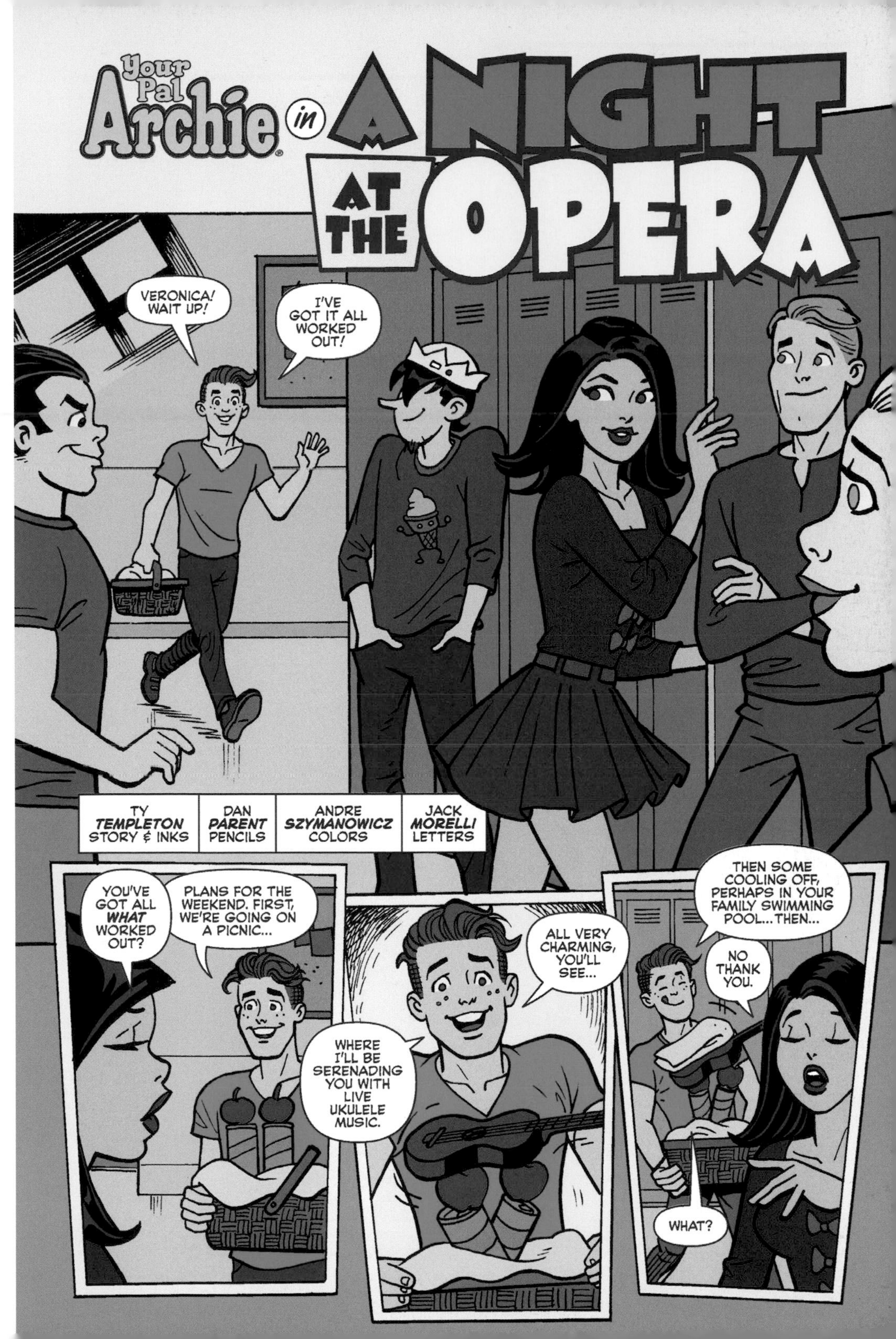
Your Pal Archie in
A NIGHT AT THE OPERA
VERONICA! WAIT UP!
I'VE GOT IT ALL WORKED OUT!
TY TEMPLETON STORY & INKS
DAN PARENT PENCILS
ANDRE SZYMANOWICZ COLORS
JACK MORELLI LETTERS
YOU'VE GOT ALL WHAT WORKED OUT?
PLANS FOR THE WEEKEND. FIRST, WE'RE GOING ON A PICNIC...
ALL VERY CHARMING, YOU'LL SEE...
WHERE I'LL BE SERENADING YOU WITH LIVE UKULELE MUSIC.
THEN SOME COOLING OFF, PERHAPS IN YOUR FAMILY SWIMMING POOL...THEN...
NO THANK YOU.
WHAT?

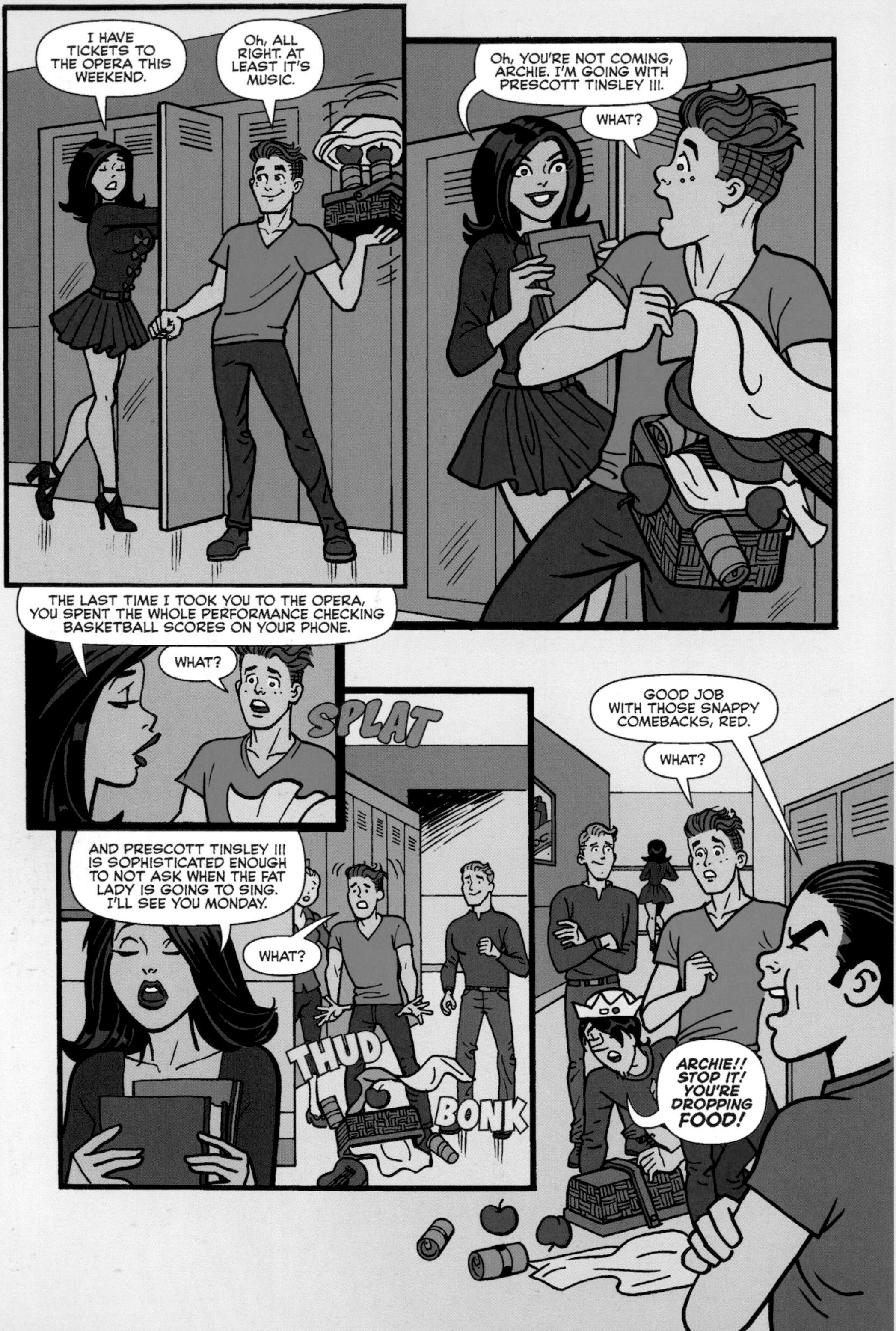
I HAVE TICKETS TO THE OPERA THIS WEEKEND.
Oh, ALL RIGHT. AT LEAST IT'S MUSIC.
Oh, YOU'RE NOT COMING, ARCHIE. I'M GOING WITH PRESCOTT TINSLEY III.
WHAT?
THE LAST TIME I TOOK YOU TO THE OPERA, YOU SPENT THE WHOLE PERFORMANCE CHECKING BASKETBALL SCORES ON YOUR PHONE.
WHAT?
SPLAT
AND PRESCOTT TINSLEY III IS SOPHISTICATED ENOUGH TO NOT ASK WHEN THE FAT LADY IS GOING TO SING. I'LL SEE YOU MONDAY.
WHAT?
THUD
BONK
GOOD JOB WITH THOSE SNAPPY COMEBACKS, RED.
WHAT?
ARCHIE!! STOP IT! YOU'RE DROPPING FOOD!

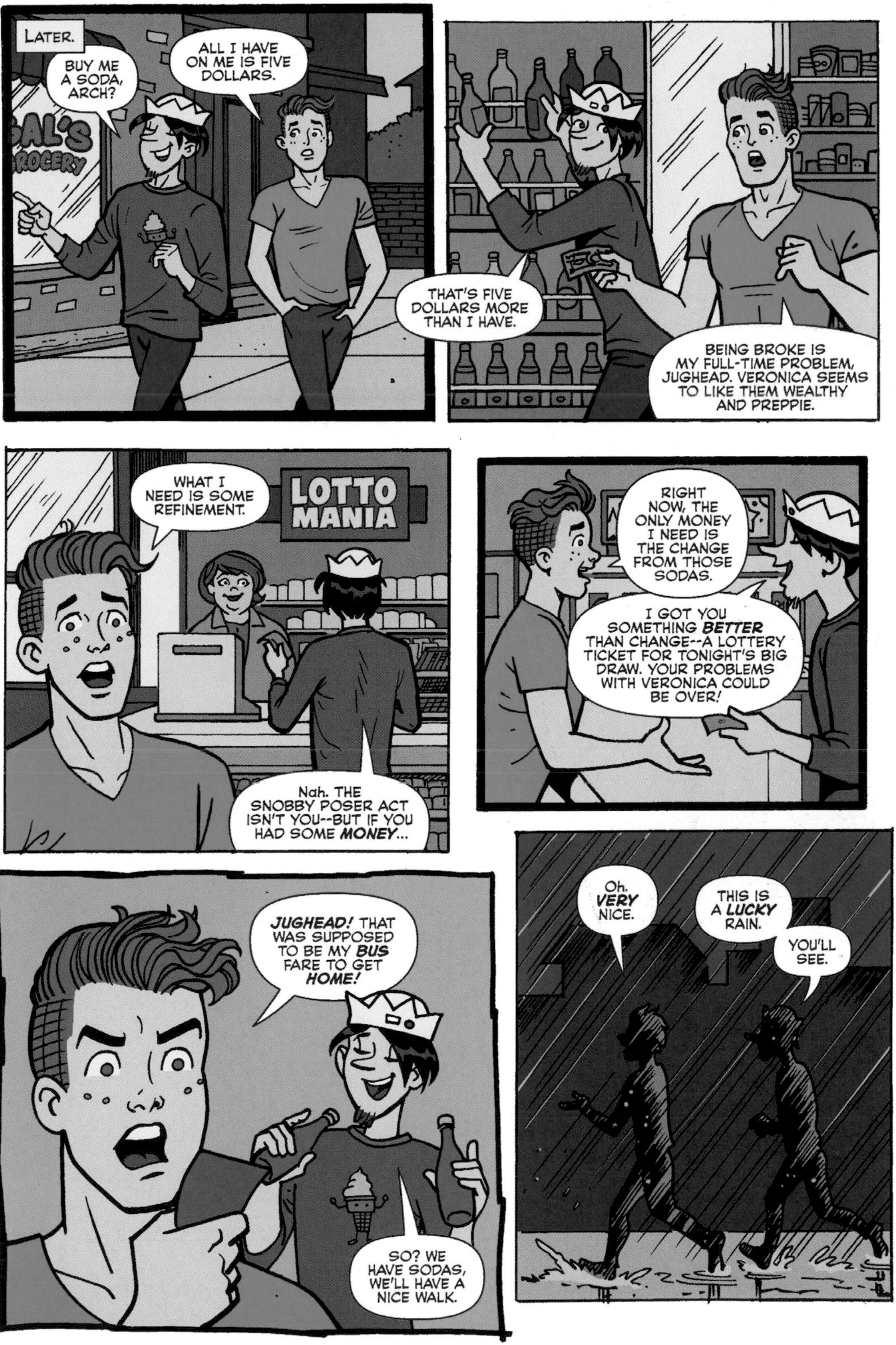
LATER.
BUY ME A SODA, ARCH?
ALL I HAVE ON ME IS FIVE DOLLARS.
GAL'S GROCERY
THAT'S FIVE DOLLARS MORE THAN I HAVE.
BEING BROKE IS MY FULL-TIME PROBLEM, JUGHEAD. VERONICA SEEMS TO LIKE THEM WEALTHY AND PREPPIE.
WHAT I NEED IS SOME REFINEMENT.
LOTTO MANIA
Nah. THE SNOBBY POSER ACT ISN'T YOU--BUT IF YOU HAD SOME MONEY...
RIGHT NOW, THE ONLY MONEY I NEED IS THE CHANGE FROM THOSE SODAS.
I GOT YOU SOMETHING BETTER THAN CHANGE--A LOTTERY TICKET FOR TONIGHT'S BIG DRAW. YOUR PROBLEMS WITH VERONICA COULD BE OVER!
JUGHEAD! THAT WAS SUPPOSED TO BE MY BUS FARE TO GET HOME!
SO? WE HAVE SODAS, WE'LL HAVE A NICE WALK.
Oh. VERY NICE.
THIS IS A LUCKY RAIN.
YOU'LL SEE.

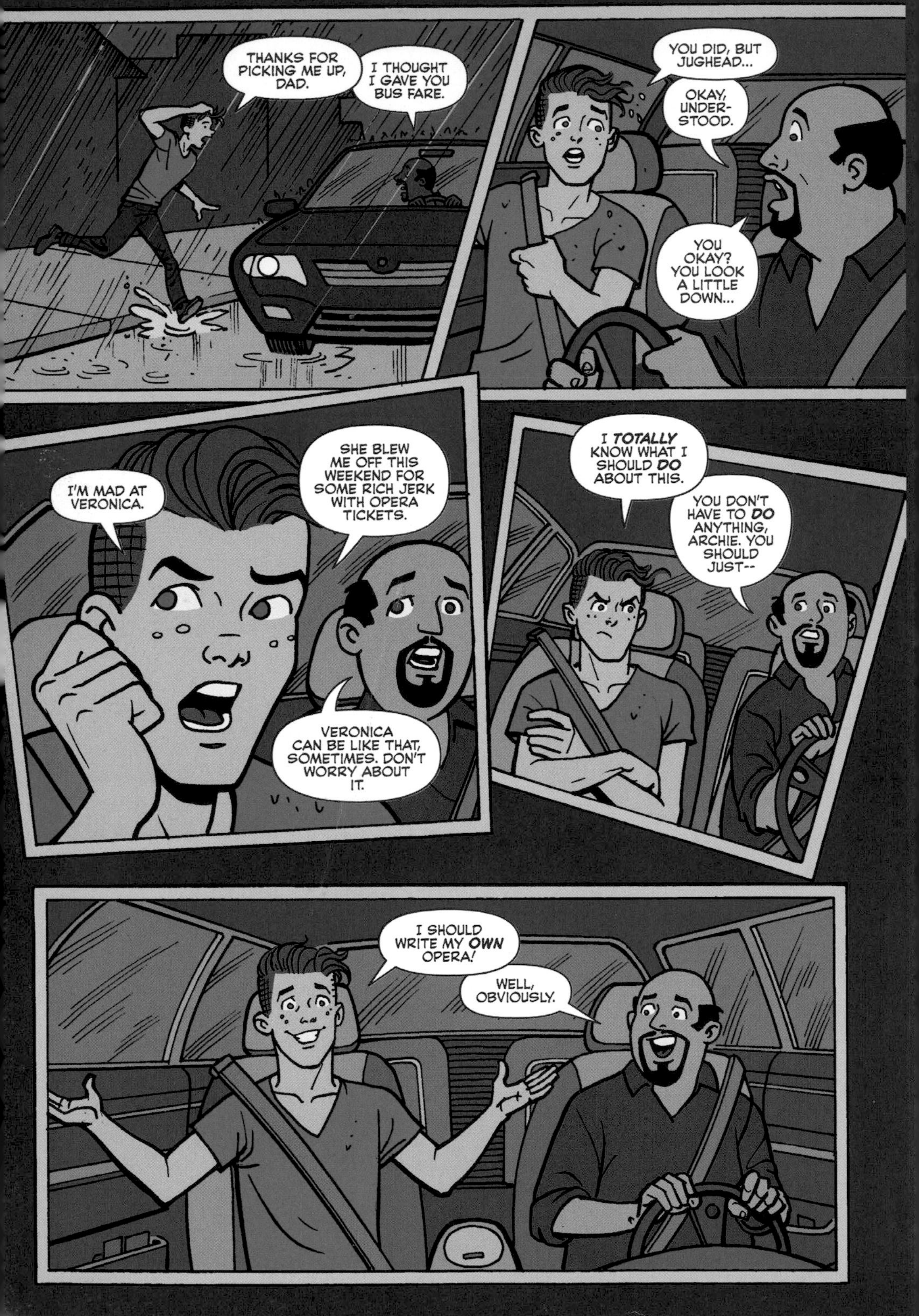
THANKS FOR PICKING ME UP, DAD.
I THOUGHT I GAVE YOU BUS FARE.
YOU DID, BUT JUGHEAD...
OKAY, UNDER-STOOD.
YOU OKAY? YOU LOOK A LITTLE DOWN...
I'M MAD AT VERONICA.
SHE BLEW ME OFF THIS WEEKEND FOR SOME RICH JERK WITH OPERA TICKETS.
VERONICA CAN BE LIKE THAT, SOMETIMES. DON'T WORRY ABOUT IT.
I TOTALLY KNOW WHAT I SHOULD DO ABOUT THIS.
YOU DON'T HAVE TO DO ANYTHING, ARCHIE. YOU SHOULD JUST--
I SHOULD WRITE MY OWN OPERA!
WELL, OBVIOUSLY.

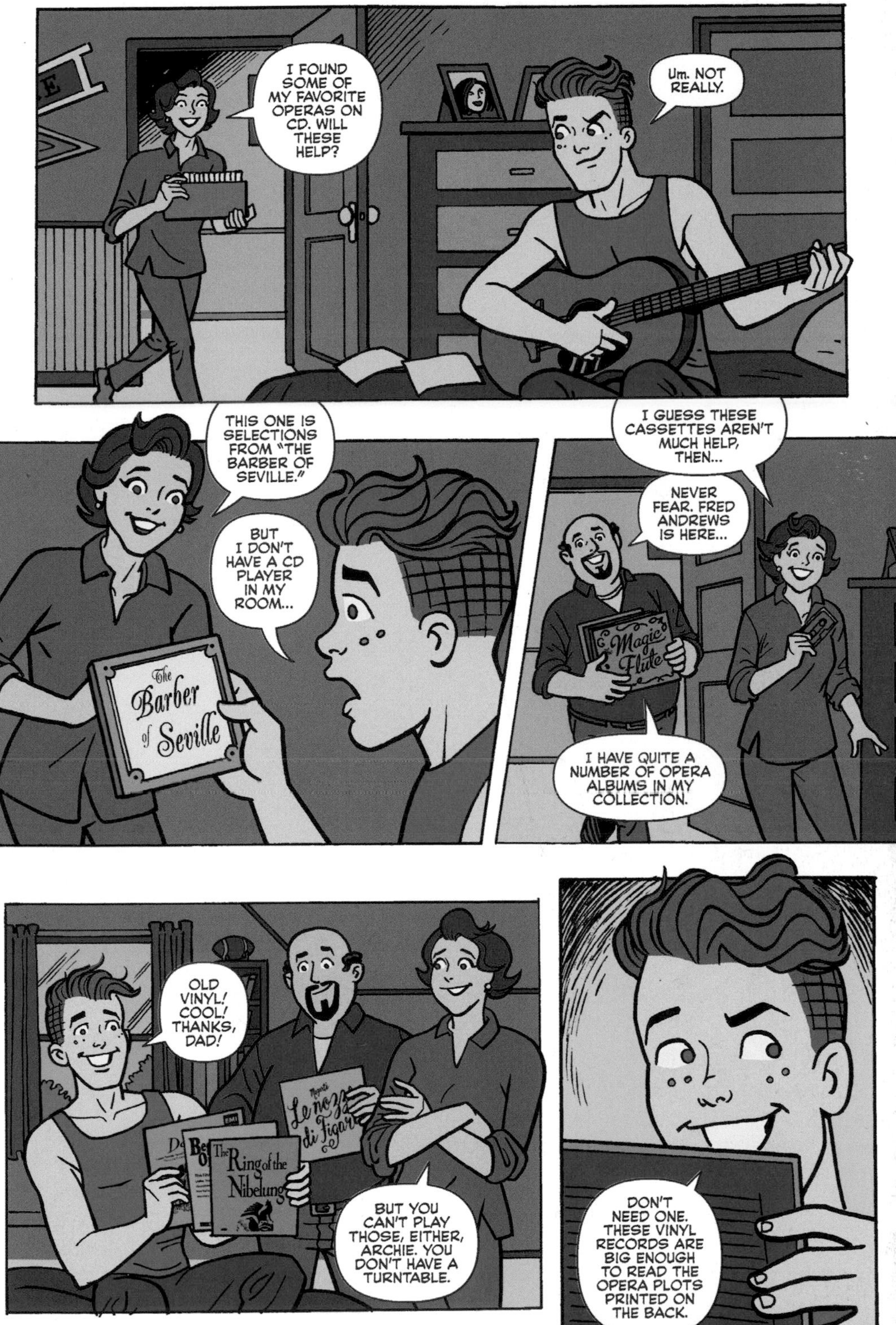
I FOUND SOME OF MY FAVORITE OPERAS ON CD. WILL THESE HELP?
Um. NOT REALLY.
THIS ONE IS SELECTIONS FROM "THE BARBER OF SEVILLE."
BUT I DON'T HAVE A CD PLAYER IN MY ROOM...
The Barber of Seville
I GUESS THESE CASSETTES AREN'T MUCH HELP, THEN...
NEVER FEAR. FRED ANDREWS IS HERE...
Magic Flute
I HAVE QUITE A NUMBER OF OPERA ALBUMS IN MY COLLECTION.
OLD VINYL! COOL! THANKS, DAD!
The Ring of the Nibelung
Le nozze di Figaro
BUT YOU CAN'T PLAY THOSE, EITHER, ARCHIE. YOU DON'T HAVE A TURNTABLE.
DON'T NEED ONE. THESE VINYL RECORDS ARE BIG ENOUGH TO READ THE OPERA PLOTS PRINTED ON THE BACK.

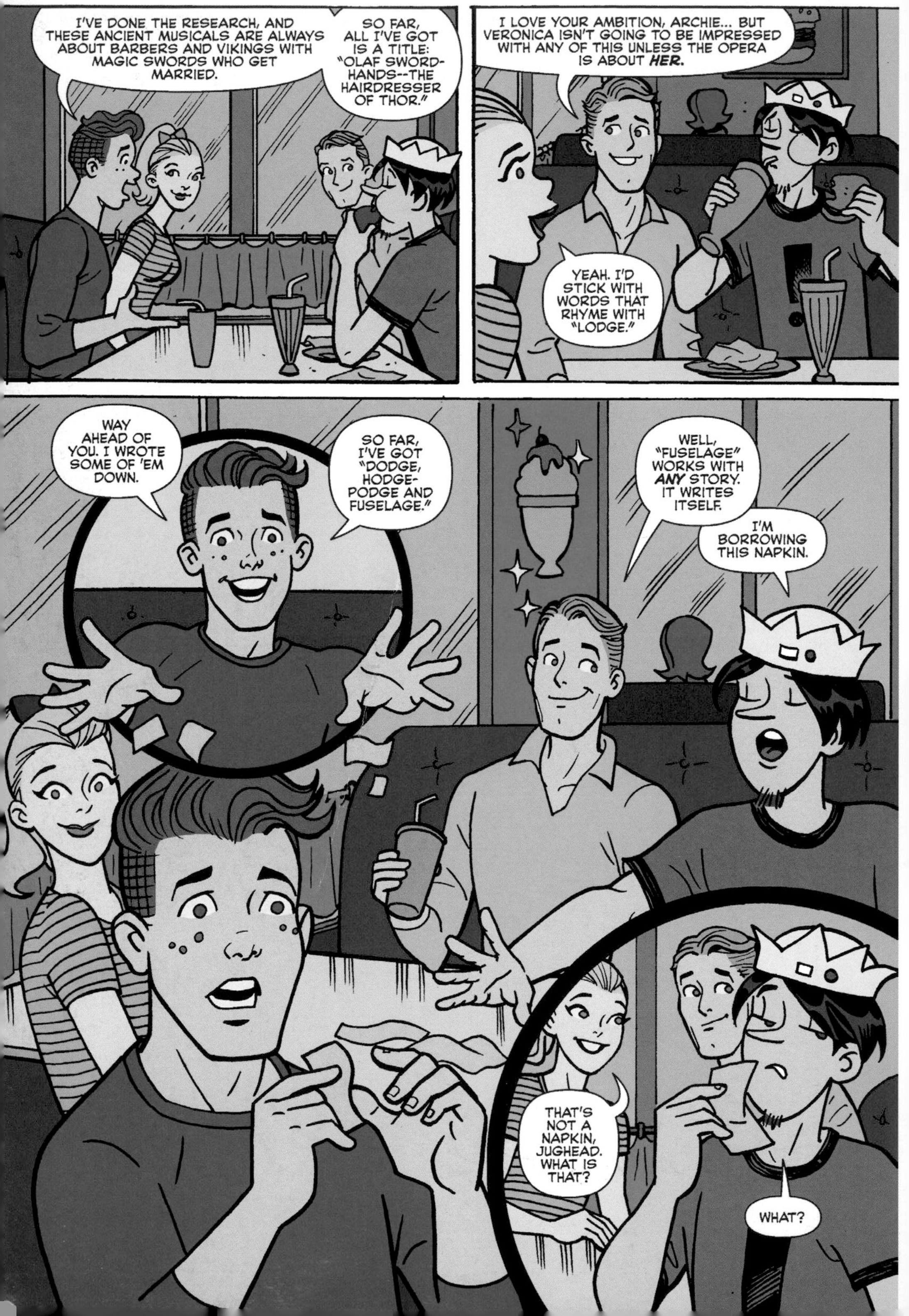

I'VE DONE THE RESEARCH, AND THESE ANCIENT MUSICALS ARE ALWAYS ABOUT BARBERS AND VIKINGS WITH MAGIC SWORDS WHO GET MARRIED.
SO FAR, ALL I'VE GOT IS A TITLE: "OLAF SWORD-HANDS--THE HAIRDRESSER OF THOR."
I LOVE YOUR AMBITION, ARCHIE... BUT VERONICA ISN'T GOING TO BE IMPRESSED WITH ANY OF THIS UNLESS THE OPERA IS ABOUT *HER.*
YEAH. I'D STICK WITH WORDS THAT RHYME WITH "LODGE."
WAY AHEAD OF YOU. I WROTE SOME OF 'EM DOWN.
SO FAR, I'VE GOT "DODGE, HODGE-PODGE AND FUSELAGE."
WELL, "FUSELAGE" WORKS WITH *ANY* STORY. IT WRITES ITSELF.
I'M BORROWING THIS NAPKIN.
THAT'S NOT A NAPKIN, JUGHEAD. WHAT IS THAT?
WHAT?

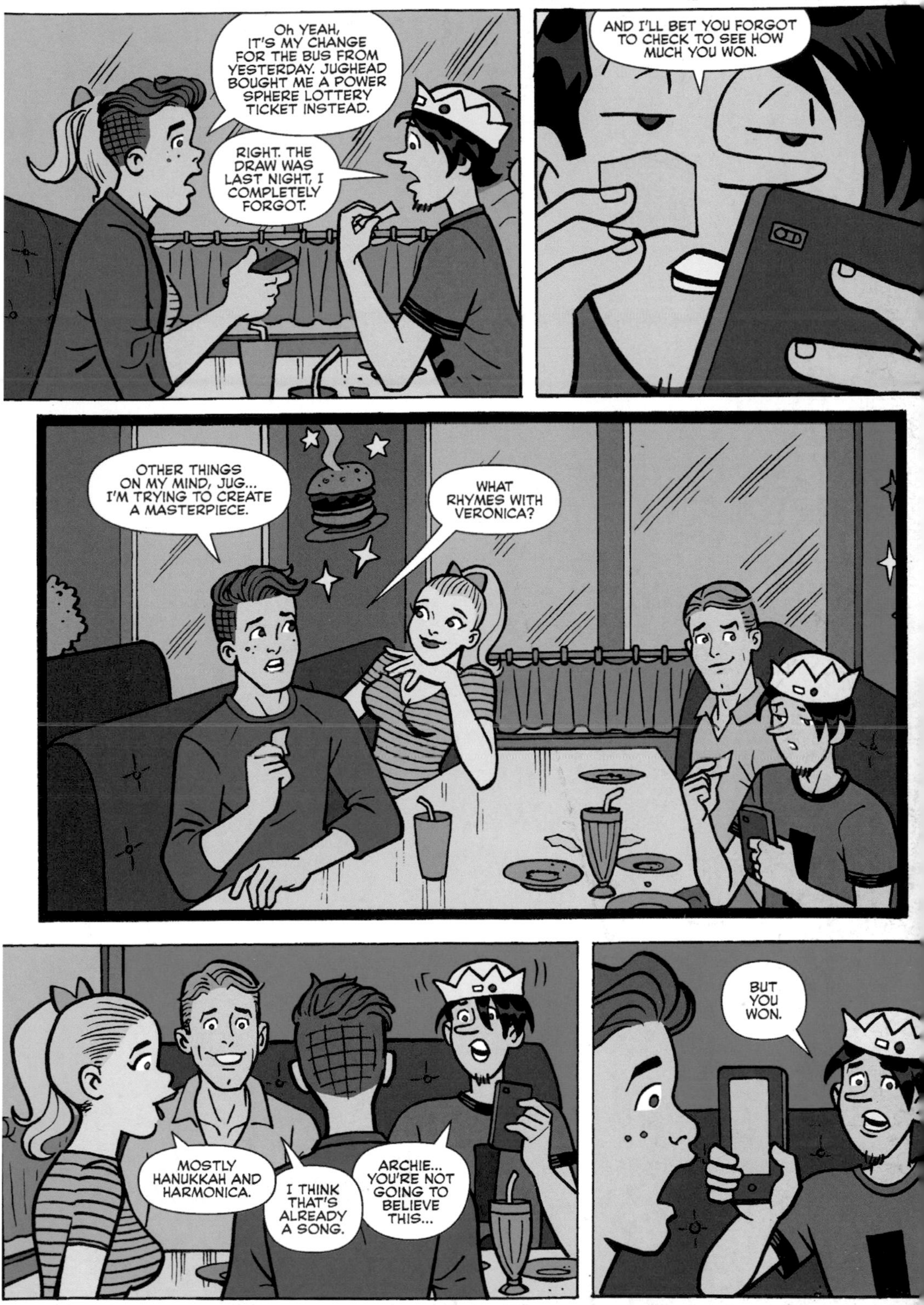
Oh YEAH, IT'S MY CHANGE FOR THE BUS FROM YESTERDAY. JUGHEAD BOUGHT ME A POWER SPHERE LOTTERY TICKET INSTEAD.
RIGHT. THE DRAW WAS LAST NIGHT, I COMPLETELY FORGOT.
AND I'LL BET YOU FORGOT TO CHECK TO SEE HOW MUCH YOU WON.
OTHER THINGS ON MY MIND, JUG... I'M TRYING TO CREATE A MASTERPIECE.
WHAT RHYMES WITH VERONICA?
MOSTLY HANUKKAH AND HARMONICA.
I THINK THAT'S ALREADY A SONG.
ARCHIE... YOU'RE NOT GOING TO BELIEVE THIS...
BUT YOU WON.

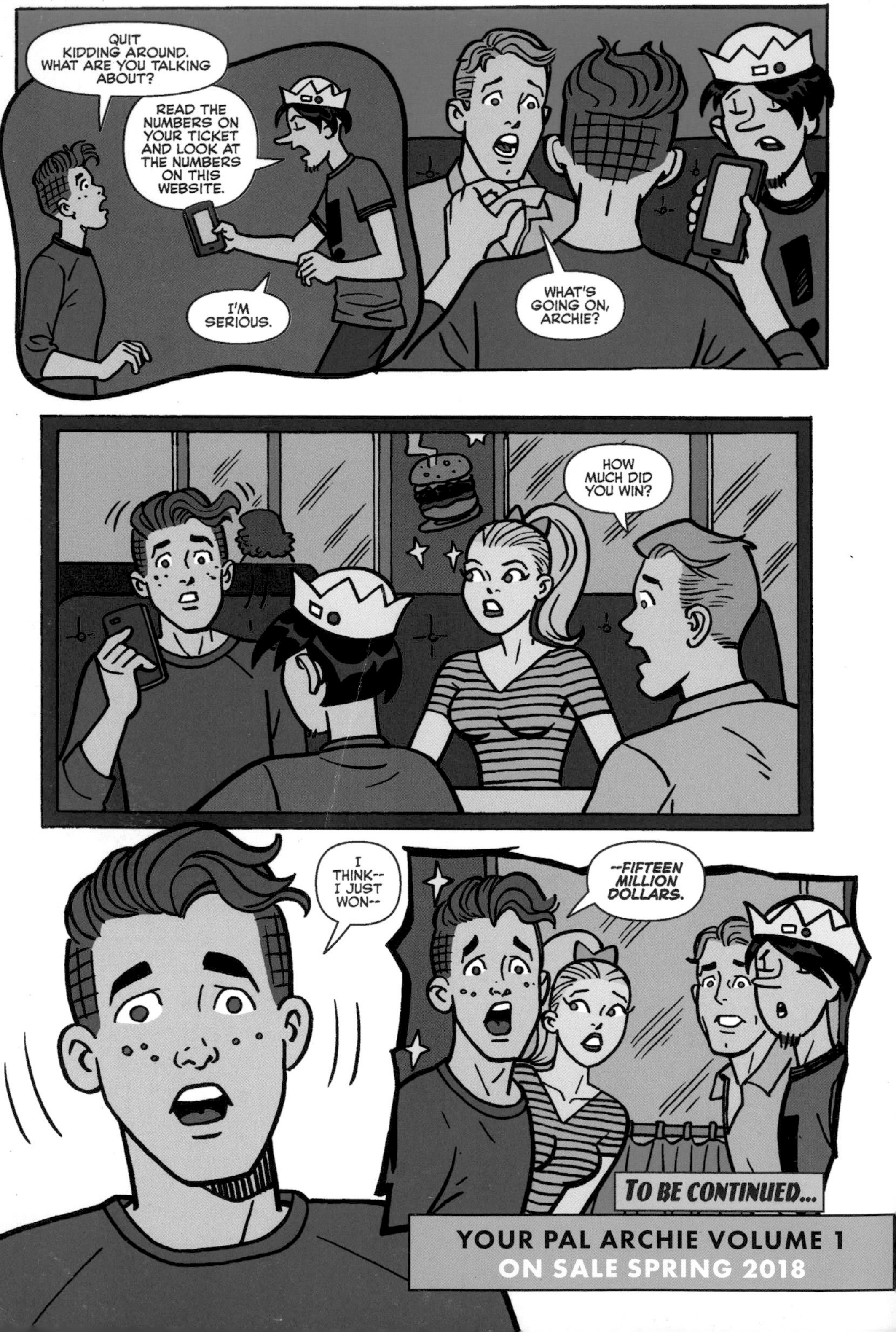
QUIT KIDDING AROUND. WHAT ARE YOU TALKING ABOUT?
READ THE NUMBERS ON YOUR TICKET AND LOOK AT THE NUMBERS ON THIS WEBSITE.
I'M SERIOUS.
WHAT'S GOING ON, ARCHIE?
HOW MUCH DID YOU WIN?
I THINK-- I JUST WON--
--FIFTEEN MILLION DOLLARS.
TO BE CONTINUED...
YOUR PAL ARCHIE VOLUME 1
ON SALE SPRING 2018